In This Book

Not only...
CLEAR, CONCISE, FULLY DETAILED "HOW-TO" ADVICE
FOR EVERY STEP UPWARD ON THE CAREER-BUILDING LADDER

But also, on page after page...
A LOT OF BEHIND-CLOSED-DOORS , INSIDE INFORMATION
THAT MANY ACTORS NEVER LEARN UNTIL IT'S TOO LATE!

✎

Right and Wrong Ways To Start; Things To Avoid; How to Survive and Stay
Publications and Services the Actor Should and Should Not Rely Upon
The Right Kinds of Professional Materials and What To Do with Them
Self Promotion, Self Publicizing, Self Advertising the Actor Can Do------
Preparing and Handling Your Own; How to Work with Press Agents Later
Getting and Keeping the Ideal Agent for You
What Small and Large Agencies Do and How They Do It
Audition Tapes and Audition Scenes, Good and Bad
Interviewing for Roles------How To Get or Lose Them
Mistakes Actors Make in Interviews that Hold Them Back
Casting Directors-----What They Do; How They Do it
The Performing Unions The Actor Must Join
The Film Job, Step by Step----What To Do Before, During, After,
to Appear an Experienced Professional Film Actor in First Jobs
Complete Details of Working with the Camera and Film Crew People
How Roles, Billing and Salaries are Advanced by Agents and Actors
The Many Different Contracts and What their Small Print Clauses Mean

First Printing 1992
Fifth, Revised Printing 1996

THE FILM ACTOR'S
COMPLETE CAREER
GUIDE

ISBN: 0-9615288-9-3
Library of Congress Catalog
Card Number: 91-73555

Acknowledgements

This book is dedicated, first and foremost, to the following agents, casting directors, producers, directors, press agents and other entertainment industry people who've contributed immeasurably to the information contained in these pages with their frankness and candor, either as close acquaintances or as discussion panel guests in some of the author's over thirty *"Actors' Career Seminars"* over the years, or have otherwise been of help in the gathering of the information all actors can use to more rapidly promote their careers:

Talent agents **Hal Gefsky, Steve Stevens, Wally Hiller, Edgar Small, Tom Jennings, Alex Brewis, Maurine Oliver, Bob Colvin, Mike Greenfield, Len Kaplan, Sid Craig, Ernie Dade, Rickey Barr, Jack Fields, Jim Gibson, Maggi Henderson, Fred Spector, Don Gerler, Dan Moulthrop, Don Schwartz, Joshua Gray, Lou Deuser, Vic Sutton, Lew Sherrell** and the late **Herman Zimmerman** who until his death in recent years was one of the most staunch and determined developers of new talent that Hollywood has ever known....

Casting directors **Ross Brown, Mike Fenton, Eddie Foy III, Milt Hamerman, Al Onorato, Tom Palmer, Pam Polifroni, Sally Powers, Joe Reich, Gary Shaffer, Lynn Stalmaster, John Crosby, Bob Edmiston, Rachelle Farberman, Geno Havens, Phil Benjamin, Joe D'Agosta, Caro Jones, Terry Kerrigan, Bill Kenney, Susan McCray, Michael McLean, Dodie McLean, Jane Murray, Marvin Paige, Barbara Remsen, Doris Sabbagh** and the author's former NBC-TV boss **Al Trescony**....

Producers **Perry Lafferty, David Friedkin, Mort Fine, Chuck Fries, Frank Price, Andy White, Hillard Elkins, Bill Conrad, Elliott Lewis, John Bennett, Ben Hecht, Ivan Tors, Everett Chambers, Wes Bishop** and **Raynold Gideon**, but first and foremost, **Jon Epstein, Maurice Unger** and **Chuck Fries**, who brought me to Hollywood, gave me hands-on training in all Departments at their studio, and taught me so much!

Directors **Fred Coe, Fielder Cook, Stanley Kramer, Roberto Rossellini, Elia Kazan, Sydney Pollack, Vincente Minnelli, Robert Lewis, Walter Doniger, Lawrence Dobkin, James Goldstone, Barry Shear, Abby Mann, Ted Post, Joe Sargent, Bernard Kowalski, Leo Penn, Ralph Senensky, John Rich, Don Richardson, Les Martinson, Gordon Davidson, John Erman, Harry Falk, Paul Henreid, Alex March, E. W. Swackhammer** and many, many others...

Critics, Editors and Columnists **Brooks Atkinson**, *The New York Times*'s Dean of New York Critics until his death; **Vernon Rice**, Theatre Editor of *The New York Post* until his death; **James Powers**, former Editor of *The Hollywood Reporter*; **Dan Sullivan**, Theatre Editor and noted critic of *The Los Angeles Times*; **Dale Olson**, former Theatre Editor of *Daily Variety*; **Deena Metzger**, former Critic of *The Los Angeles Free Press*;

Hank Spalding, fomer Editor of _Hollywood Talent News_; **Bill Edwards**, former Theatre Editor and Critic of _Daily Variety_; **Lloyd Steele,** former Entertainment Editor and Critic of _The Los Angeles Free Press_; **Hal Marienthal,** Critic of _"Theatre Beat"_ on television; **Ray Lloynd** and **Ron Pennington**, former Critics for _The Hollywood Reporter_; the late **Margaret Harford** and, later, **Sylvie Drake** of _The Los Angeles Times_ entertainment columns staff; **Andre Bercoff**, Entertainment Editor and Critic of _L'Express_, Paris, **Ugo DiCenzo**, Theatre Critic for _Corriere della Sera_, Rome; and other critics and columnists perhaps overlooked whose comments about my work have advanced my career...

Publicists **Maxine Thomas**, founder and first president of the Hollywood Women's Press Club and publicist for many top stars; **Dale Olson**, former Editor and Critic of _Daily Variety_ and more recently publicist for top stars and production companies; and **Helen Kauffman**, the author's first publicist and never forgotten because she helped make the first steps of visibility in Hollywood possible....

Theatre producers, too many to name, in the Off Broadway movement in New York in the late 1940's who patiently listened to the gofer sent by Brooks Atkinson and Vernon Rice and aided in forming the Off Broadway League...and the many, many theatre producers in Los Angeles and Hollywood who helped make the formation and quick growth of The League of Los Angeles Theatres by this author possible and who supported it with their active participations during my presidency in the early 1970's....

All the acting coaches and teachers in Hollywood, New York, San Francisco and other cities who in 1980 helped this author form the Acting Coaches and Teachers Association and continued to support it with their memberships and their efforts until in 1985 its work was accomplished...

Mayor Tom Bradley, Mayor Sam Yorty and **Councilman Joel Wachs** of the City of Los Angeles for their important contributions toward making Los Angeles and Hollywood film, televiion and theatre problems easier and for their encouragement and help given to the League Of Los Angeles Theatres during my presidency....

And...my beloved wife **Virginia Parke**, whose patience during the preparation of this book has been so deeply appreciated!

Lawrence Parke

About The Author

Lawrence Parke is one of the most uniquely qualified Hollywood film industry leaders for the laying out in this book's clear and concise terms, for actors of all career levels---whether already established in film and television acting or simply at the beginning point of deciding whether to pursue a film acting career---all the complicated *do's and don'ts*, career *musts*, information about and the ideal manners of the actor's relating with people in job-giving positions, and the wealth of behind-closed-doors and other little known information that Mr. Parke's years of experience in most aspects of the entertainment industry make it possible or him to pass on in this book.

For twenty years he has presented, in Hollywood, his *Professional Acting Career Seminars*, with guest panels of leading casting directors, agents, producers, managers, press agents, etc., appearing before his audiences to provide actors with completely candid information that is impossible to obtain---at least in so full detail---anywhere else.

Parke himself has appeared in over 200 film and television roles; has been a recognized and respected casting director of motion pictures, television series and their pilots, Movies of The Week and daytime dramas (soap operas); was a Screen Actors Guild and AFTRA talent agency head for several years representing and negotiating contracts for stars, top suporting players and talented new people; was a recognized careermaker and unofficial personal manager for a number of today's leading actors during their early years; and for thirty years has been one of Hollywood's and other cities' leading acting coaches, responsible for the training, career starts and later advances of a growing list of stars.

In his early years in New York theatre he was twice winner of the Vernon Rice Award (the predecessor of the Obie Award), appeared in theatre roles himself in New York, in summer theatre and in national tours, produced his own summer theatre, and directed Off Broadway, summer theatre and national touring productions and appeared in many "Golden Age of Television" acting roles prior to being brought to Hollywood by one of the studios in 1957.

A recognized entertainment industry organizer as well, he was the founder and first three terms' president of both the Acting Coaches and Teachers Association and The League of Los Angeles Theatres; was co-founder and first seasons' co-chairman of both Equity Library Theatre West and the ANTA Repertory Theatre West. He received Mayoral Commendations from both Mayor Tom Bradley and Mayor Sam Yorty for his contributions to the Hollywood and Los Angeles entertainment industry community.

He is currently the editor for Acting World Books of the bimonthly *The Agencies---What The Actor Needs To Know*, the quarterly *The Hollywood Acting Coaches And Teachers Directory* and the six-book *Seminars To Go* series of career guidance books for film actors.

iii

Foreword

The decision to come to Hollywood to pursue an acting career in film and television is probably the easiest of all the decisions an actor must make. Millions have made that decision and come. Some have come prepared with foreknowledge of what to expect; some simply came with nothing but blind faith in miracles. Some came with an amount of actual acting experience that fed the fires of their determination and deepened their conviction that they *could* and *should* be actors, but some came with no acting experience at all and nothing but the impression from fan magazines and tabloid fables that acting in motion pictures and television is a glamorous, exciting lifestyle that always leads to fame and fortune.

Those who've done their research ahead of time know what they have to do when they get here. The blind dreamers think others will do everything for them.

At any current moment there are between seventy and eighty thousand *pofessional* actors---union members who work at least once in a while---in Hollywood. Hollywood really doesn't need any more actors. Yet hundreds more actors and *would-be* actors arrive daily. Some will eventually make it. Many more won't.

This book is directed to those who have the intelligence to find out all they can ahead of time---even before making their big decision to come; to the actors who know ahead of time that they have talent and who have the determination to do the hard work along the way toward achieving their ultimate goals; and to those others who need to be *discouraged* early, before they waste many important years of their lives chasing rainbows and waiting for miracles.

I've tried to lay out---clearly and in enough detail---every stage and step the actor will encounter and also---again clearly and in enough detail---point out what can and should be done and how and when to do it in a manner that achieves the results hoped for.

Director John Huston, who passed away in recent years, once told his daughter Angelica, now a top star, when she decided to become an actress, "The things a film actor or actress needs to know would fill a book!" Those things are what this book is filled with.

Lawrence Parke

Contents

****

Chapter One

Don't Come To Hollywood Expecting Any Miracles!

Don't come to Hollywood if it's just to "show 'em they don't appreciate you!" back home, or to "Make 'em respect you!", or any other mixed-up emotional obsession or alibi or escape or weapon of revenge. There are thousands upon thousands of Skid Row candidates here already who came for similar reasons, stayed for the same reasons and, because they "couldn't go home till they'd made it big in the movies", couldn't ever go home, period. They walk Hollywood Boulevard and Sunset Strip, living on a daily diet of excuses, despairs, soul-sellings and daydreamings, without the foggiest notion of why they're not "making it" in Hollywood.

Fan magazine in one hand and "overnight" bag of dreams in the other, more arrive every day. They climb off planes here with their heads full of Academy Award acceptance speeches and gossip column quotes about how they've "made it in spite of everybody," or they imagine millions of their fans already cheering as they get off the bus at the dusty downtown terminal. They feel the sun painting them California gold and Hollywood silver. Their profiles shine. Their eyes gleam with anticipation as they

1

climb into a taxi for Hollywood. There are probably still a few coins jingling in their pockets, assuring them that dinner and a cheap hotel that night will see them through till a talent scout from one of the studios spots them the next morning.

As the towering palms of Hollywood come into view, silhouetted against the Chamber of Commerce orange and ultra-violet of the afternoon sky, they imagine themselves celebrity-hosting in white tie and tails at their own private swimming pool atop their own private Hollywood hill within just a few short weeks.

Passing the Pantages, the Egyptian and Chinese theatres they notice with disappointment that those theatres whose names they've read in so many fan magazines look like plain old hometown movie houses with hot dog stands on one side and hock shops on the other, in one of the seediest city sections they've ever passed through.

Hollywood and Vine---the mecca they've dreamed of since fan magazine perusing in their teens---is actually no more than traffic lights, cars, and tired, lost-looking people waiting for buses or holding their hands out begging. All the Hollywood buildings look old and tired rather than shiny and golden like in the fan magazines.

Most don't even start cold sweating yet when, getting out of the cab at a Hollywood backstreet address, their chauffeured limousine turns into a plain yellow cab with its driver's hand out for some of those last coins they're brought in their pocket.

The first real shock comes when, alone in some desolate little hotel room, with the map of Los Angeles spread out on the bed, they discover that Universal City, Studio City, Culver City, Burbank and other studio locations *actually are* cities after all, not even within walking distance of Hollywood and Vine! Without a car, and with no money for a lot of bus fare, "Hollywood" is still a million light years away as it pertains to their dreams of overnight stardom.

All of a sudden the sparkle and searchlights go off, and Hollywood becomes a shabby little hotel room with street noises flooding in at the window and a giant "Rent Payable in Advance; Checkout Time 11:00AM" sign on the inside of the door to remind them that tomorrow...that day when they were supposed to be "discovered"...has already turned sour.

The first few tomorrows in Hollywood heap one disillusionment on top of another. Studios, within a day's walk or several hours of hitchhiking, all have big gates and studio security guards at their entrances. Their walls are high and nothing can be seen through them. Hollywood itself is just a small town made up of used car lots, dime stores, hot dog stands, apartment buildings and small houses. It's not nearly as attractive or even as clean as the hometown freshly left behind to come to Shangri La. Hollywood hasn't been those glamourous film lots and those golden spas pictured in old fan magazines for many years, and the places "where the stars all go" either don't see any stars anymore or have actually---like the old Brown Derby, Ciro's, the Copacabana and other former "star hangouts"--

2

-been torn down or changed to other uses.

Those places that advertise that the stars still hang out there are now just tourist traps for the most part, living off the reputations they gained in the twenties and thirties. The stars of today have moved away to "private membership clubs" that some of them own and operate as tax writeoffs, leaving behind only their pictures on the walls of the old hangouts for tourists to gawp at and write lies about to folks back home.

"Hollywood", as fan magazines still call it, once applied to the small area centered around Hollywood and Vine, in the early days when most of the studios were located nearby and the area streets were truly boulevards of the stars. The Brown Derby and a few other places were truly the centers of everything. The Rolls Royces climbed just a few short hill streets from the studios to the palatial homes in the Hollywood Hills which have long since been torn down and replaced with high-rise condominiums and supermarkets or now---with their windows out and their lawns weed-buried---usually house transients for the nights that interrupt and punctuate those unfortunates' daytimes of pandering for handouts on Hollywood Boulevard.

The Avenue of The Stars---and that's its official name---is now located far out west toward the ocean in Century City, nextdoor to 20th Century-Fox Studios. Universal City Studios are in North Hollywood. Burbank Studios, where Warners and Columbia and many other production companies are located, is in Burbank. Metro-Goldwyn-Mayer is far southwest in Culver City. Paramount is still in Hollywood thus far, at Gower and Melrose...but it's the only film studio still occupying the same lot down through the years in one strictly "Hollywood" location.

The television networks' studios too are scattered over the horizon in all directions. Fox Channel is actually right in Hollywood, at Sunset and Gordon, and CBS Television is the closest to Hollywood, on Beverly Boulevard at Fairfax, just over the border into Los Angeles. ABC Television tapes most of its programs far over on Prospect in a low-rent housing district. NBC Television is far out in Burbank, around the corner from Disney Studios.

The stars, with few exceptions, haven't lived in Hollywood for years. The word "Hollywood" made it the first stop and starting out place for many, but as soon as their careers made it possible they acquired gate-enclosed estates in exclusive and gate-guarded Bel Air, easily a half-hour or an hour's drive from Hollywood. And the Hollywood to which a million fanatically optimistic midwest malcontents, disillusioned Broadway attempters and egomaniacs of all varieties migrate each year has become a small "border town" catering to its specialized daily menu of tourists and transients. The fan magazine photos datelined "Hollywood" aren't really taken there anymore.

To an actor, though---in spite of all these discouraging current day realities, Hollywood is still the "status" address from which to write the folks back home and a first settling place, because of the town's name, from which business can be conducted and a career started in one of the quite low rent apartments there---with a certain amount of diligent effort and some luck. If Hollywood represents anything other than a place to start a long, hard trip that in the end may or may not bring you success and happiness, don't come to Hollywood.

Very few stars are "made overnight" these days by being discovered on stools in drugstores (like the Lana Turner legend) or driving a truck (like the late Rock Hudson) or pumping gas on the corner next to one of the studio lots. Very seldom these days does that "talent scout" who zooms in at the curb, jumps out and hands you his phone number and promises you the moon, turn out to be a talent scout after all. Talent scouts, too, have disappeared, since no studios maintain contract players anymore. Those few still building contract player stars until recent years found them through agents and managers for the most part.

Even the studios that once maintained ultra-lavish Babylons inside their high gates have more recently been taught by young television upstarts (who now chair most of their Boards of Directors) that it wasn't ever necessary to waste all that money and go bankrupt so often. Since the advent of television filming in Hollywood most of the old studios...once giants of lavish pomp, splendor and money-wasting...have come to grips with the realities which determine the operations of the television production companies that have taken over the major portions of their acreages.

No longer are talentless "overnight sex symbols" pampered through thirty-nine takes of expensive studio sound stage and union crew time. (That actually happened in the first film job of one of those mentioned earlier.) No longer do they build museum-size dressing rooms for stars with private zoos for their pets and running champagne at nearly every tap. (That's what Gloria Swanson had in her heydey.) Most of the great grandaddies of Hollywood's "glamour days" have passed on or retired, and their sons and nephews and the television producers who dominate their lots now really pinch space, time, money and personnel instead of wasting them.

Logistics is the word now. Budget. Efficiency. Schedule. There's no time for dream-indulging in the stepped-up maelstrom of television series production. Even the major film companies...now mostly landlords and second-class citizens on their own lots...have caught on.

There's little market currently for the pretty girl or handsome fellow who has nothing but looks to offer. There's too much at stake, and too many bank financing eyes watching over everybody's shoulders. Even the talent searchings have turned more to workshops, coaching establishments, small Hollywood-area theatres and reputable agents for what used to be called "studio talent scouting".

Even the casting directors now have little time in their own rat race for seeing newcomers in those once popular but often time-wasting "general interviews"....unless a few promising newcomers are forced upon

4

them by agents with top clout on the lots.

Most casting dirctors are now actually "independent", simply because the studios don't keep them on salary long between pictures or television series shooting cycles and they too have to sweat the job market much of the time. Those who most feel the pinch of having no job security and the need for added income...which includes most of them...advertise themselves as teachers of acting, whether they're qualified or not. or charge exorbitant fees for attending "showcases" where actors must pay to appear in audition scenes, hoping to have their talents recognized by those casting people earning between $200 and $300 for just being there to watch. In some cases they're the same casting people who once watched such scene presentations in their offices during working hours, for nothing, as part of their jobs.

"Producers" and "agents" who used to walk up to pretty girls or handsome fellows from the Midwest on streetcorners and wave their powerful "instant star" wands and their private, late night telephone numbers at them would now be laughed out of the business quickly for what they really are. Even those agents who in earlier years got by with buying and selling "special services" to industry bigwigs have been forced into going straight and dealing with real talent and known commodities most of the time.

It's an investors' market now, run by banks which loan production budget money to companies at high interest if they have faith in the drawing power of the stars who've been committed out front to do their pictures. Some production companies still make money if they get lucky, but the time is so long between start of production and finishing shooting, editing and ultimate releasing of pictures that the interest on those huge bank loans coming due regularly along the long haul of pre-production, production and post-production totals up to the point that budgets are increased tenfold for most companies. There are simply too many eyes on the pot of film production now for any of the old-time nonsense!

So...face it. Just *wanting* to be an actor won't cut it anymore. Everybody back home in the little town you're coming from has at least thought they'd like to become an actor. Like you perhaps, every time they've walked out of a movie theatre they've thought they could have done as good a job as that fellow or that girl on the screen they've just watched. Almost *everybody, everywhere,* has daydreamed about an acting career at one time or another!

Unless you've done at least something to prepare yourself for becoming an actor, and are willing to do the hard work to become an increasingly better one, you're no better off and stand no better chance than the cab driver who drops you off at your little first night hotel here---who was probably brought here years earlier by the same dream, or the waitress who serves you your breakfast---and shows her profile and proportions just in case you may be somebody yourself, or the tired desk clerk who hands you your room key---who himself probably tried for a while many years back, then gave up, but stayed in Hollywood simply because he too "couldn't go home a failure".

Don't come to Hollywood unless you've decided that you _are_ an actor, and that you _have to come here_ simply because this is where the industry is, where the jobs are.

Even if it's only community theatre you've been able to do, that's better than nothing, and perhaps all you could find back home. Or college theatre. There are some fine college drama departments across the country that yearly turn out actors who at least know they _have to be actors and nothing else._ And there are bound to be summer theatres somewhere near you, wherever you live, where you can either pay your own way as an apprentice or work in some capacity for room and board while getting a little early experience---even if most of it is backstage, on the chance that you may get one or two small roles during the summer season in support of a star or two and find out whether you're laughed back to the farm or given a glimmer of encouragement by people who know the difference between talent and ego-gratification.

And there's always New York, where there are some good acting coaches, Off and Off Off Broadway productions where you can flex your creative muscles in public either for pay or for free, and all kinds of opportunities for your talent to acquire some technique and for your personality to acquire more professional polish.

Still better---from the standpoint of a beginning toward a film career, is to not overlook the possibility of doing "bit roles" or trying for at least "extra" work in location films---those films of Hollywood production companies that go _evrywhere_ to film---to both the smallest back country villages in this country and everywhere else in the world.

Almost every state has one, two or several talent agencies and even one or more casting directors---usually with their offices in the states' larger cities---who are contacted by Hollywood film companies when they're scouting locations for filming in even the most improbable, out of the way, small villages and hamlets. Such location filming is done year round and, although the stars and important role players are brought from Hollywood, there are usually many small "bit" roles of one or a few lines left to be cast locally.

When the producer and/or director are ready to see local actors for some of those small roles, the casting director (or on occasion the talent agencies) will call local actors they know who seem right for each role. The actors are interviewed initially and a few are singled out for "callbacks" (second interviews for final choosing among the standout contenders for the roles). Generally, these roles pay what's called "SAG minimum" or "scale"...which at this book's publication time is over $400 for each day worked, which isn't a bad day's pay for so little work!

You shouldn't be afraid to try for these "location filming" roles. They're quite unchallenging, with just a few speeches if any, and one or two of them could be yours if you simply "look right". If you've read for a casting director or a talent agent and been considered by them to have enough talent, you might well be called in for one of these golden opportunities to obtain a first acting job, modest though it be---and for pay!

In addition to perhaps nine or ten of those "bit" roles remaining to be cast locally, there are usually many *Extras* hired at between $40 and $60 a day as "background" on city streets, in stores, at playgrounds or town meetings, in offices, etc. Sometimes these "townspeople" are hired for several days, even weeks, because they're established as being residents who should appear waltking through or standing around in many scenes.

You certainly could check your state's larger cities' phone books for listings of "Talent Agencies" or "Theatrical Agencies" and make appointments. Have a photo of yourself printed in black and white, glossy, 8x10 form and supply it, with your contacting information, to each such agency, telling them you'd like to be called for any "extra" opportunities at least. If you feel you're already a good actor, ask them to call you to try for some "bit" roles...but don't rule out being called for "extra" work as well.

Should you eventually get even a one-speech role in one of those Hollywood films that are shot under Screen Actors Guild contract (and all with stars in their casts are), you can then join the Screen Actors Guild immediately. In most states it costs far less to join the union there than it would later in Hollywood, and you'd arrive in Hollywood someday with your Screen Actors Guild Membership card already in hand!

Once you're a SAG Member, you stand still better chances to be cast in location filming, because your SAG card tells directors and producers that you're "a professional". In addition, you'd have experience on actual film location sets, watching how everything's done and becoming familiar with procedures and film set terminology. You'd have valuable foreknowledge of what it's all about, and you'd be able to enter each role's information on a growing resume even before coming to Hollywood when the time seems right.

Consider these three examples: Two actresses and one actor, totally new but with some expert film training in acting classes taught by a former Hollywood acting coach who had moved to their city and established acting classes there, were called for interviews for three of the tiny "bit" roles in the first episode of a television series preparing to film there. All three were cast in what are called "recurring roles" (roles that are brought back in a number of series episodes). They kept working in episode after episode for the run of the location filming! Such unexpected windfalls happen regularly, and they can happen right nextdoor to your own hometown area if you go looking for them.

Bottom line: To start on any decent level at all in Hollywood short of begging for the kind of "handouts" and "help" that usually come with some kind of price tag, you're expected to *already be* an actor before you come. Behind every door you're able to get through there's going to be somebody asking "What have you done?" Do yourself a favor...have some answer other than "Nothing."

And don't come to Hollywood unless you have enough determination to take rejection after rejection; enough maturity to keep your goals in mind in spite of the many distractions; enough objectivity to know that you still have a lot to learn (about film, at least, even if you're experienced in theatre); enough intelligence to avoid some of the human quicksands that abound here; enough money in your own or somebody else's available bank account to buy a car upon arrival if you can't drive one to Hollywood in the first place; the ability to pay your own way for a length of time; and if possible some other ability or skill which will enable you to get a job so you can continue to live here long enough to complete your preparation, get your bearings, give somebody a chance to see your work and make the contacts that will help you get started.

And *don't* think you can effectively "give Hollywood a six month try", as some newcomers do. It never works. Any respectable talent agent in Hollywood would laugh you out of the office if they hear this. If you're coming to Hollywood, fine...come. But plan to stay if you do.

Come equipped with at least those home town, college or other *reviews* of your acting performances very neatly pasted up in a book, along with any pictures you have of actual productions you were in (especially any that involve professionals in their casts). Bring any *letters of referral* and introduction you can get to people in the industry, and the *telephone numbers of friends of friends* here who might be willing to help you get settled and make some first contacts. Bring every stitch of *wardrobe* you can lay your hands on before coming. Bring your *Social Security card*, so you can get a parttime job without delay. Carry plenty of *insurance* on the car you bring. Freeways are notorious and it's easy to have accidents when you're confused about offramps when you're first arrived. Bring *travelers' cheques* enough to set up your first checking account here...because Hollywood is a little wary of out-of-town checks and the bank might put a hold on that big check from Dad, leaving you without funds for a few days. Another reason for travelers' cheques is that there will be down-and-outers watching where you carry your wallet or purse.

And pack enough faith and hope for what may turn out to be a very long siege before things start to break for you.

In short, don't come to Hollywood because you think you'd *like to be* an actor. Come because *you already are* one. Recognize, too, that you're still not a *film* actor and will have to learn how to work before the camera here in the film production center where people know how to teach film acting technique...*before* you start looking for agents or acting jobs and spinning your wheels.

Those who come with nothing but shiny dreams and optimism---with no prior background, without the basics outlined above to enable them to stay long enough for something to start----and when they get here fail to take all or most of these sensible "beginning" steps----stand little chance of causing anything to happen for themselves.

Don't come to Hollywood expecting any miracles! There's enough blood on Hollywood sidewalks already.

Chapter Two

When The Plane Lands...
You're Just Taking Off!

If you really feel you're ready, let nothing you dismay. Buy the plane or bus ticket or take a long term lease on the family's second car and drive, which is better when you get here and find you need one to get around. Long ago swarms of actors migrated here via their thumbs on highways, but watch your television newscasts and you'll decide that's no longer the way to go. However you come, getting here is the easiest part.

The late Sir Cedric Hardwicke, before his death, wrote a letter article which was partially reprinted in *Variety* some years ago, saying that in his early days in England it was enough to just be a good actor, but during his later years in Hollywood he had found that an actor must be a business executive...to handle the details of his career; a bit of a cheat...to cope with taxes; a check-grabber in restaurants...to appear successful whether successful or not; a glib raconteur and after-dinner speaker with all of *Joe*

Miller's Joke Book at his fingertips...to be invited more than once to important social gatherings; an aspirin or reducing diet salesman on television...to pay rent and eat when between engagements; enough of a lothario to keep his name in gossip columns and on everybody's tongue...so producers and casting people would think of him when roles come up.

If you have some latent talents and aptitudes in these areas, this book may prove very helpful to you.

GETTING AROUND

First thing...even while you're reading this chapter, whether you're already here or not...is to somehow get hold of *a map of Greater Los Angeles!* Not just Hollywood...Greater Los Angeles! The movie colony is just that...a colony. While "Hollywood" is its imaginary monarchy, the empire and its colonies stretch across a bunch of pretty vast provinces called cities that together make up what's called a megalopolis.

Santa Monica Boulevard extends from downtown Los Angeles all the way to the Pacific ocean. That fabled boulevard, Sunset, starts far east of Hollywood and stretches westward through Echo Park, Hollywood, West Hollywood, Beverly Hills, Century City, Westwood, Brentwood, Bel Air and West Los Angeles to far out past the Pacific Palisades almost to the gateway of Malibu. Be smart. Get a map.

WHERE TO LIVE

There's no use kidding ourselves...no matter what you read in this book, you'll probably opt to start off living somewhere in Hollywood itself, like every other newcomer does. It's the magic city name. It's where the picture postcards have to be sent from for impact on the family and neighbors back home. Who back home has ever heard of Brentwood or Westwood, Pacific Palisades or Bel Air...where most of the wealthy stars live now? So get that little apartment in a Hollywood back street. Your heart's probably set on it. It's as good a place as any to start from.

From a rent standpoint, Hollywood isn't a bad idea anyhow. For years now it's been one of the "low rent" districts, but you don't have to tell folks back home that.

Expect to pay at least four hundred dollars a month or more if you're really particular, but you can pay much less if you'll settle for comfort without any show at all. Only the wealthy arrivals should plan on Beverly Hills, Brentwood or Malibu. Others with slimmer purses should walk the back streets of Hollywood, North Hollywood, Burbank, Studio City or parts of Sherman Oaks even, checking out not only the "For Rent" and "For Lease" places but also the little cottage courts where the rents are usually pretty modest. Be careful of Encino, Tarzana, Woodland Hills and other West Valley areas. They're farther away from all studios and much more expensive anyhow.

At least in the first above mentioned cities for slimmer purses you're closest to the main hub of studio locations; rent is as high or as low as you want---varying from block to block usually; the coaching establishment you'll need to check yourself into is probably nearly; many casting directors and agents are close by at the end of their busy day and therefore might come to see you in small theatre productions in your area once you get started; and you're in the *"actors' community"* ---where you can often pick up gossip and casting information from the new friends and neighbors around you there. Also, you'll be saving gas money.

More specifically, in <u>Hollywood</u> try the backstreets south of Sunset Boulevard all the way down to Beverly Boulevard; from Virgil Avenue all the way west to about Doheny (where Beverly Hills and high rents start).   Some nice, clean, small residential hotels and motels are available in those areas and you might want to roost there at least temporarily while you look around. Or try north of Hollywood Boulevard from Vermont Avenue on the east to Laurel Canyon on the west. If you choose Central Hollywood in that particular area, however, lock your door securely at night and be careful wandering around after dark. It's the roosting place for a lot of prostitutes and hustlers and other temporarily hungry folks.

Eating places abound in the Hollywood area, from starvation to feast level, and at like prices. After all, it's a tourist haven area.

In *North Hollywood* (which is closer to Burbank Studios, Universal, Columbia, Disney, NBC and CBS-Fox Studio Center), there are more single family dwellings and fewer transient residences like apartment buildings of the low rent kind. If your taste runs to having your own house immediately they're there in profusion and at fairly affordable rents. Motels dot the main avenues such as Ventura Boualevard, Lankershim Boulevard, Cahuenga Boulevard, Tujunga and other boulevards and avenues in that neighborhood. Some are high rental; some are fairly low.

Likewise, <u>Burbank</u> and <u>Studio City</u> are desirable and close-in locations for starting out. Again, there are plenty of motels and single family houses and enough apartments with "For Rent" signs out most of the time charging fair rents in the main.

CAREER AIDS YOU'LL NEED IMMEDIATELY

You can't even begin to do anything without some form of telephone service. If you're hard pressed, at least sign on with a *Telephone Answering Service*. It will cost anywhere from $5.00 a month up to have such a service receive your calls on their board after you've given that number out for contacting you and leaving messages for you. With this kind of service you have to call in regularly to pick up any messages left for you. Most of these services have higher rates escalating upward with each level of service provided, such as locating you at other numbers or your home, 24-hour pickup of your private home phone, call-forwarding, wake-up calls, etc.

If you can afford it immediately, have a phone installed in your apartment or house. You'll have to pay a one-time, quite heavy deposit in this notoriously transient community at the time of installation, and you'll still need to have either an *Answering Service* or an *Answering Machine* attached to your line. The answering service will run anywhere from $30 a month upward. It will make you sound important to callers, if that matters to you. It's definitely the classiest way to begin if you can afford the extra cost. To add even more appearance of "being somebody" you might consider a *Paging Setup*. There are several manners of incorporating this into your phone hookup to the outer world.

On the other hand, there are fine answering machines which you can easily hook up to your own telephone at home for recording of messages. The minimum cost at the time of this book's preparation, for anything worth having, is about $99.00. A word to the wise, however: If you're recording your own message on your own phone pick-up machine, don't be "cutesy-pie" clever with your message. Busy industry people become impatient with the "off the wall", tongue in cheek, cute recorded hellos and often hang up rather than listen to rock music or your Jimmy Stewart imitation before they can leave their short, businesslike message.

As mentioned earlier, you'll delfinitly need *A Car!* If you can't borrow one of your family's cars indefinitely till you can afford your own, the Hollywood and Los Angeles streets swarm with fairly low-priced transportation car lots where you can pick up a $100 piece of junk that may or may not see another day or a good, fairly new used car costing perhaps several thousand dollars less than it did new. If your credit's excellent you may be able to lease a nice get-around car from one of the leasing and lease-to-purchase lots. In any event, plan somehow to have or get something to get around in. It's a bunch of miles for the walker to MGM and 20th Century-Fox from Central Hollywood.

Don't even consider picking up the morning or evening paper and starting to look for either acting jobs or acting study availabilities! The Classified Sections of the dailies are filled with misleading ads that offer blue sky come-ons for the gullible...some advertising "Casting!" which turn out to be ripoff schools of the assembly line type which offer nothing but receipts for your money every week or month and seats where you can sit among a lot of others who've fallen for the same ad hook. Some offer "Screen Tests!" but are in reality small offices where they impress you with videotape equipment, have you tape whatever kind of monologue you want, tell you they're considering you for an important role in something, then call back later (after taping some other gullible patsy's "test" right over yours) to say that before they can consider you for that juicy starring role you'll need to take some "coaching" from their coach.

Really, it's disgraceful how many "acting study" ripoff programs there are that are out for the easy mark's money. There have even been two that advertised in bold print that they offered GI Bill training and Government Student Loans; then so disappointed the registrants that those people quickly left but the teaching organizaion kept receiving and cashing those

Government checks long after the students for whom the Government was paying had departed. Later both organizations got into trouble with the Attorney General for doing it but somehow managed to avoid going to jail and in one case---a location on Wilshire Boulevard---got right back into the same Government-supported program and is still pulling its scams today.

The other of the two was the scene of the shooting murder of the head of the organization by a former student who resented being taken and one day simply walked into the organization's office with his gun. Nobody but the taxpayer is against the Government underwriting acting study for deserving people, but you should investigate such a program thoroughly before you plunk out Uncle Sam's money and your own time. Read the contract they'll hand you---a contract to enable them to start collecting your benefits....every word of it!

There are many excellent places for studying acting for film and television. You'll want to start acting study for film and television almost as soon as you arrive in Hollywood. Accept as a rule of thumb that the ones you should consider never advertise in the daily newspapers' Classified Sections. That kind of advertising is for suckers. A scad of good ones do advertise, though, in the pages of the weekly _Drama-Logue_, the actors' legitimate newspaper. The problem is that the good coaches' ads appear side by side with so many other ads that it's devilishly hard to choose which ones to even investigate. At least most of those advertising in _Drama-Logue_ aren't after the "easy marks" among beginning actors like the two organizations mentioned above. These folks offer their coaching and teaching to actors and actresses of all professional levels from Beginning to Intermediate to Advanced, rather than to innocent prey for quick dollars.

The best source we know of at the present time for learning of acting study programs, finding out about their coaches and teachers and the reputation of their organizations, is the Acting World Books publication, _"The Hollywood Acting Coaches And Teachers Directory"_. which costs $12.50, is published quarterly (Spring, Summer, Fall and Winter editions) with constant updating, and which is available at most Hollywood actors' bookshops or by mail order direct from Acting World Books, P. O. Box 3044, Hollywood, CA 90078. In this publication you'll find the coaches' biographies and as complete details about their teaching programs as is possible.

Rather than "flying blind" from the start and trying to pull an acting job miracle out of the hat, you should, out of fairness to any future hopes for a meaningful future for yourself, sign on quickly with a reputable acting teacher or coach. The two are the same, by the way, with some preferring the first label while some prefer the other.

Even if you have a good theatre background from somewhere (even New York), remember that many of New York's finest legitimate theatre names have run back to New York after finding out they didn't understand film acting's technical requirements.

Once you're with a good coach, his or her help and knowledge and contacts may---if you deserve them---be doled out to you and you'll learn the things you need to know before actually starting and making mistakes.

So...you should include in your arrival budget the cost of at least a decent period of being coached in film acting. A later chapter will be devoted to finding the right place to study. Its searching out and selecting is not an easy process for the newly arrived and uninformed.

THE NON-CAREER BUSINESS DETAILS

The business side of living anywhere, Hollywood and California being no exception, must get under way immediately. You've just "migrated". Get the details you'll need for just plain *living* organized before you start trying to spread your wings.

Pick up a *Tax Record Book* someplace. The "venture capital" you're spending in starting out in Hollywood won't be tax deductible until some income is realized from your profession, but what if you're one of the lucky ones and through some fluke of luck start actually working as an actor during the current fiscal or calendar year? If you should make even the tiniest amount of money *as an actor* during the year you'll be able to charge off much of what's been spent in relocating and equipping your "business" (acting). If you've already earned money *as an actor* before coming then it's even better. Your expenses will need to have been recorded and the receipts and sales slips held onto, just in case, toward the filing of *an actor's tax return*, with its marvelous spectrum of allowable deducions. Appropriate tax record and daily expense books that can fit the actor's needs are available in many drugstores and stationery stores in Hollywood.

Your *Out of State Driver's License* is okay for the first eleven days only, if you play by the rules. Either then, or as soon as you go to work at any job of any kind (if it should be sooner than the eleven days) you must apply for a *California Driver's License*. The Department of Motor Vehicles maintains an office for this purpose (and for registering that cheap car you've just bought or brought with you), at 803 North Cole Avenue (at Waring Avenue, below Santa Monica Boulevard) in the south edge of Central Hollywood.

If you're eligible for *Unemployment Insurance* from an out-of-state source, go to the Department of Employment (Human Resources Department is the classier new title) for the area in which you're setting up housekeeping. There's the usual waiting period before receipt of your benefits, so go there immediately if you do qualify. The right office for your area is listed in the Yellow Pages, in the Government pages.

Believe it or not, you're likely to glimpse your first movie star or very familiar film actor face there. They stand in line all around you there, quite unabashedly...not because they're poor and need the money badly, but because they know they've paid plenty (more than most, by average) into the coffers of the State when they've worked---perhaps just last week they were costarring or doing a featured role in a picture), so some feel they should certainly collect even this "cigarette money" when they're again between jobs. It's surprising how many at least recognizable faces you can

14

see in these lines if you look around. You may not know their names, bu you know you've seen them in films or on television.

If you're not entitled to unemployment insurance---because you left that job back home in an emotional huff, threatening to get even by becoming a movie star, and if you don't have a private gold mine constantly feeding your checking account, *get a job*! Any kind. Nights might be best, if you can get one of the coveted waiter jobs (which fit actors' needs nicely, therefore are hard to get anywhere in the Greater Los Angeles Area) or a nighttime taxi job...so your daytimes can be free to start things going professionally. Or you might opt to start with nighttime acting classes, in which event a daytime job is the answer for the first period.

Part-time work is plentiful in Los Angeles just as it is in any other industrialized, commercial, major market and career center...if you have some of the skills which are most in demand. Look them up in the Yellow Pages of the Telephone Directory. Wordprocessors, secretaries, bookkeepers and all other manner of office jobs are especially welcome at these Temporary Employment agencies.

You'd need to register, be tested and accepted for representation by the agency and then be on call for assignments. Such agencies collect paychecks from the employing companies, then pay you what you've agreed to accept when you registered, regardless of how much they can get for your services...and you'll seldom know how much that is. What you get is of course substantially less than they receive, but it's handy and easy as jobs go, and there's no long-term obligation or commitment. You can beg off from accepting jobs when you have "actor" things going.

Pick up a *Loose Leaf Notebook (standard size)* and plenty of filler paper and index sheets. The reason for the "standard size" suggestion, rather than a small pocket size one which many actors mistakenly start with, is that many of the union regulations, casting information, organization listings and other papers which you'll be obtaining for your use are that size and many of them are three-hole-punched for convenience.

Start a record in this notebook of people, places, things of all kinds involved with the profession...perhaps all West Coast theatres, coaching establishments, photographers for the profession, production company locations and personnel, casting offices, talent agencies, all kinds of professional information pamphlets, etc. Who knows, at dinner tonight you may accidentally meet a casting director, an agent, a producer, a writer, or even the secretary of somebody very important, and your "*Information Book*" will get its first entry. He or she will also belong on the *Mailing List* you'll also start putting together---in the same notebook---for occasional follow-up purposes as you go forward.

If you haven't already picked them up, the best advise we can give you is to immediately pick up from one of the actors' bookstores or newsstands that handle them the two publications, *The Agencies---What The Actor Needs To Know* and *The Hollywood Acting Coaches And Teachers Directory*. Both of these periodically updated publications are from Acting

World Books. Already having the book you're reading right now, you won't need to pick up the six-book *Seminars To Go Series* of publications from Acting World Books which includes *"How To Get, Work With and Keep The Best Agent For You"*, *"Increasing Your Success Ratio In Interviews And Readings For Roles"*, *"The Film Actor's Career Building Stepladder"*, *"The Film Job, Step By Step---Before, During, After"*, *"Self Promotion, Self Publicizing, Self Advertising For The Actor"* and *"Audition Tapes, Audition Scenes And Showcasing"*...since most of the information contained in those six books is included in the book in your hand.

It's best that you get all of these "business" details under way immediately. It will save you time and many problems later.

Too many young people drop everything suddenly when the whim strikes them to try Hollywood. Too many haven't done any research or study of the conditions they'll be encountering. Too many know little or nothing about the film industry. Too many may not have any kind of business or even blue collar labor background or skills to fall back on when they've exhausted the pennies they thought would be enough to bring with them. Many of these folks are headed for trouble or quick disillusionment and a call to Dad or Mom for bus money to come home, or bail money because they've joined the panderers and hustlers on Hollywood Boulevard in order to stay here.

To eat, have a place to sleep, a car to get around in and money to get by on it's usually necessary to have some kind of job. To expect an *acting* job within the immediately foreseeable future is sheer self delusion. Be one of the smart ones. You'll be here longer.

Chapter Three

Don't Waste Time
Stargazing!...

There's no getting away from the fact that the first few days in Hollywood will be spent by most newcomers buying those *"Maps To The Stars' Homes"* (which are available on many streetcorners in Hollywood for the tourists) and driving around endlessly in the hills trying to peek over high hedges or beyond tree-hidden driveways to get first glimpses at how the stars live or perhaps even actually see a star or two as well. It's really not worth the bother. Those maps are usually long outdated; the stars can't afford to stand out in their front yards for you to gawk at; you'd have to set up camp for a long time at the electronic gate of your favorite to catch even a fleeting glimpse of him or her as the shaded-glass limo windows of their car whisk past you.

And forget about hoping to meet those actors and actresses who are busy all the time. Maybe you didn't know that the people who either have television starring roles or who go immediately from one major motion picture to the next usually get up about 5:00 AM and whisk off to the studio or some location in the early dawn for a 6:00 AM or 6:30 AM "call" on the set; that they seldom see the daylight except from in front of a camera; that they get off from shooting usually well after sundown...sometimes much, much later at night; that they have dinner anytime between 8:00 PM and midnight; and that they have to study the next day's lines till they fall asleep.

On weekends you might see the ones who aren't currently busy, ever so briefly, at one of the celebrity watering places, but not even then if they have a heavy day coming up the following Monday. They're probably---even on weekends---studying lines at home, between magazine interviews, publicity appearances, hair stylists' appointments, business conferences with agents and managers and accountants and producers and press agents and directors. The last place you'll find them is in a well known "stars' hangout" heavily publicized in fan magazines, where they would too often be jostled by opportunists and tourists demanding their autographs while they're trying to eat their dinners before they get cold.   When   they're between engagements you might catch one or two shopping along a main stem street in Beverly Hills---if their maid or valet doesn't have to do their shopping to enable them to avoid the fans and sycophants who follow them waiting to pounce on them once they're recognized. They might be in the Polo Lounge or the Lanai Room at the Beverly Hills Hotel visiting with another star from out of town, or having dinner out (oh, rare occasion!) in the dining room of the exclusive Bel Air, Beverly Hills or Beverly-Wilshire Hotel. Those who don't have permanent residences here sometimes stop at the Sunset-Marquis, Le Mondrian, the Beverly Hilton, the Chateau Marmont or at one of the larger hotels which specifically cater to stars and celebrities by offering well nigh impenetrable fortifications of private, secret entryways and security guards.

It might surprise you to learn that some of the most likely places for bumping into some stars are the leading "workshops", where they can sometimes be found polishing their craft still further on their nights or days off. There are some of these study programs where a star or two might go to prepare and perform---for their workshop peers and the noted coaches with whom they're working---those roles that they wouldn't normally be cast in, or to simply continue growth activities among friends.

Others who aren't continuing their studies sometimes hang out in some of the eating and drinking places where they can hobnob with people they know and enjoy being with...but they're usually tucked away out of sight of main rooms, even there, to avoid hassling. Until you're one of the established elite, what you'll find in these "actor hangouts" is more probably just a lot of unknown actors there to table-hop and exchange tips and gossip and contact-importune in every manner possible. Those same "actor hangout" actors are often there hoping to run into some important person who can do something for them.

Be one of the smart ones. Spend your evenings in workshops or acting classes in order to grow, or stay at home watching the current television series, just in case you get lucky with an interview for a role on one of them at some point.

Chapter Four

Watch Out For
The Newcomer Traps!...

The first and most obvious scam-trap a newcomer to Hollywood may fall for is the *"Free Screen Test"* ad with those words prominent at the top of the ad or in heavy bold type at the top of a flyer dropped along several "dream street" boulevards.

Long ago a screen test meant the magic door...being "discovered" and whisked off to a contract player magic carpet kingdom. The fan magazines were full of those stories...some of them at that earlier time quite true. Not so anymore. Nowadays it simply means that you've picked up a flyer somewhere or read those words in a Want Ad column; rushed to the address given; were shoved in front of a videotape camera; were told afterward in hushed tones that you are ideal star material; and were offered the opportunity to star in an upcoming film or pilot...*if* you were willing to pay a paltry amount (anywhere from a few thousand dollars to whatever amount they could smell in your checkbook) for some "preparation" in their acting classes. Unfortunately, there are still some newcomers who can't pass up such a golden opporunity and are ripe for the taking.

Actual screen tests...the genuine article...used to be used after someone was talent-scouted somewhere, so that the studio could see them on film and judge their potential. If they got contracts afterward their classes were furnished by the studio in excellent training programs; they began in small roles and were swiftly elevated into starring roles to justify their continuing paychecks from the studio. Those honest screen tests are no more.

However, the magic contained in the *"Screen Test"* tabel still impacts upon the minds of the fresh arrivals from small towns who don't know any better and want to believe. That label is unequalled by any other words, and the quick buck operators know that.

Even some unscrupulous acting workshops use those magic words as sure come-on lures. If they do, it probably means that they simply have videotape equipment and will put you in front of a camera, tape you doing or saying a few things, then tell you that "With their training..." I'm sure you get the general idea.

Occasionally there surfaces another *"Video Casting Service"* of the kind that quite soon fall under the City Attorney's investigation and get out of town with large bank accounts just before they're caught. These shysters usually tape you and promise that your tape will be shown to casting people for roles. Of course you must pay them...usually between $100 (low for most) and $350 (about average) to be taped and supposedly shown. When lawyers and State offices begin calling they move and change their names and get going again in new cities in the Los Angeles vicinity. These operations are scarcer now, but one or two pop up from time to time. Beware!

Similarly, those acting schols which advertise that you can *"Work while you learn"* should be shied away from just as determinedly because of the obvious "sucker bait" approach they employ. A catchphrase like *"Casting!"* or *"Now Casting!"* usually appears at the top of their ads in the Los Angeles Times and Herald-Examiner Classified Ads. *"All Types!"*, they also proclaim...just in case you're between 8 and 80 and have some cash in your pocket. Don't fall for any of this garbage.

There are often ads in those same columns for *"Non-Union Extra Work"*. If you answer such an ad you'll find that there's a $200 or larger fee for registering, which amount is promised you in such work over a period. You may in fact receive enough paying extra work through such an organization to pay back your investment, since they're usually cagey enough to try to avoid legal action. Some actually do try to get you such work...for the latter reason only. Why not? They have your $200-$300, and when you do manage to walk in the background of a shot on a film set you're paid by the producers, not the company that advertised and rooked you in. You could probably do just as well on your own if you want to seek extra work.

There are also worthless *Agencies...Talent Agencies...Modeling Agencies, etc.*, that aren't franchised by the Screen Actors Guild and can't represent you for films at all! They'll probably ask for money out front to "represent you".   Such agencies are often quite within the law...as *employment* agencies at least.   It's when they advertise to represent *actors*...for *film, television, commercials*, etc. (all requiring union membership of the actor and contract negotiation by agencies franchised by the Screen Actors Guild) that they're on the wrong side of the tracks for any thinking actor.   Unless you're a stripper, a club act, a circus clown, a rodeo performer or a Las Vegas dealer, they can't do you any good.   The minute such an agency asks for evem *one red cent* out front in return for representing you you should guess pretty surely that they're not one of the SAG-franchised agents, put in a call to the Agency Department of SAG at (213) 856-6732 and inquire about them.   If they *actually are* a SAG-franchised agency they'll be out of business in five minutes!

Anyone who promises you work in exchange for money is duping you. Be it a personal manager, an agent, a casting service, an acting coach or teacher, a producer or one of the *"We'll Help You Get An Agent"* advertisers.

This latter category of newcomer trap is a booming business! Actors know they need agents.   Both experienced professionals from star level down to bit players and new people just arrived in town know the importance of having agency representation. Top people are sought after by agencies because they promise quick and large commissions, being in demand. Similarly, players of co-star or at least established levels have little trouble getting agents to represent them.   But newcomers with no background, often not even ready to work in film, want agents too. Hundreds of them respond to those *"We'll Help You Get An Agent"* ads. Why not? By paying between $300 and $500 to a person who advertises himself or herself as a "Casting Director" or "Casting Consultant"---those words by themselves being a newcomer come-on even if there is no record of the person having ever cast anything, the naive newcomer is promised that he or she can be signed with an agency...just like that!

What the newcomer, so desperate to have agency representation, doesn't find out until later is that an agent who eagerly signs all people referred by such an agent-procurer probably has a fee-sharing arrangement with the agent-procurer as the main reason for signing all those referred.

If the agency-procurer were able to obtain---for those newcomers who feel they must resort to such a service---an agent or agents of unquestionable reputation and quality who would help them, it would be different. But statistics suggest that this is probably not possible in the first place.

Any agency worth its salt is deluged in every morning's mail and by phone calls throughout every day with requests for representation from a goodly portion of the approximately 40,000 actors needing agencies.   Many of those applying for the agents' consideration have extensive credits and good industry recognition.   An agency that eagerly signs all newcomers sent by an agency-procuring service is doing so not for any 10% commissions expected from those newcomers working at any time in the near future. That agency is probably receiving a goodly share of the $300-

$500 paid to the agency-procurer!

If an actor does employ such an agent-procuring service and later feels the referral, the resulting agency association and the agency's practices to be questionable, suspicious or worthy of complaint to proper agencies and bureaus, not only the Screen Actors Guild and the Better Business Bureau of Greater Los Angeles would be interested; also, the actor can more importantly address formal complaint to the State Labor Commissioner, Division of Labor Standards Enforcement, 525 Golden Gate Avenue, San Francisco, California 94102. That office is where all talent agent licenses are issued.

Similarly, if in order to get an agent you're required to have photographs taken by a specific photogapher or attend a certain acting study program, the agent requiring this, if franchised by the Screen Actors Guild, is violating the SAG Agency Agreement and should be reported. There is the chance (indeed, the probability) that there is a *"kickback"* operation involved....the photographer or the acting coach sharing what the actor pays them with the agent that refers the actor.

When you're new in Hollywood it's difficult to find the right person to advise you when something seems questionable...or even before that. As mentioned earlier, the first person who will know enough to give you good, sound advise will probably be your acting coach or teacher.

Getting the right coach or teacher is the best place to begin. You need an advisor, a mentor from the start...someone who knows the industry and the right manners of going about first steps as well as the things you need to know about film and television acting.

It would definitely be to your advantage to obtain the then current quarterly issue of *The Hollywood Acting Coaches And Teachers Directory*, mentioned earlier. In it you'll find not only details of most of the available programs and contact information but also in most of the listed cases the biographical information about the instructors which can help you select the teaching programs you wish to investigate first, to save time and telephoning.

It gives details of the kind of training offered, the kind of scheduling available, qualifications for entry, whether they're training programs exclusively or perhaps also offer showcasing for the industry and/or public performances. It is the best such publication available regarding Hollywood, Los Angeles and Southern California acting study programs....and usually the only one that won't be found to be out of date!

Chapter Five

Finding The Right Place
To Study Acting

The teaching profession in Hollywood, which at one time was dominated by five or six leading teachers with long established reputations, is now so glutted with new ads appearing all the time and with people beginning to teach for the first time that those seeking the best place for their continuing development are totally confused. They sometimes become victims of unqualified promoters, waste trial periods and monies paid for them, have to go looking again, and often repeat the unhappy process several times over.

First, it is impossible to tell from only a name or an organization title what is actually offered, but there are some fairly general definitions which can be trusted:

An **Acting School or Academy** is generally an institution with departments and a variety of subjects and disciplines, usually with a large staff of instructors. Such institutions often conduct their teaching in semesters rather than with ongoing classes available for entrance at any

23

time. Bearing that identifying label in its advertising usually implies that it has many different kinds of instruction in addition to acting. Often such an institution is more directed toward stage than toward film and television.

An *Acting Teacher* usually conducts private classes in his or her own private studio or in a rented space, whether for professionals only or for beginners and for intermediate levels as well.

Professional Classes usually indicates that the coach works only with professionals in private classes and is hesitant to bring any new people into classes. Some make exceptions after strict qualifying tests of some kind or where there is enough background or some union menbership to recommend consideration for entry.

Acting Coaches who advertise themselves with that title are usually teachers of reputation who also---if there is any difference at all from an "acting teacher"---often have smaller classes, allowing more individual "coaching" rather than mass teaching...perhaps about 15 attendees tops for acting technique but possibly more for scene study groups involving less intensive teaching. They often offer private coaching, and sometimes act as dialogue coaches for film and television productions. They are often consulted by established professionals for special help as well.

An *Acting Workshop* can mean anything! It may be scene study exclusively, or scene work in combination with occasional showcasing of talent, or it can be strictly technique classes for all levels, or scene study, or any number of other programmed activities combined with technique classes. It may be videotape-oriented, a fraternal group with little moderator supervision, or practically anything.

A *Videotape or On-Camera Workshop* may teach camera acting technique, or it may simply tape prepared scenes with little or no duplicating of actual filming conditions, little or no direction in terms of camera technique for the actor, and may offer little of worth. It is the kind of workshop that should be observed carefully ahead of time, since some, recognizing the actor's fascination with film acting, offer little but very poor work, poorly taped and poorly supervised, mostly catering to the ego gratification of attendees who don't know how little they're getting.

A so-called *Master Class*, very fine sounding, depends on the prestige and reputation of the person heading it. The teacher of a Master Class should have a long established prestige---as a Master Teacher---which can be easily verified. Investigate thoroughly.

A *Commercial Acting Workshop or Class* is usually conducted by either a commercial casting director or an experienced commercial actor or actress. Usually offering limited term programs of from six to twelve weeks, these workshops often have commercial agents and casting directors present at some of their sessions to either instruct on a "guest instructor" basis or to observe the work of the workshop group...at the same time scouting for talents, by the way! It's not a bit uncommon for a newer actor who's having difficulty obtaining a SAG or AFTRA card with a first job to come out of one of these sessions with a commercial and a SAG card.

A **Voice-Over Workshop** is for those who plan to specialize; who can do a number of voice-type characterizations and who enjoy the equivalent of "radio" acting. These offerings are usually ongoing, rather than term-oriented. Some even help prepare "voice tapes" for use in acquiring agency representation or for submitting to prospective employers looking for special voices for "voice-over" (off camera) work in commercials, for animated characters in the various media, public service announcements, dubbing of voices in film and television and foreign language dubbing for both. Common program offerings for such workshops include Copy Interpretation, Character and Cartoon Voices, Narration for Industrials, Audition Techniques, Radio Commercials, Film and Record Promos, Techniques of Voice Production, Re-voicing of Foreign Films, etc.

Children's Acting Workshops or Classes must be thoroughly investigated prior to placing a child in one. Some have been hailed into court by disillusioned parents. Best to consider one of these for children up to about 10 or 12 years old, no older. Young people older than that won't get much out of working with the young-young kids. Parents should ask to observe a class prior to enrolling a child in one of these, since their child probably wouldn't be able to accurately or objectively judge the quality of the program.

There are also the two phenomena that sprang up in the 1980's...**Casting Directors' Cold Reading Showcases** and **Casting Directors' Acting Classes.** Unfortunately, most of these are exploitative if they offer any kind of "acting study" because most casting people aren't qualified to teach and are simply teaching to augment the earnings of the positions which are more temporary and unpredictable in the current industry practices.

Actors, on the other hand, tend to view these classes as opportunities to "pay to audition" for these folks and if the actor is ideally ready to be judged perhaps in some cases it can help. As a manner of studying acting, though, it has been reported to be terribly disappointing in too many cases. If it's simply a **Cold Reading Showcase** that advertises a casting director's name as being scheduled to observe actors' readings of assigned script roles, *auditioning* for that casting director is exactly what it is. The casting director is receiving a fee to come and conduct the session. It may or may not help the actor.

If it's advertised that the casting person will be *teaching* in some manner, try to find out ahead of time whether the casting person has a good acting background, not just a casting job. A few---but very few---do. What should be borne in mind when considering this avenue of "study" is that many casting people are simply last year's receptionists and secretaries who've taken over their former superiors' jobs by undercutting their salary demands.

If you're one who feels ideally ready to be judged by casting people, and are willing to "pay to audition" for them in these offerings, fine. For any kind of actual "studying"....think twice.

25

A **Musical Theatre Workshop** is just what it claims, probably. While fewer in number than other kinds of study programs, these usually include some preparation of musical numbers, movement for the musical theatre, perhaps dance and movement training, maybe even some acting study of the kind appropriate for musicals. Most of these are on an ongoing basis, but the larger ones tend to be term-oriented.

While most study facilities and programs of whatever kinds must be experienced for at least some time to discover their worth, much can be learned by asking industry people about them. Ask agents, casting directors and other actors to recommend study facilities they respect. Some names will crop up more often than others.

INTERVIEWING A PROSPECTIVE COACH OR TEACHER

When you've chosen the coaches or teachers and programs to investigate further, you might carry a list of the following questions which can help gain fullest information in the interviews:

Fees, Minimum Schedule Required, Study Materials Provided or Required To Be Purchased?

Fees charged by study programs vary widely. The most expensive are not necessarily the best. Some require materials to be bought or supplies purchased, whether through the facility or otherwise. You might also consider the gas mileage costs before making your decision, if you're pinched financially. Be sure that you have the amount of time and the hours available if there is a minimum schedule required.

The Approach Taught? The Goals of the Teaching?

There are many, many teaching approaches. Many are valid and have result goals. Some are "preparation of roles" oriented. Some are more "freeing of the actor's instrument" oriented. Some prepare the actor more for film than for theatre; some vice versa; some for both. Some are "method" of one kind or another; some are "no method". Some would be simply repeating what the actor has already learned; some are different and unique and highly contributive. Judge for yourself whether you feel the teaching offered is what you most need.

Who Will Teach You?

Will you be working with assistants or substitutes rather than with the person whose name drew you to the program? Make sure you're going to get what you're there for.

By Semester, Term or Ongoing Pogram with Entry at Any Time?

Some programs are offered in semesters of six, ten or twelve week cycles. Others are "ongoing", with entrance into classes at any time because the teacher enjoys a longer, more personalized involvement with each individual's development.

How Are Classes Conducted? Exactly What Takes Place In Sessions?

Are the sessions mostly scene work or improvisation, and why? Is there time spent on "exercises" you may have had or feel you don't want to have? Are there definite "technique, methodology, approach" items taught, so that your ability to prepare roles and experience them excitingly is being developed? Is there a lot of "therapy" and "behavior modification" work? Some of the latter is qualified; some isn't. Is critique handled by the teacher alone, or are class members allowed or encouraged to comment on each other's work whether ideally qualified to do so or not? (The latter manner of working is so timetaking and often confusing!)

How Many Members in Each Class?

Class sizes vary widely. Technique classes of most types wherein approach items or systems are taught average about 15 members tops, while scene study groups (where preparing and performing roles for critique is the main activity) are often larger and sometimes too large for you to work as often as you might like to. Larger classes would certainly seem to be less personalized, but the total effectiveness depends upon the abilities of the teacher. It's wise to consider the size of the class you're considering, since the amount of personal attention you're hoping to receive is an important concern when you're paying for devlopment.

Is Preparation of Roles Taught?

No, this isn't a silly question to ask. It is probably what you're there for. If it's not included in the work the teacher probably has a good reason for its exclusion...based on their own preference of emphasis. Find out.

What "Level" Class Will You Be Put Into?

The terms "Beginning," "Intermediate" and "Advanced" can mean different things in different situations. If such labeling of different levels is based on your background prior to entering the class it's one thing. If it's based on the fact that a definitive technique and methodology is taught, the coach or teacher may insist that you learn that approach from the ground up, as you will probably want to anyhow. "Advanced", in the latter siuation, obviously means ahead of those others in use of that approach.

May Other Classes Be Observed?

Some teachers---those intrested in the most rapid progress for their class members---allow observing of their other class sessions once you're enrolled in one, and this can help you become acquainted with new terminologies and manners of working more quickly. If you're permitted to observe the work of the more "advanced" groups it can help tremendously. Often the "advanced" groups are working on other facets of the technique of the program and the early exposure to what lies up ahead of you can be helpful in speeding your early development toward those work goals.

Is Auditing Allowed Prior to Registration?

Many of the best tachers don't allow auditing, but some do. Especially coaches concentrating on teaching different technique items in different sessions avoid "auditing" like the plague. They feel that "Class Looky-loos" will fail to fully grasp the fact that such single, individual classes' work is not representative of the over-all work or the total technique. Most who do allow auditing make a charge for same.

Requirements For Acceptance?

Teaching standards vary also. Some teachers will take anyone who applies...for obvious reasons. Others are far more selective. Most legiimate teachers will require some qualifying interview...perhaps a scene or monologue; possibly some reading from a script; usually some personality exchange dialogue. If refused by one teacher, ask them for other recommendations. They generally know enough about other teachers' approaches and offerings to at least recommend with intelligence. It can save you having to go back to the confusion of ads and starting fresh.

Is There Promised or Implied Employment or Help With Job-Geting?

Even a hint of helping you find employment as an actor is a big danger signal! Most legitimate teachers will reply with a resounding "No!" You should be there inquiring about teaching or coaching. Don't expect any legitimate coach or teacher to be your agent.

Help With Photos, Résumés and Advice?

Many will help in all counselling areas in which they feel amply qualified, but if they require or recommend a specific photographer whose price turns out to be quite high there may be a "kickback" scam involvd. Some offer such help as résumé preparation or changing, scene preparing, etc., free of extra charge, while others (those whose time is more valuable) usually make a small charge for such time and help if they have the time to offer it at all.

Will Your Personalities Mesh?

This ability or lack thereof for certain personalities to work with each other without clashing is sometimes called "chemistry". If you feel instant rapport or instant concern, it's still not the most important thing one way or the other...the teaching is. But any long term association should be comfortable in order to be ideally producive. There are other coaches, after all.

* * * * * * * * * *

If you think of other important questions to ask, ask them. Except in the case of top people who are most selective and who may decide *they* can't accept *you*, you're the one who must decide whether they're what you're looking for.

IF YOU ENCOUNTER PROBLEMS OR MALFEASANCE

If a situation you encounter suggests that advertising has been misleading or that some "ripoff" or scam is afoot, there are things you should do about it to help others like yourself.

There are agencies and bureaus set up to deal with any such complaints and actors and actresses should certainly consult with them in questionable cases.

If the complaint is ***definitely of legal nature*** there is the Office Of The City Attorney, City Hall, Los Angeles, Califonia 90012, as well as the Office Of The Attorney General, State of California, Capitol Mall, Sacramento, California 95814. There are lawyers, also, who'd be happy to help you.

If it's regarding ***questionable business practices*** or what appears to be *possible* violation of law, deliberately misleading advertising or something similar, you could address a letter of complaint to the Office of Private Postsecondary Education, 721 Capitol Mall, Sacramento, California 95814, reporting the details. (Most teaching of actors is that..."Private Postsecondary Education"...and this office will know what to do about your complaint.)

In any of the foregoing circumstances, also request the Better Business Bureau of Los Angeles form for filing of a complaint with them. Their form is required. Letter complaints are not accepted by them. Send a self-addressed, stamped, business size (No. 10) envelope and a letter of request for the form to Better Business Bureau of Los Angeles, 639 South New Hampshire Avenue, Suite 304, Los Angeles, California 90005.

If the complaint is with regard to a teacher who is also an agent or sub-agent franchised by the Screen Actors Guild (which is a violation of SAG's Artist Managr regulations to begin with), send a letter to the Agency Department, Screen Actors Guild, 7065 Hollywood Boulevard, Hollywood, Califonia 90028. They will take prompt action of several kinds...perhaps even including revocation of the agent's franchise.

If you were lured into a misleading situation in the first place by a newspaper or magazine ad, you should also send a complaint letter to the publication. You may still see the same ad later, but if you do you can then write a Letter To The Editor and it may be published. Also, the publication

29

might, upon consulting its Legal Department, consider its own vulnerability in case of legal action and refuse to run the advertiser's message in the future.

Also, for pusposes of its own regular and ongoing reportage regarding teaching programs in *The Hollywood Acting Coaches And Teachers Directory*, Acting World Books would appreciate such information as may be contained in any of the foregoing complaints for its file in its Actor Information Service Department which responds to specific requests for information from actors with regard to teaching programs' reputations and known quality.

So much for the "seamy" side of the teaching and coaching profession in Hollywood! Like in any other professional field, there is one. The problem is that would-be actors are among the more gullible and the most often victimized, because they're more desperate to believe the pie-in-the sky promises made by some scam artists.

If you observe the foregoing cautions and corrective measures that are available to you when mistreated or misled, I'm sure you can avoid the pitfalls and obtain the ideal preparation you need in one of the reputable establishments or with one of the reputable invididuals who simply and qualifiedly want to help with your career.

The bottom line, of course, is for the actor to find the acting study program which provides his immediate needs, then his ongoing development and finally any career help the teacher can and will provide in the acting marketplace of agency contacts, introductions, information about opportunities and all the other things an involved coach / teacher can provide to those whose talents have earned them.

Chapter Six

Image Tailoring...
Sooner Is Better Than Later!

Okay, you've been accepted by a well known, highly respected acting coach and have studied for a while. You've found out in your classes that you actually do have talent and you can feel yourself growing swiftly in how to act before the camera. It's not uncommon for new actors and actresses at this early point---long before even their talents are well developed---to go out and get expensive photos made, start grabbing any and all kinds of showcasing opportunities, start agent-hunting and casting director mail-outs....without any thought of *what they are or have* that should interest the industry people they're trying to impress.

It's never too soon to start thinking about *your professional image*! Start tailoring yourself---your general appearance, your outstanding qualities and everything about you that needs to be consciously considered and perhaps consciously adapted toward presenting yourself in your most employable manner.

If you don't, you'll waste a lot of money on early photos that you'll have to throw out later, clothes that you'll later realize are killing your acting role prospects---because they confuse people and distract from your personality, and expensive faddish hairstyles that quickly turn off casting and other production people---because they're often so patently unprofessional...and probably wrong for your features and personality to begin with.

Start thinking like a casting director, a producer and a director. Look in the mirror. Really examine yourself. Is there _anything_ about your appearance that will whet industry people's interest to meet you and will help them actually remember you afterward? If what you see in the mirror doesn't suggest some general casting category and some types of acting roles then it's time do start doing something about it.

Don't delude yourself that your acting talent alone will get you into agency offices or casting interviews. Everyone in Hollywood is assumed to have talent.

Like a product on a supermarket shelf, there has to be some kind of special "packaging" that will make it stand out from all those other brands. In manufacturing it's called "product engineering", "point of sale appeal" and other very clearly sales-oriented things. Every possible device is used to attract buyers. That's what film and television industry people are...buyers. And you the actor are the product.

Manufacturers are wise enough, calculating enough, to not have their products displayed on shelves before all those buyer-oriented devices are designed and in place. Actors should do the same....sooner, not later.

Following are some items that actors and actresses should consider, should do, should obtain and should painstakingly prepare before even thinking of having expensive professional photos taken, before any kind of showcasing, before asking agents to consider representing them and before sending out mailings asking for any kind of film and television industry employers' attention:

INTERVIEW YOURSELF IN THE MIRROR

This should be step one. In your mirror appears an actor whom you as a casting director must find interesting. You have all kinds of roles to cast day after day and there are always a few of them small enough that you can dare to cast in almost exclusively physical appearance terms with little consideration for talent. Like most other casting directors, imagine that you maintain reminder files of different "types" for such "bit role" casting opportunities. As you look at the actor staring at you from your mirror try to decide where in your casting reminder files that actor's photo and résumé should be filed.

Is the actor there in the mirror athletic, outdoorsy? Extremely handsome? Unattractive? Scroungy? Hard, mean and streety? Executive suite? Skid Row? If his appearance doesn't suggest being dropped into one of your files the photo may well go into the wastebasket with all those others that don't suggest something.

Is she glamorous and high fashion? Tomboy? Flashy and cheap? Executive suite? Frumpy? Natural beauty? Frazzled housewife? Librarian / Spinster? Prison matron? You should hope one of these is staring back at you.

TAILORING OF MEN'S IMAGES

If you're obviously _athletic and outdoorsy_, keep your body in shape with some muscles or get it that way. Muss your hair slightly. Keep about half a tan. Stock up on plaid and plain blue denim shirts, jeans and work pants. Go to a corner barber, not a Rodeo Drive hair stylist. Throw away most of your ties, especially the school stripe kind. Keep a few shirts and jackets unpressed. If you've studied speech, perhaps gotten rid of a regional accent, get rid of those perfectly aspirated and dotted t's and d's, popped p's and b's, and any other speech sophistications that don't fit that wide range of middle class, Middle American, blue collar types that appear in every script.

Unless a beard or mustache sets off your features and adds to a slightly rough-around-the-edges masculinity, don't grow either. If you have one or both of them already and are sure it's a plus, keep it or them, even though either or both can keep you out of the running for some roles. But certainly---even if you love that long Santa Fe and Taos ponytail hanging down your back---realize that it's poison for your professional image and don't waste any photography money before you have your corner barber cut it off for you to hang on your bedroom's memorabilia wall. There aren't that many westerns nowadays, and those there are aren't shot in Hollywood.

If you're extremely handsome all of the foregoing apply equally for you with the added awareness of expert color coordination and the colors that set off your particular hair and eye colors.

If you're basically unattractive don't let it bother you in acting terms. Notice how many of the current top stars are fairly unattractive. Simply make sure that you can peg some casting areas where your lack of attractiveness can be a plus. Many producers and directors look for and value the "offbeat" looks. If you have it flaunt it. Make sure your shirt color doesn't go with your pants color, that your hair is just as unattractive as you feel your facial features are. Never go to either interviews or photo sessions dressed up.

If you're definitely the Executive Suite type, subtly say so with what you wear. Just don't go overboard and appear too selfconsciously dressy. Keep your hair well groomed and avoid the faddish longer hair at the back of the neck. Again, beards and mustaches will limit you.

If you're one of the Biker, Pusher and Street Gang types, play it to the nines. Remember, we're talking appearance. You may be a well bred intellectual inside. The outside is what counts in visual entertainment mediums and you should keep your Socrates and R. D. Laing hidden in a pocket when you're with industry people. Certainly have long, unkempt hair or some weird hairstyle. And if you're mean and hard appearing, simply follow most of the tailoring suggestions above for the athletic and outdoorsy type. You don't need to go overboard.

TAILORING OF WOMEN'S IMAGES

If you're glamorous and a high fashion type, which of course includes the height consideration that you're probably minimum 5'9" or 5'10", quite thin and graceful of manner, you're somewhat limited in casting terms of any category but what your appearance and manner so obviously suggest. If you want good dramatic roles those "runway model" items need to be downplayed. Your height alone limits you for leading roles opposite many top male stars. All the regimens taught at modeling schools apply for you, and you should certainly learn them and in every way aim to include top modeling among your career goals. Many top models have later become top film and television actresses....after they've been scouted as top models. There isn't much hope for you to make much of a mark in acting roles until you're found by a producer, director or casting director accidentally watching you as a game show hostess, a Clairol spokesperson or a Paul Mitchell hair tosser in a commercial. You won't be expected to be a good actress at first. The fact that you're that as well as a top model will help when the chance comes to work in the same scene of whatever size with a tall leading man. You won't generally be cast to work with a shorter man.

If, try as you always have to hide it, your mirror tells you that there's a cheap, flashy or streety look about you, no matter how much or how little makeup you wear or avoid, go for it! Don't try to be like all the others. Fill your closet with fairly low-cut necklines, bright colors that may even clash, jewelry that has to be Home Shopping Club CZ because it's too flashy to be real and higher than comfortable heels.

For most women, regardless of type, simple, conservative dresses are best at all times. Learn what colors compliment your hair and eyes. Don't wear more than a bit of jewelry....jewelry categorizes you.

Most women should consult hair stylists and try different hair styles and different lengths until they have what they know sets off their features. But one precaution applies to all: If you're not expert at putting long hair up, be careful of keeping too much or too long hair. Hairstyles that are close to the outlines of your head can compliment your features without distracting by their mass. Bangs should be kept to a minimum and the forehead should have some open space to lengthen the face.

FIRST IMPRESSIONS ARE LASTING ONES

Tailor your image early, folks..._before_ you get photos, start showcasing, seeking agents' or casting directors' appointments. You'll spin your wheels forever if you don't do this.

Chapter Seven

Publications Of Special
Value For Actors

Some newer actors and actresses, upon first arriving in Hollywood, don't know of the many publications which can be used to stay informed on casting, locations of industry companies and people, practices with which the actor should become acquainted toward best creating of and capitalizing on opportunities, available services, etc. Some excellent, reliable publications are available in theatrical bookstores and on some newsstands catering to actors, and in some cases by subscription. Some should be avoided, while some should be considered a must.

Always available on newsstands (especially) are some publications which are utterly worthless, in spite of their bannered hype titles like *"Casting Calls"*, *"Complete Casting Information"* or *'"Acting Jobs"*, etc. They're designed to grab your dollars while they provide little or nothing of what they promise once you've opened the usually stapled shut pages. Something with a title like *"How To Make It In Hollywood Overnight"*, you can be sure, is designed to yank from $5 to $25 out of your pocket in exchange for woefully out-of-date lists of casting and agency people and tips that are suicide in the profession because in most cases they've been written by amateurs.

Stick to the publications that give what they say they do. Actors who've been in Hollywood for some time come to recognize them as "the source", but folks new to the scene need to be told about them:

Drama-Logue (available on newsstands, in actors' bookstores like Samuel French and also by subscription) is a weekly "must"! Pick it up on Thursday mornings on most newsstands in the Hollywood, Beverly Hills, Burbank, Universal City and other locations. It offers actual casting news (very conscientiously) for film, television and theatre; also variety and technician opportunities in those fields, along with informative articles, interviews and general news that the actor needs. Although some casting people decline to have their information published---because of contracts of exclusivity with the Breakdown Service (which publishes the information for agents and managers only and which brings casting desks piles of submissions daily), some upcoming productions do allow this publication to list their casting needs. This particular publication evolved from its conscientious publisher Bill Bordy's long-ago *Casting Hotline* and is now *the* publication most used by actors in the know...justifiably. It's far and away the leader in *job finding* for actors!

Especially valuable for actors to get and to keep handy throughout the year is the **_Special Christmas Issue_** of this paper. In that issue _Drama-Logue_ lists all theatres, large and small, union and non-union, in Southern and Northern California, with information as to who should receive pictures and resumes for casting consideration; acting coaches and teachers, with their addresses and phone numbers if available; many services to which actors must go from time to time; etc. It's a valuable resource and remains fairly accurate throughout the year.

The Agencies---What The Actor Needs To Know, a bimonthly publication of Acting World Books, is available at actors' bookstores throughout the Central Area. For out-of-towners not yet in Hollywood, it can be ordered through Samuel French Theatre Bookshops, 7623 Sunset Boulevard, Los Angeles, CA 90046, or direct from Acting World Books, P.O. Box 3044, Hollywood, CA 90078. It costs $10 and is ussued February 1st, April 1st, June 1st, August 1st, October 1st and December 1st each year, with Updates on the first day of each of the interim months delivered to the stores that carry it and inserted in the book by the stores for subsequent purchasers. Yearly subscriptions, direct from the publisher, cost $40.

This is the only publication which details the names of the agents and sub-agents, the kinds of people they represent as well as their levels (starring down to newcomers), appraisal of their established reputations, longevity and manners of working with their clients and some casting panel members' comments. For anyone seeking agency representation it's a "must" too!

And for "Everything you've wanted to know about actor/agent relations and processes but were afraid to ask", get our friend Edgar Small's wonderful book **_"From Agent To Actor"_** (Samuel French, $14.95)! It will help you understand what's involved in *getting* an agent, *keeping* an agent, *working with* an agent....also, what agents go through for their clients.

The Hollywood Acting Coaches And Teachers Directory, another Acting World Books publication (described earlier), is a quarterly issue, available through the same sources as *The Agencies*, above, and sells for $12.50. It's issued in Spring, Summer, Fall and Winter Editions, and contains most legitimate coaching and teaching programs, with as complete description of them as possible and with biographies of the professional backgrounds of the people who teach. Someone new to the Hollywood scene or planning to come here will find it invaluable and the only source of so much information available anywhere.

The ***Seminars To Go*** series of six guidance publications, also published by Acting World Books, is also available through the same sources as mentioned above. It includes separate booklets on *How To Get, Work With, and Keep The Best Agent For You....Increasing Your Success Ratio In Interviews And Readings For Roles....The Film Job, Step By Step---Before, During, After....The Film Actor's Career Building Stepladder....Self Promotion, Self Publicizing, Self Advertising For The Actor* and *Audition Tapes, Audition Scenes And Showcasing*. Each separate publication costs $10 in the bookstores that carry them, but the complete series of six booklets may be ordered direct from Acting World Books for $43., which includes all handling and mailing costs. Anyone coming to Hollywood or seeking complete career guidance information after getting here should have these books!

(We should add that for readers of the book you're reading right now these publications aren't necessary, since most of the information covered in these booklets is included in the book you're reading. For those who don't have the book you're holding right now you should recommend either it or these six *Seminars To Go* books. They'll thank you later.)

The CD (Casting Directors) Directory is another must. It's available either at Samuel French Bookstores, like the other standard actor reference publications mentioned here, or by direct order from Breakdown Services Ltd., 1120 S. Robertson Blvd., 3rd Floor, Los Angeles, CA 90035. This publication can be subscribed to by calling (213) 658-5684. It, like all the Acting World Books publications, is constantly updated to keep track of where the casting directors are currently located (since they move often from one production office to another). It's published by the Hollywood organization which issues "breakdowns of all roles" being cast to the agents and which maintains daily contact with casting people, knows where they are and what they're casting. The new issues come out each January 1st, May 1st and September 1st, but it's constantly updated for subscribers each fortnight. For building your own mailing list of casting people's addresses it's *the* publication!

The Studio Blu-Book (published annually by *The Hollywood Reporter* and available on newsstands, at Samuel French and other bookstores and at the publication office, 6715 Sunset Boulevard in Hollywood) is of course quite expensive, but it's also the most thorough directory of all studio, production company, guilds and unions, trade infomation sources, agencies, services and equipment and other information anyone in the industry may become involved with or need. For those who can afford the price (usually around $45) it covers almost everything imaginable.

The ***Academy Players Directory***, published by the Academy of Motion Picture Arts and Sciences, at the Academy Players Directory offices on the 6th Floor of the Academy at 8949 Wilshire Boulevard in Beverly Hills, is too expensive for actors to buy each issue or perhaps ever. The full set of all categorized pictures of all actors (or most) in Hollywood usually costs about $75. Actors really don't have any need to own the Directory...but they _need to be in it_ just as soon as they can! It's furnished without charge to casting and production people, and it's the absolute *Bible* for casting. Your picture and how to locate you (your agency, personal manager or phone number) should be in every issue if you want hiring people to think of you.

To insert your photo and information, SAG membership or an agent or manager is necessary, but the price of insertion is small change for its value. It's the publication most continuously referred to by casting people for reminder purposes, and producers, upon a casting director's recommending of an actor, don't even ask if the actor is *in* the Directory. They ask *"What page is he on?"*....on the asumption that if he's worth being in their production he's in this book! It's the one advertising expense no actor in Hollywood can afford to bypass.

The Screen Actors Guild Appointment Book is another publication you should have. It's available only at the SAG office, 7065 Hollywood Boulevard. It's a yearly appointment book / diary usually put out in December, with not only diary pages for the applicable year but also condensations of SAG employment contracts, minimum salaries and union information of all kinds, list of franchised agencies, organizations and services actors need to know about, etc. It's a handy size for carrying around. It's usually about $15. At the time this is written you must be a *SAG member* to go in and buy a copy.

There are other publications, of course. They come and go, and they cost money which is sometimes found to have been wasted after opening them or after receiving piles of returned mail from their long outdated listings.

The problems which keep so many of those publications out of date are of course publishing problems, in that even if they do honestly try to be up to date at the time of their publication they're almost immediately out of date because agencies change their staffs so often; casting directors move from one production company or studio job to another so often; theatres, coaches and teachers and actor services move or cease operation. If the publication you're considering isn't a weekly, monthly, bimonthly or quarterly periodical, stating continuous updating, it's certain to be full of old, unreliable listings.

The attempt of this chapter is to guide you to those publications which are _completely reliable_. Be careful of most of the others!

Chapter Eight

Showcasing Your Talent...

Who, What, When, Where, Why and How?

During the early stage of your career in Hollywood it's important to find or create the opportunities for casting and production people to see your work, and for reviewers in trade and daily press publications to write some glowing words about your performance and talent which can be used by you and the first agent you'll be getting about this time.

There are good showcasing opportunities and bad ones, just as there are actors who want to show their talents without any concern about their readiness to be judged by those who will or won't hire them as a result.

When you've built some confidence that you're ready to show your talents, the next step is probably to look for the most promising opportunities for doing it.

Hollywood small theatres used to be devoted almost exclusively to that---showcasing actors' talents for film jobs. What was called "theatre" in those early years was too often just two or three actors on a bare stage in front of a black velour drapery or a roughly painted four wall set...with no concern for the many elements of theatre....just concerned with the performances of the two or three people on stage and nothing else. It almost ruined the chances of Los Angeles ever becoming a theatregoing community with an eager, building audience at boxoffices. In more recent years---although 99% of the actors appearing in these Hollywood Area productions are still in them for the showcasing they offer toward interesting film and television producers, casting people and agents, the theatre producers themselves, their directors and many in their casts have become more conscientious about at least combining "good theatre" with the goal of effectively showcasing their talents. Now, even casting people and agents, at the end of their busy day, can look forward to seeing a good, well produced theatre production in most of these theatres while checking out the talents being exhibited, rather than just going as a favor to some actor and considering it a casting director's obligation.

If you're new in town, from wherever (including New York's Off Broadway and Off Off Broadway, by the way), a good theatre production is always a good showcase if your talents are worthy of one. You're the **_Who_** for whom showcasing can work. Also, if you're an outstanding talent who's still quagmired in small roles it can't hurt to be seen in a large, meaty role in a small theatre somewhere where people from the industry do actually come because of the quality of the theatre's work having been established over a sufficiently lengthy period.

But consult your agent first if you have one, since there are agents in Hollywood who say a flat "No!" to showcasing almost anywhere but in a large theatre production or at only one or two of the smaller Hollywood Area ones where important work is done...where they know the quality that can be expected and they're confident casting and production people will come in large numbers. You have to consider that your agent may be trying to get you interviews for _important_ roles in casting and production offices and won't want you to do small roles in unimportant small theatres and reduce the probability that you'll be considered for those larger things in film and television.

If you don't have an agent, then it's good to ask your acting coach or working actor friends whether and where you should try to showcase.

As to **_What_** to showcase yourself in....what type of role, type of production, etc., there are some obvious but sometimes overlooked pro's and con's.

Be sure the role is essentially your type in terms of casting. Don't even consider doing roles that are older or younger than you appear. Don't take a small role if your agent is putting you up for large roles exclusively. Don't do environmental theatre or experimental theatre productions for showcasing purposes; stick to more conventional stuff which offers you one decent role instead of many varied roles that are small in a production which highlights lighting, sound, music and effects more than the actors' performances. You can take your chances on doing roles established and remembered as masterworks of stars, but it's very chancy to do it, since most people in Hollywood either saw the original and will compare you unfavorably or will be looking for the same qualities.

Some original works are excellent showcasing, but some of those will garner reviews more for the new work than for the cast members performing it. This often happens. There's the tendency on the West Coast for reviewers (where we have so few excellently qualified critics) to treat new works in precisely that manner. Recent plays from Broadway which haven't been overdone are good. They're fresh to most viewers, and most will also be fresh from the standpoint of predecessors' performances not having been seen. Remember, we're strictly discussing _Showcasing_ here; not theatre in the over-all sense.

When to showcase yourself is something few actors bother to think about, much less understand fully the implications of this aspect. There is, after all, a seasonal aspect to film and television work for actors. It's good to bear this in mind.

Between April and late June or so, many casting directors and even many agents are _on hiatus_ and take vacations and getaways from Hollywood if they can afford to. There are layoffs at studios until resumption of filming for television series around June or July or August. Many of the casting directors seek other work during that period and even your showcase's invitations may be missed in the mail. During the same period the wiser agents aren't disposed to take on new clients because employment is down for those clients they already represent, with the resulting pressures on the agents representing them. Lower budget films are shooting during this period, to take advantage of the television stars not busy on series at the time, but those low budget films are hard to locate for the sending of invitations.

Fall is by far the best time, therefore, to shoot for a good showcase production. The casting directors are still adding recurring roles to the new television series; agents are scrounging around for people of types they don't have or need more of; everybody's in town and probably looking for more categories of prospective clients then than at any other time except at television pilot time, which also starts just about then and continues throughout the winter. Most pilots...with all the new roles they bring...are _"in the can"_ (finished) and being peddled to networks by March at the latest, since networks usually set their next season commitments by some time in April.

Doing a showcase production of any kind during the hot summer months can be less productive---especially in a hot, un-airconditioned theatre which everybody in Hollywood knows from past experience is unbearably hot and a place to avoid.

Where to showcase? Where industry people can get to it, certainly! Centrally located theatres get their fair share of industry attendance during the busy season if they have good reputations, while theatres in outlying areas are always very poorly attended by Hollywood folks whether they're good or not.

Industry people work hard and fast, under pressure, and at the end of busy days they're too tired to go out to small theatres where they may or may not find exciting talents after traveling to and from, perhaps foregoing dinner to make curtain time and getting home to bed at late hours. Only an agent they trust wholly and unwaveringly, who can visit them and badger them into going, and who perhaps takes them to dinner before the show as well as chauffeuring them there, can usually persuade them to make any long trip.

Often the industry people will call to reserve seats, honestly planning to attend, but many simply don't show because something has come up, and usually forget to even call and cancel their reservations. The closer the theatre is to the centralized, many studioed area, the better. They're aware that they may be doing you a favor by coming...and they may doubt that they'll find anyone exciting enough to make the trip worthwhile. So forgive them if they're not anxious to travel a bunch of miles to see you.

Also consider the reputed quality of productions at any theatre you consider as a place to show your talent. Some have excellent industry attendance because they're predictably excellent, while some are quickly written off because they're predictably mediocre when even that decent. Agents can advise you as to who's good and who isn't. As mentioned, if you don't yet have an agent your coach or teacher can probably tell you. They'll warn you away from even that meaty role if it's at one of the poor quality places where poor production could mess you up in the industry's eyes rather than help you.

There are a few commercialized "Showcases" in Hollywood, also, which advertise their organization's showcasings and for a time made a booming business of (1) auditioning actors in scenes, then (2) choosing which pairs of actors would be afforded the opportunity of paying between $60 and $100 for each person allowed to participate---in exchange for the showcase organization's presenting their scene as one of about seven or eight (or more) scenes to invited audiences of industry people, (3) giving those chosen some direction to polish the scenes and at the same time cutting their length to about three minutes each, (4) then sending out invitations to industry people and (5) on a studio work day showing either the ten scenes or perhaps half of them to invited audiences just before lunchtime, (6) serving the industry guests cold cuts and cheap wine for lunch and (7) showing either the same ten scenes again after lunch for a new audience or the other five or so scenes for the same group.

Even at $60 per person, times two for each scene, times even just ten scenes...$1,200 is a nice little chunk for the showcase producers...minus minimal space rental and the cold cuts, the wine and the large advertising campaign.

A disadvantage actors encountered, and still may encounter, is that although there are often more sitcom television series than dramatic series, many actors better suited for dramatic work may out of desperation to be showcased in this manner allow themselves to be poorly showcased because most such showcases insist upon "light" material. These showcases usually insist that casting people wouldn't come to see "heavy" pieces at that time of day. It's a moot question, but some casting people feel exactly the opposite.

These days such showcases apparently draw fewer casting and agency people. Especially the casting people are more involved now with their own appearances at Cold Reading Showcases where they're paid quite well to be there, conduct readings with attendees and make a few suggestions to the people---which qualify their labeling of their appearances as a manner of "teaching". The Casting Society of America, of which many casting directors are members, doesn't condone its member casting directors receiving payments to simply attend and observe audition scenes or readings, but the majority of the Society's members still do. If there's "teaching" involved they're permitted to, and usually do, charge a nice fee to appear.

In fact, many casting directors appear to be "booked solid"---spending as many as possible of their weeknight hours making the aforementioned "teaching" appearances at the many such "Casting Showcases" and "Cold Reading Showcases" that need their names for drawing attendees.

Why showcase? Because you know you're ready to be seen and judged desirable for roles or for agenting. Some people already started up the ladder do it to get better agenting than they currently have; show themselves in categories of casting for which they haven't previously been considered; or to help aspiring young friends by appearing in scenes with them.

Commercialized showcasing can be embarrassing at best, since casting people and agents in attendance know you've paid for the opportunity; the props and furniture are less than ideal; the lighting is often dreadful (because it's set to handle all ten scenes in the same lighting setup); and any direction you may receive from the people who've turned to making money in this manner may be less than ideal as well.

The final disadvantage of commercialized showcasing setups is that, while in earlier years many industry people showed up for the free wine and cold cuts and opportunities to say hello to equally busy peers they might never see otherwise, some showcases have been so dismally inferior that most industry people stay away from them now. While ads appear from time to time thanking a huge list of industry people for their support and attendance, many of the names so listed are from the 1970's or so!

As for those Casting and Cold Reading Showcases which feature casting people auditioning actors in cold readings, many actors maintain that there are advantages in such pariticipation in that, having more or less replaced "General Interviews" in the casting people's own offices (which have all but disappeared now), they offer just about the only opportunity currently available for the casting people conducting them to become acquainted with so many actors' talents, and they sometimes result in immediate call-ins for roles in whatever projects the casting people are currently casting.

To paricipate in these sessions actors should expect to pay $20 or $30 for each participation. The calendars of some regularly producing showcases of this type are available in actors' bookstores, usually naming the casting people who'll be conducting the sessions. Bear in mind that when a well known, highly respected casting person's name is listed for a certain

43

session it doesn't mean that he or she will be there. The practice is rampant of cancellations for various reasons and the sending of alternates, sometimes even the casting person's secretary or a totally unknown subsitute rung in to fill the vacancy at the last minute.

The Screen Actors Guild tried to end this kind of showcasing sometime back, but was unsuccessful in its arguments and finally compromised because many SAG members supported the concept and because there was really no legal ground on which SAG could base its stand.

Finally...**_How_** showcase? **_Professionally, or not at all!_** That's the bottom line. It's your head on the block if you do a half-ass job, even if the director lets you get away with it. Whether it's in a commercial showcase somewhere or in a theatre production, make sure you'll be shown to best advantage in every respect.

The most dignified manner of showcasing is and always has been a good theatre production in a good, well thought of theatre whether it's large or small. A new theatre just starting out isn't too wise because its quality isn't yet known and industry people tend to wait and see. By the time they've "waited and seen"---from reviews of a first producion or word of mouth---the production may have closed. It happens all the time.

If involved with a theatre production and thinking of it strictly as showcasing (as most in Hollywood do), and not "theatre for the love of doing theatre", be cruelly objective.

Since it's possible that some industry people may come, judge with absolute objectivity the quality that you see coming along as rehearsals progress. If it's obviously going to be less than the best, find an excuse--- soon enough that you can be replaced without hurting the production---and get out. If you find yourself at loggerheads with the director over interpretation or something else, also find an excuse to leave. It's _Showcasing_ you're after or it's the director's version of theatre and acting. Use your own career as the determining factor. If others in the cast are embarrassing as performances approach, do the same coldhearted, selfish calculating as to the risk for yourself by being seen with them.

If totally satisfied and sure the production's going to work excellently, there's more _How_:

Send out invitations to casting, agency and production people, offering free tickets at the boxoffice in the invitees' names---two tickets rather than just one, by the way, in case they may want to bring a guest (who will probably be another industry personage). It makes the offer more attractive to these folks if they have this option of bringing someone with them. You may have to pay the production for the seats, but is that so bad?

Invitations should have your picture included somehow. An offset printing is wise. The custom in New York is smart here too, and has become common procedure in Hollywood too in recent years: Have postcards printed up with your photo printed at one end and with blank space over much of the card. Have them printed in sufficient quantity that part of the print run can be imprinted with the invitation information for that current

44

showcase and a major portion of the print run can be kept by you for future use. With only your photo appearing on these held for later, you can also send thank-you notes to those who have actually come and still have many more of the same photo-only cards left over for personal messages and notices later on for other things.

It's not a bad idea to reprint some quotes (or have a group of review quotes typeset to save space) on either these cards or on a special flyer, to send along with any invitations, to encourage industry people's reserving and their actually showing up after doing so, attracted by the good comments about what you're doing.

Be sure to pick up all the local papers and magazines which customarily review productions of the type you're in. You might otherwise miss an absolutely sensational review about you in one of them. Every word of praise counts! A bad review should simply be forgotten as quickly as possible. Console yourself with the knowledge that not too many industry people will have read it anyway.

If the production is a very good one stay with it to the end. You can never tell who might finally come to see it the last night.

In the weekly _Drama-Logue_ issues there are many reviews of performances at such theatres, sometimes indicating in so many words that the work at the theatre is customarily excellent. That should be at least some assurance and point you in the right direction when you're looking for a good theatre for showcasing in or at least help you avoid the customarily inferior houses.

For those who don't know, there's seldom much if any salary paid to either the union or the non-union actors in these small Hollywood area theatres. The union (Actors Equity Association) until the Fall of 1988 simply declared a hands-off stance with regard to theatres of 99 or fewer seats, allowing its members to work either with other Equity people or with non-union people, without salary of any kind and with an almost total relaxation of the customary union working conditions, representing quite a remarkable opportunity to newcomers, in such theatres. A few theatres do now pay the minimum amounts to cast members, as directed by the Actors Equity Association's new stance enacted by membership vote in 1988, and certain other conditions for use of Equity members now apply to these theatres. But don't expect to make much more, even now, than what may cover your gas to get to and from performances.

For those who aren't yet in any union, the possibility increases yearly that if you've chosen one of the very top small theatre productions and it enjoys a huge success it might be selected for adapting into a television or feature movie, as a number have, and often many members of the original cast are reemployed for the new, union signatory (and union salary) version required for such translation. You would then be allowed, in fact required, to join AFTRA (American Federation of Television and Radio Artists) or the Screen Actors Guild---depending on the manner in which the new version is produced.

The final advantages of showcasing in theatre, as opposed to showcasings for which the actor must pay to be shown, are that it's more dignified, is more apt to expose the actor's talents in a fully prepared and attractively presented manner, and offers the opporunity to gather some printed comments in trade and daily publications which are read by those whose business it is to seek talent and offer opportunities.

Simply remember---regardless of the kind of showcasing you choose, if it's in Hollywood or in any major film and television production center, that it's best to make sure that the role you accept presents you, your personality, your current age range, your good points and your particular type of acting talent or specialization in the best light possible. Anything else is not showcasing and, for exposure to film and television industry people, is quite unwise.

Acting is a business like any other business. Corporation boards spend months preparing any campaign that's to "go public". The product must be refined in every aspect; it must be appropriately and attractively packaged; its promotion and advertising must be effectively designed and, finally, any favorable reactions and comments must be fully exploited.

Showcasing your talent shouldn't be looked upon as a "just do it" activity. It can be done, well or poorly, and forgotten immediately by those who've seen it...or, with some thought and calculated promotion on your part, turned into a productive career advance!

Chapter Nine

The Tools Of Your Trade

First off, you'll need ***Profesional, Black and White, 8x10, Glossy Photos***, even before getting an agent. You need them for sending in response to casting calls in *Drama-Logue* or some other paper for theatre roles, student films, AFI (American Film Institute) films, etc., and for submitting to agents in the hope of getting one to represent you.

Don't get a friend to take photos intended for professional use. You can waste a lot of money and time trying with friends---even though you may just pay for some rolls of film, developing and printing. And sometimes it's chancy to even have professional photos done in your own city before leaving for Hollywood. Too many of the photographers available in outlying cities are more accustomed to taking family photos or modeling photos, etc., and they may as a result like certain types of shots that are absolute no-no's for actors. It's probably best to wait till you get to Hollywood before getting them made. Get here. Ask around. Get recommendations as to the best and most often recommended photographers that you feel you can afford. They know what they're doing, and they know the industry preferences and requirements for whatever type of work you're seeking.

47

In choosing a photographer, probably the first consideration is their charge. It varies widely from photographer to photographer. Don't expect to pay any less than $50-$150 for a sitting fee for theatrical portraits (just head shots) and perhaps (but not always) a few prints included, and the most reliable commercial photographers usually charge between $100 and $350 or so for "commercial" shoots with many different types of characters, several wardrobe and prop changes, etc. Some require deposits ahead of time. Appointments for shooting should be made at least a week ahead of time, and in some cases there may be quite a wait.

You'll want to inquire about the fee; any deposit; the amount of time afforded at that price for a sitting (either commercial or theatrical or both combined); whether they shoot indoors or outdoors or both and in what kinds of locations; what amount is payable at the sitting or when the money is to be paid: the number of proof pages (there are about 36 or 72 to a page usually) or the number of total shots that are included; how many original 8x10 prints come in the package at that price; the cost of any 8x10 original prints over and above the number included in the price; and whether they release the negatives to you (most don't); how soon proofs may be expected; how long any ordered prints should probably take; what kind of wardrobe the photographer recommends; any other questions you can think of.

Any photo taken for professional purposes should suggest your personality. Don't use (or even have *taken* in a "*theatrical*" photo session) any wild expression stuff! For *Commercial* photos, on the other hand, you do need different expressions, along with wardrobe and props which suggest different roles you feel you're right for in commercials.

Don't have the top of your head cut off in the frame. Don't wear a hat. Casting people and others want to see your total head. Backgrounds of medium greytones, whether leaves of trees or buildings or whatever else, are best. No dramatic black and white contrasts to distract from your face. There should be a little brightness (sunlight or artificial light) in the pupils of the eyes. And don't have the photo "raked" or "airbrushed" to take out your moles or lines or wrinkles or dimples. Both eyes should be visible to some extent, whether in a three-quarters angle (turned a little sideways) or fairly straight front.

Dress for photos as you see yourself most useable in roles. Don't let patterned material of any kind dominate the shot and distract from your face. Keep your hands and any props out of face shots. They distract even more.

There are different casting potential categories....straight leads, heavies, characters, street people, executive suite people, etc. Your appearance and personality automatically place you in one or two of these categories whether you like it or not. Each category certainly requires the basic likeness and exploitation of your own unique personality, but there are other considerations in addition:

Ingenues (pretty young women) shouldn't select "cleavage" (low or nonexistent bodices) unless that's what they want in terms of roles. Such photos won't generally produce any other kind of job consideration and sometimes bring unwanted kinds of telephone calls. After all, it's logical that some people are going to consider these kinds of shots "sales pitches" of a certain kind. If body shots are taken in your photo session because you do have an outstanding body, okay. In some manner you can point this out subtly, but don't let the wardrobe or the pose attract too much attention from your face, and be careful to not have on too much makeup. The last is a common mistake of so many young actresses in their first photos.

Young men should be even more aware of their casting potential categories. Film and television haven't yet advanced out of the imbalance between male and female roles in scripts. Young women are sometimes chosen simply because of their appearance as much as their talents, while in any script there will probably be many different kinds of male roles. It's a fact of contemporary film life.

If you're a healthy, outdoorsy-looking, sports-bodied type, say so subtly in your photos. No dressed-up businessman wardrobe shots. Rough, medium-tone and maybe even wrinkled or blue denim shirts are ideal, or soft plaids, suggesting your category. Otherwise, still plain and undressy photos, no matter what your type. Few should dress like lawyers or junior executives. If they do, that's what they'll be thought of for by casting people.

Leading women who are beautiful have the problem that there are so many former starlets and ingenues already established by name and public recognition who are now growing into the 35-50 years range.

First, women tend to be immediately categorized photographically by their choice of wardrobe; even more than men. Express your own taste and personality, with some indication of social level in your choice of what to wear. Not too much makeup. And resist the temptation to have the photo retouched to eliminate any small problem of which you're selfconscious. Too many women do this; more than men.

Leading men of the "handsome" type have the same problem when they reach their forties and fifties. Too many others in their handsome category have publicly recognizeable names and much background, therefore are first on the tongues of casting people and directors when roles come up.

Don't try to be handsome unless you're strikingly so. Your uniquenesses are far more important in the casting pool of men in your age bracket with whom you must compete, both talent-wise and in photos aimed at selling you. Unless you're aiming at comedy, a serious expression is best, hopefully conveying some hint of your ability, depth and---most important, your personality.

Character people usually need at least three or four different shots suggesting their various categories. Agents usually request several different photos in order to submit their best shot of you for specific roles. Character roles are so varied. And character people should exploit anything which

49

makes them different and special. If they have any facial, body or other features which are unusual or even abnormal in their own estimation, those things they may hate about their own appearance are probably what they should exploit most prominently in their professional photos. Character roles, by their very label, demand characters!

Get some help with choosing your proofs for printing up. Order three or four 8x10 originals, at least...as many as you can afford, before making final choice of the one or more for quantity printing. Then take the chosen shot or shots to some photo reproduction shop for a "dupe neg" (duplicate negative) and order at least 100, perhaps more copies in your first print run.

If you like your name professionally and definitely want to keep it (after checking with the Screen Actors Guild and AFTRA to make sure you can use it as a union member since no other union member has the same name), then you may want to have your name set into print at the bottom margin of the prints while getting the quantity reproduction done. It's not too wise to have anything else typeset and printed at the bottom of your photos. Those who put their agents' names at the bottom are in trouble when they later decide to change agents!

At this time, **_Duplicate Photo Labs_**, located one block north of Sunset Boulevard on Highland Avenue, is fine for quantity reproduction. So is **_Quantity Photo_**, at 5432 Hollywood Boulevard, and there are others. Those are the two that seem to this writer to be the most often used, and they're both excellent for 8x10 glossy black and white photos...your standard "headshots".

If you're having **_Commercial Composites_** done, after a prospective commercial agent has selected the shots desired for inclusion and has helped lay out how they should be arranged on your multiple-picture composite, you'll probably be told to go to **_Anderson Graphics_** in Van Nuys to have them done offset.

While most actors have to choose their own shots for their standard "headshots", all good commercial agents will insist upon seeing your proof sheets (not prints) and making their own choices. They like to designate which standard headshot is to appear on the front of the composite and which wardrobe, props and character action shots shall appear on the back.

YOUR RESUME IS YOUR "AD COPY"!

Next, you'll need a **_Professional Résumé_**. After it's prepared it should be rubber-cemented onto the back of all your photos so it won't tear off when stuffed into casting or agency files. Have it typewritten or word-processed neatly, along the lines suggested below, then cut to 8x10 size so it won't stick out past the photo when pasted onto the back of it.

There is a standard form recommended by the Casting Society of America which has been adopted industry-wide and is now the form in which producers, directors, casting and agency people expect to see it:

Your name should run across the top center in large type---perhaps a pasteup strip from your personal stationery, or a special typeset version in heavy bold type, so the name stands out, or you can simply type your name there in capital letters and perhaps underline it to make it stand out as much as possible.

One of the first principles in advertising---which is what a résumé is---is that the name of the product should appear in larger size type than anything else around it, and this is equally true in any "advertising" the actor does---including later opening or end credit listings in film and television casts. So start observing that principle with your résumé.

Just below the heavy print name line, at the top of the left side of the sheet, list, one after another down the margin, *Height:, Weight:, Hair:* and *Eyes:,* with the correct information shown for each item.

While height and weight should simply be accurate, it can be a nice attention-getter to describe brown hair as "Prairie dog brown" or "GQ brown" or some other adjective-enriched version of "brown" that can even suggest your own personality. You might describe blond hair as "Surfer blond", "Golden blond", "Alley cat blond" or something else...any phrase that is more specific and that offers the opportunity to in addition suggest your personality.

Either leave the upper right corner area with empty space for your agent's imprint and contact information (if you have an agent) or to simply pen in the manner of contacting you if you don't yet have agency representation. In this top righthand space, until you have an agent representing you (to whom all calls about you should be directed) you might just write in an Answering Service number. In any event, there should be some manner of contacting you shown at that spot on your résumé, but it's wise to use some phone number other than your own home number, for obvious reasons. There are still a few of the wrong types of people in the industry, and once your photos and résumés leave your hands you never know whose hands they may fall into.

In the center, at the top, just under your name, if you're a member of one or more of the unions---SAG, AFTRA and Equity, you should enter that information. Just "SAG" or "SAG / AFTRA / Equity"...or whatever applies.

Then drop down about five or six lines to start your listing of your credits.

If you have no motion picture or television credits yet, then list any theatre background under the centered, all capital letters, bold type heading THEATRE. Perhaps underline that title so it stands out. Then drop down two more lines and at the left margin show the first play title; in a centered column across from it name the role and (some do) in parenthesis add (Lead) or (Starring) or (Featured). Across from these entries, at the right, list the theatre and perhaps the city; the year if you like.

But if you do have some (any kind of) film or television background---this being Hollywood, the first centered title should be the one of those two in which you have the most credits---either MOTION PICTURES or

TELEVISION. List all your credits, down the page one after another, under each title, using the same basic layout as described for theatre, except that in the case of motion pictures the right hand column should show the studio or production company and, if you like, the year in which produced. Some like to also give the name of the director.

For television, if the appearances are in episodes of series, the left hand column should name the series in bold caps and the episode (also bold) in parentheses; the middle column should name the role you played and if you like, in parentheses, the billing---(Starring), (Costarring), (Featured)...or you could, as some do, after the episode and role names put in a one, two or three word description of the character...like (The nasty nurse), (The kidnap victim), (Slinky's Boyfriend). The latter entries make even a bit role appear to have been more important, and also give opportunities for you to subtly advertise the kinds of roles you'd like to play more often.

The foregoing titles sequence...first MOTION PICTURES or TELEVISION, then the other of those two, then THEATRE (last because this is Hollywood), should be followed by other centered titles for COMMERCIALS AND INDUSTRIALS, if any, then OTHER.

Under the Commercials heading the usual entry is simply "List Available Upon Request" (whether there's been even one commercial to list thus far or not). The reason for this very common phrase is that if people have actually done several commercials it signals potential hirers that they should check with the actor's agent to make sure there hasn't been a "conflict"...a commercial job for a conflicting product...for example, a previous commercial for a soft drink of any kind when someone's being considered for a Coca Cola or 7-Up commercial.

Under the OTHER title should go entries of Variety experience, Dance, Musical Groups, etc.

At the bottom left corner, list SPECIAL SKILLS or call it MISCELLANEOUS, and under that list things like Swimming, Skiing, Skydiving, Gymnastics, All Field and Track Sports, Snakedancing, etc.

Across from that, at the right margin, under the title TRAINING, list the names of the best known coaches or training establishments, what was studied with each, and where the study occurred. Of course list any Hollywood, New York, London or important other coaching or study first.

If you have any ability with dialects or speak an additional language or two, list those in the bottom center, under the title LANGUAGES AND DIALETS. Be absolutely objective by not listing any language or dialect with which you're not expert. You might add in parentheses after a listed language or dialect a word like "fluently" or "fair".

AN ALTERNATIVE TO LISTING CREDITS YOU DON'T YET HAVE

If you have absolutely no credits at all as you and your coach or teacher decide that you're ready to make your first moves, it's possible that your coach may be willing to supply a paragraph or two for reprinting over his or her name in the empty center of the résumé (where all the credits would otherwise be listed). This has been an effective first-doors-opener for many people whom the author has personally coached. Such recommending entries over the coach's signature or name, perhaps printed in a box or border right in the center of the empty middle area, could be worded something like this:

"Miss Bagnold is ideally ready to start in excellent dramatic roles. She is a magnificently talented actress and is experienced with all aspects of working before the camera. Her talents deserve your consideration."

If your coach has any reputation and credibility with industry peers this kind of quite unusual résumé entry will open doors more quickly than a small list of working credits that indicate only "bit player" or semi-extraing experience.

READY, GET SET, GO!

At this point, with your photos and résumés ready, you'll probably want to start using the publications listed in the earlier chapter for sending out your photos and résumés to casting and agency people. If your coach feels you're ready perhaps he or she will suggest some first agents for you to start contacting. Some are willing to provide this extra help and advice; some may even be willing to write a few letters or make a few phone calls to introduce you and request interviews for you. Or, if you ask, your coach may be willing to give you a note over his or her signature (somewhat like the one in the previous paragraph suggested for your résumé), for you to send out yourself to encourage people to afford you your first important interviews.

Later, after you've had some jobs, enter each of them in ink on the typed résumé. Being in ink, they more vividly call attention to the fact that they're <u>very recent</u> additions, implying that you're getting under way. Established people do this too, for the same reason---recent roles meaning increasing popularity.

A good idea sometimes not thought of by actors is to call your agent after each new job and offer to go in to the agency office and make the new ink entry of the new credit on each copy of your résumé that is held in the agency office for sending out when submitting you for more roles. Sometimes the agent is too busy to make the new entry and the agency staff person delegated to make such entries may also be much too busy or may simply overlook this menial task. Such new entries are very important for you, the actor. The agency of course knows about the new credit, but the casting and production people to whom your résumés are next sent won't know about them unless they appear on your résumé. And the agency will no doubt appreciate your helping with this task. It's very much in your own interest, so it's a good idea to do it.

If you don't yet have an agent when there's a new credit to add, burn some midnight oil and make the entry on all your résumés immediately at home, in ink as mentioned above.

From time to time check your agency, asking whether more photos and résumés are needed. If they are, you're being submitted regularly. If the agent's supply isn't going down much at all, your materials aren't being used much and you might start being concerned.

Chapter Ten

In Hollywood
You Need An Agent....

You won't get far in Hollywood until you have an agency representing you. That's the simple fact. The agents are the only ones able to visit casting offices and suggest you for roles or even for general interviews. They receive the "breakdowns" (lists and descriptions of all roles, delivered to agents immediately as soon as casting is announced). Some of them are even in on preparation of scripts and their roles far ahead of time through their own literary departments, long before any general casting begins. They know where casting offices, director and producer offices are and have at least limited access to all offices involved in the casting processes. Some have an amount of "clout" in production and casting offices that insures their actor clients top priority consideration. Having an agent pushing for you indicates that somebody whose opinion matters thinks you're worth their pushing for you.

You can find out who's a franchised agncy (an agency authorized by the Screen Actors Guild, by AFTRA and by Actors Equity to represent those unions' members) in several manners. The Screen Actors Guild and AFTRA have available at their front desks lists of the currently franchised agencies, but to obtain a copy of such list you may need to show a membership card...and you may not have one yet. And the problem of relying on these desk handout lists is that some agencies will have closed, some will have moved their offices or even had their franchises revoked soon after these lists are printed and prior to the new lists being printed..usually several months later, with a lot of changes having taken place.

The most reliable and up-to-date listings of all the talent agencies franchised by the Screen Actors Guild, AFTRA and Actors Equity are found exclusively in the Acting World Books bimonthly publication _The Agencies---What The Actor Needs To Know_, described earlier in Chapter Seven. This publication is updated the 1st of each interim month following the month of its publication. With it you can be confident that you won't waste postage or phone call money on outdated information. We know of no other publication that can assure this.

The best manner of making a first contact with a prospective agent, or at least trying to, is for your coach or teacher---if he or she thinks you're ready---to make a call or write an introductory letter that the agent won't be likely to throw in the wastebasket. If they won't do this for you yet, then you can still on your own write very short notes (note, _very short_ ones) to the agencies you think might be most interested for some reason.

There are many kinds of agents. There are those who represent only for "theatrical" (motion picture and television roles); those who represent only for "commercials" (because it's a different field and involves different offices all over town for the agency to cover regularly); those who lean toward representing established or even starring people only; those who have "mixed levels" lists (including middle-to-top level people and usually a few newcomers in whom they believe who have fewer or no credits); those who represent mostly "day players" (people who seldom have large roles but who work often in smaller ones); those who are known for good representation of mostly "character" types (the not pretty folks who usually work more often than the pretty ones because they add color---"character"---to roles); those who mostly represent the "pretty people" and try to build them to boxoffice stardom; and those who represent only "new people" whether union members or still non-union, simply because the agencies themslves are new and haven't much to attract the regularly working people to them yet.

To find out _who is what_ and _what kinds of people they represent at the moment_ is a drag, but it's an important concern. You can waste a lot of phone calls and letters and shoeleather on the wrong agents who couldn't possibly be interested in representing you for some of the foregoing reasons. Ask your coach or teacher or a good friend who knows which agents specialize in what...or, again, get a copy of _The Agencies_ and find out more quickly and more surely. Then make up your list of whom you want to contact. If all on the first list "bomb out" because of no interest or response you can go back and make up a second list, and so on till you hit someone who's responsive to you.

Certainly it's not going to be easy. At any time like the present there are between 75,000 and 85,000 actors who hold SAG cards. Of those approximately half usually have current agency representation. That means that all those other 40,000 actors without current agents are bombarding the same agents to whom you'll be sending your photo and résumé. That's why it's especially ridiculous to answer an ad of a "talent agency" that's *advertising* for clients. With all the submissions they'd be receiving every day if they were worth anything they certainly wouldn't need to be advertising.

REQUESTS FOR APPOINTMENTS

A one-paragraph request for an interview is best for sending with your photo and résumé. If you write a long, wordy letter to an agent which boils down to just a request for an interview they won't even take time to read it. The whole submission will go into the wastebasket immediately. Just a short, businesslike request for an interview regarding representation...that's all you need, and that's what works best.

Often if an agent is seeing anyone at all for possible representation it's upon the enthusiastic recommendation or persuasion of someone they respect---a producer, a director or casting director, or a coach or teacher they know won't send them someone unqualified.

The best times to call agency offices, if you call at all, is at the end of the day, around 4:30, 5:00 or 5:30. Agents are in the field (at studios and production company offices) the rest of their busy days, and only come back to make phone calls and receive next days' appointment calls from about 4:30 on, up to around 6:00 or 6:30. They may not be available to see anyone even then, but it's the best time---especially if you're dropping the picture and résumé off in person, because they'll probably be there, even if you don't get to see them, and will probably be handed your photo and résumé immediately by their receptionist.

Many actors drop off their photos and résumés and leave it at that, figuring the agency obviously isn't interested. Others understand the agency business more and understand that agents are always so busy that, even if they've planned to call an actor, they've simply put it on the back burner. A follow-up call can't hurt. Even if you get one of the standard answers---"We're not interested at this time"..."We're not taking anyone at this time"...or "You'd be in conflict with several of our other clients"...or something else equally discouraging, at least you'll know you've tried to the exent that it may do any good.

THE APPOINTMENT WITH AN AGENT

If you do get an appointment from a mail-in request, you may be asked to read from a script or perhaps get a scene ready to come back and do for them at a later time. If you're approaching them with limited or no credits, accept whatever conditions they impose for any further steps...up to a point, of course. They're basically doing you a favor if they're willing to have you come back for another appointment, and you must recognize that if they do there must be some interest.

What impresses agents most, according to many who've appeared on my Seminar panels discussing such things, is a personality which seems confident, an outlook which hasn't become bitter or discouraged, an air of friendly and intelligent appreciation of what their particular agency is and what it can do for them, and something which suggests that the actor might fit many roles within their general category of interests.

For instance, there is always a certain amount of call for attractive girls and good-looking fellows, since they have series pilot and groupie fan-mail potential in the current marketplace. There are always roles, albeit usually supporting ones, for young "police / detective / junior executive / clerk / factory worker" types among the men; "office employees / waitresses / sales ladies / bar hangers / girlfriends" and other such roles for good-looking young women....and without much background these are the roles you'd probably be sent out for at first, until you make some headway into heavier roles.

On the other hand, there is always call, also, for the extremely unattractive or special-stangeness people of all ages. They have their special niches in casting potential. Yes, they're "character role" people, but these folks are often easiest for casting people to remember because of their unique qualities and appearances, and they often start moving up the ladder in those offbeat roles more rapidly than their pretty and handsome counterparts.

The bottom line of an agent's interest toward possibly representing you is that you should have _something_ that's a little special and all your own that they feel they should be able to sell.

If it's a one man or one woman agency, with perhaps only a secretary-receptionist in the outer office (if even that), it doesn't necessarily mean that they're no good. There are many highly respectable and very able agents in those one person offices. Some of them even represent a small list of stars and top players.

You can check for many signs as to the worth and standing of the agency in the very first visit to the office. Note the way the receptionist relates with the agent. Note the number of phone calls that come in from casting offices. Note how the agent relates with whoever's calling. Listen to the quality of any negotiation you overhear in those phone calls. Observe how busy or idle the receptionist is, since receptionists do much of the paperwork, submission notes and letters, picture-pulling, new credits' entries on resumes, etc.

It's not the location, size or decor of the office which should concern you. The rapport or lack thereof should matter to you, though. An agent who may be excellent for some may be wrong for you. Likewise, an agent who works only halfheartedly for some may with great belief and enthusiasm for you as a new client work his or her tail off for you.

Don't expect a royal welcome in a busy agent's office, ever, until you're earning big salaries and offering to bring that agency big commissions. Until then, and certainly in a first meeting, you're fortunate enough that the agent is taking his or her time to even meet with you---especially if you're a new, inexperienced actor with few or no credits.

Starting new actors is a terrible burden for an agent to assume. You're not yet known. There's always a period of trying to get first interviews for you when others with more background and credits are up for the same roles and are called for instead of you, no matter how hard the agent may try. The agents know this, and a newcomer---no matter how impressive---is a big obligation and demand on their time. Agents, like any other businesspeople, prefer those clients for whom phones ring often and jobs come by telephone without any effort on the agents' parts.

The larger the agency the less desirable it can be for anyone whose name and face are not yet known. The reason is that larger agencies with five, ten or in a few cases up to 60 or 70 agents on staff divide up the Hollywood studios and production company offices as to area or influence group and each agent covers only a small portion of the total territory. Also, in a very large agency there may be only one of the agents there who even knows you exist or cares about you. Bear in mind that that one person may be covering just one or at the outside two or three studios. You essentially have no *representation at all* in the hundreds of other offices!

SIGNING WITH AN AGENCY

When the moment of signing contracts for representation comes, if the agency holds SAG, AFTRA and Equity franchises, then all three contract categories may be presented for your signing.

There is now the new combined agency contract form of SAG for television and theatrical (motion pictures), by the way, and a separate SAG contract form for television commercials. Retain one copy of each contract for your own file.

The first-time contracts are for just one year, however they may be renewed after your first year for three years if both the agent and you are happy with each other.

In lieu of the standard contracts, there is now also in use a "Client Confirmation" form used to confirm *verbal* agreements between agents and new clients for representation, covering all three areas---television, motion pictures and commercials or, if marked to so indicate, any one or two of the three areas.

The agency will forward one signed copy of each contract to the unions (SAG, AFTRA and Equity), but it's a good idea for you to check personally by phone call to the Membership Office of each union involved within a few weeks at the latest, to make sure the union has received the contract copy from the agent, so you'll be recorded in the union's records as being with the new agency and easy to locate for casting. Sometimes when agents are busy---and when are they not?---they forget to send the copies until much later.

The agent will probably want you to make up a list of people who are most apt to help you. Even if there are just two or three people you can put down, do it. The agent needs any help you can supply at this early point.

Check Authorization Forms and a _Power of Attorney Form_ will probably be handed you for signing at the same time, along with the contracts. This happens in most agencies these days. The check authorization forms are later sent by the agency to production company payroll offices when you work, instructing them to send your salary checks to the agency rather than direct to you. The agency, upon receiving your salary checks, endorses them with their "Clients Account" stamp and deposits them, deducts the agency's commission from the salary portion of the checks, then makes out its own checks to you for the balances. That's what the "Power of Attorney" form is required for.

SAG and AFTRA require that the agency's checks to you be sent or delivered to you within three days from date of receipt at the agency office.

In a first meeting try to obtain a clear understanding of how often you may call the agency office and when it's best to do so---if at all. Some agencies don't want you to call in to check at all, since if there's anything to tell you they'll call you immediately. And the worst possible thing to ask an agent if you do call in is "What's happening?" Agents absolutely hate that question. If they're working for you at all they've been submitting you for roles. If no interviews have been produced by their submissions they're already unhappy enough. To have to take the time to tell you what you've been submitted for is a bother, since it bothers them especially that their efforts in all those cases have been unsuccessful. That particular question is a first step toward lessening the agent's enthusiasm about continuing to represent you. Never ask it.

Find out immediately whether they plan to send you out on any "general interviews" (first meetings with casting people, which will be discussed later). Many don't believe in them, knowing that little impression can be made by an actor in a so brief meeting. They prefer to wait for role opportunities for which you can be sent in, to make such first meetings more productive by interviewing your _talent_ rather than just your _office personality_. In fact, some agencies feel that if you've had a lot of general interviews with casting people before coming to see them and still haven't worked for those people at all your chances are minimal at best.

Supply your new agent with several phone numbers where you can usually be reached when not at your own telephone or available by beeper. Worse yet would be to suddenly take off for somewhere without telling your agent how to get to you quickly.

As an example of this....once during the author's talent agency years one of his favorite clients with quick, top star potential had just been fired from the cast of a Hollywood theatre production because his talents far out-shone those of the leading lady...and the leading lady was also the producer! In a fit of depression over being fired he got into his van and headed for Mexico to lick his wounds without even a word of warning to his agent (this author).

The very next morning came a call from Columbia. A director for whom he'd done two fairly good costarring roles at another studio wanted him---for one of the *top Guest Star roles!*...in *"The Quest"* series. The studio was prepared to sign him immediately without even an interview because the director was insisting on him. It was the break that would have catapaulted him to instant stardom! Every effort was made to find him. I had to keep alibi-ing to the production office for not being able to confirm him for the role while frantically trying to locate him. Finally it was found out, through a brother across town, that he'd borrowed some money for the trip and was enroute south. The production finally gave up, realizing that for some reason he couldn't be confirmed. You can imagine the new anguish that actor experienced when he got back from his wound-licking trip and heard the news. Keep your agent informed! You never know when they may suddenly have to get to you.

You might watch out for this, in case it comes up in one of these contract-signing meetings: A few small agencies insist that you pay to have your photo and resume printed in their *Clients Photo Book.* Don't fall for this if it's suggested or requested. Such books are of no use to casting people, and at best are usually a moneymaking scheme of the agent for office rent-paying purposes. Not many agencies would attempt this, however.

The SAG contract, although for one year the first time, is really only for 90 days should the actor foolishly (or even intelligently) decide to terminate the contract at that time for some reason. You needn't even stay the full 90 days if you feel for some reason you must leave earlier. If you haven't worked through the agency's efforts during the first 80 days of the contract period, or at any other 80-day period, you may leave the agent on the 76th day, since they will not be able to provide you with 15 days of employment during the remaining period, as required to prevent your leaving them.

Agents hate that 90-day clause and always have. They may begin in earnest trying to help a newcomer and after all their hard work may find that they have a client who is impatient and unintelligent enough to not recognize all that hard work and decide to leave the agency after so short a time. Don't utilize the 90-day clause, ever, if you know your agent is working for you and there's no better agent clamoring to represent you.

An agent makes a decision almost immediately as to the best manner of handling your particular talent. Often, if the decision isn't an easy one, the agent feels they shouldn't take you on as a client.

In some cases the avenue chosen is to try for as many small but slowly building roles as possible---the quite practical thinking in such cases being that each small role gains that much more casting director recognition for you and sometimes begins to produce second and third calls for you from either casting or directors for whom you've worked.

In other cases the agent may have enough appreciation of your talents and the dogged foresight to decide that you should not be sent out for any role which is less than a worthwhile cameo scene or a costar billing level. It takes a lot of belief to establish your talents in the agent's eyes on the latter level, but it does happen occasionally.

Whatever the agent decides, let them go the way they believe to be best. They usually know what they're doing, and they understand the market for your type at the present time and the advantages of building you slowly by getting you exposure around town in small roles or refusing to submit you for or let you go in for small roles, holding out for much better and more important opportunities.

Remember, the agency pays its office rent---and sub-agents' salaries, if it has sub-agents---from commissions earned from its actors' employments. There are the times when the agency must pare down its list in order to bring in others who promise more commission income for the agency. Don't feel too badly when you get a dismissal letter from an agent, and don't take it as a put-down of your talent. There is simply often someone more established and better known in your category, in financial terms and commissions potential, whom the agent wants to sign or may already have signed just before sending that dismissal letter to you. If it's anything else causing the dismissal no doubt you'll be told what it is or will know without being told.

If, on the other hand, you at some point decide to leave an agent, then later find that you weren't so bad off there after all and want to come back to that agent, bear this in mind: *The love is gone.* The former agent who worked so diligently for you earlier and perhaps for a very long period, then experienced your rejection of them for another agency, is a human being. What was a labor of love before will never be the same again. Most agents say this, by the way, although a few say that they'll happily take back someone who by then justifies the return with enough promise of large commissions. They feel they've earned those later dividends with all that earlier hard work, but that's it the second time around....simple financial consideration on their part by then. And you'd better earn your keep during a second term with an agent. It's not love anymore.

Also, be careful about signing with a _Personal Manager_ out front, before seeking an aglent. Agents consider too many of them absolute anathema! It's understandable. A personal manager has the right, through his contract with you, to insist that if you have an agent the agent must check with him before sending you out for an interview, and the manager has the right to refuse to let you go. The agent must check salary negotiation with the manager, and there is always disagreement. The agent is closer to the job market and knows what you can get in job terms, while the manager, to earn his keep, must insist on more, more, more...and perhaps different kinds of jobs that the agent knows aren't open to you.

Managers, to be worth considering, must be able to do things the agent can't do---have entré to more top producers' offices and studio heads' offices, etc. There are some fine personal managers in Hollywood, but there are, for every good one, a thousand no-good ones who simply sign young actors to long term contracts at 15% or more of the actors' total salaries from all sources---whether the managers have done anything to get those jobs for the actors or not, then do nothing except sit back and collect the money, leaving all the job-getting aspects up to the agents!

Simply get an agent as quickly as you can, and let that agent handle your career beginnings.

To try to "go it on your own"---without an agent representing you---is pure folly. While a few casting people might come to know you and call you in for tiny bit roles---for which you'll receive only SAG minimum pay, there'll be nobody really pushing you; nobody asking for a little higher salary or better billing when you work for the same people several times and they begin to value you. There'll be nobody receiving the Breakdown Service's breakdowns of roles each morning to know what's casting, who's casting it, where they are, and submitting you for any role you're right for.

Without an agent you can't possibly keep up on the things being cast and how to get to whoever's in charge of casting. You need an agent!

AN OVERVIEW OF THE HOLLYWOOD TALENT AGENCIES

There are many different categories of talent agencies in Hollywood that are franchised by the Screen Actors Guild. They range in size, clout and specialization from the behemoths---that handle all types of performing, writing, directing, producing, rock group, club and variety, animation, art design, cinematographic, choreographic and all other kinds of talent--- down to the one man or one woman office that often does an excellent job of representing a smaller, select list made up exclusively of actors and actresses.

There are "talent" agencies---usually representing actors in the main; "literary" agencies---mostly representing writers, directors and producers; "commercial" agencies---usually representing people exclusively for commercials; "modeling" agencies---specializing in high fashion, runway and print models; "voice-over" agencies that handle people for off-camera voice work, radio commercials, cartoon and animation voices, etc. There are also agencies that try---usually unsuccessfully if they're too small---to handle *all* areas.

There are at all times about eighty percent of the total list of currently franchised agencies that are highly respected, vastly experienced, efficient and dedicated. Most of these have gained position and different degrees of "clout" for their well established quality of representation over many years.

But there are also at all times about twenty percent (a rough estimate) of the SAG franchised agency list that aren't worth their salt; that are new and inexperienced or that simply *pretend* to be agents for one reason or another, which may include exploiting actors through photography, workshop and other "scams".

For the most up-to-date information---about what agencies do what, how well they do it and for what categories and types of talents---we recommend the purchasing of the current issue of _The Agencies---What The Actor Needs To Know_, at Samuel French Bookshop or one of the other booksellers that carry it, mainly because agencies so frequently change, move, cease operation, merge with others or simply change their categories and manners of representation.

However, following is a rough "overview" which attempts to present a "categorized" picture of the agencies as they're perceived to be operating at the time of this book's publication. Bear in mind that by the time you're reading this book there'll have been so many changes that to put together a mailing list or find the agencies that might be interested in you and that you feel would be right for you you should pick up that booklet _The Agencies_.

The Global Agencies

Some agencies have offices in Hollywood, New York, Paris, London, Rome and elsewhere. They represent mostly top international stars and often, also, represent top international producers, directors, screenwriters and playwrights, top novelists, politicians, designers, cinematographers, lecturers, rock groups and other musical artists, etc.

Among the mightiest and those with the most branch offices scattered around the globe are **The William Morris Office, Creative Artists Agency** and **International Creative Management (ICM)**.

There are others, somewhat smaller and less departmentalized than the first group, that nevertheless have important and highly respected offices in several other capitols of the world. These include, for example:

Paul Kohner Inc.---the agency that comes to mind first because of its history of total involvement in the international scene for so many years, also **Agency For The Performing Arts, The Artists Agency** and a few others less broadly known to belong in this category.

Most of these agencies would not be interested in any performing, writing, producing or other talents until they are well established, until their names are fairly well known in the broader talent marketplace, and until a top boxoffice history or at least easily perceived potential for one is broadly recognized.

One major film starring role in a successful picture, or at least one season of starring in a top rated television series or a long and critically-acclaimed starring engagement in a Broadway or London theatre production would probably be the minimum to make the actor attractive to such an agency. But in spite of this admonition to save your postage and phone calling in trying to interest this kind of agency the author knows that many actors with little to offer in the way of interesting one of these or the other agencies mentioned in this section will try for them anyway.

Both Coasts" Agencies

Many top agencies in Hollywood maintain both New York and Hollywood offices but are still a little more accessible (than those listed earlier) to some talents who come with fewer and less impressive credits. Some also have offices in Toronto, Miami, Chicago and Dallas and some have affiliations with top agencies in other countries rather than maintaining their own offices there.

These agencies usually have many television stars, many top national and some international film stars, top directors, producers and writers on their client lists. Few of these will represent newer people whose backgrounds have only potential and few major credits to offer yet.

Among this much larger group: **Abrams Artists Agency, Actors Group Agency, The Agency, Agency For The Performing Arts, Alliance Talent Inc., Ambrosio/Mortimer & Assoc., The Artists Agency, Baumann, Hiller & Assoc., J. Michael Bloom Ltd., Don Buchwald & Assoc., Inc., Cunningham/Escott/Dipene & Assoc ., Elite Model Mgt., Epstein/Wyckoff & Assoc., Flick East-West Talents Inc., The Gage Group Inc., The Gersh Agency Inc., Henderson/Hogan Agency, Paradigm, HWA Talent Representatives, Innovative Artists, Honey Sanders Agency, David Shapira & Assoc., Silver, Kass & Massetti, Michael Slessinger & Assoc., Susan Smith & Assoc., Sutton, Barth & Vennari** and **Writers & Artists Agency**.

The Powerful "Mostly Hollywood Only" Agencies

Many long established, influential and powerful agencies have their offices and their total operations only in Hollywood. Some are even more powerful than quite a number of the ones mentioned above. They've earned their positions and power over many years. They too represent many top stars, many top directors, producers and writers as well as other celebrities, simply because Hollywood is the center of most importance to the majority of their clients.

Some of these agencies occasionally sign newer talents in whom they have faith, but it usually takes some respected industry friend's persuasion to obtain consideration by such an agency. With smaller staffs than some of those mentioned above, they have less time available for the large amount of promotion required to get a new talent off the ground and upwardly mobile to the point where the agency's commissions justify the hard work and time spent on that newer talent.

These agencies range from "never take any new talents" to "one or two new people once in a while" attitudes. They usually require extensive and encouragingly important backgrounds.

At the risk of unintentionally overlooking a few who belong in this category, here are at least the majority of them:

Amsel, Eisenstadt & Frazier, Badgley • Connor, Metropolitan Talent Agency, Eric Klass, Bresler/Kelly & Assoc., Century Artists, Gold/Marshak/Liedtke & Assoc., Kazarian-Spencer & Assoc., H. David Moss, Progressive Artists Agency, Irv Schechter Co., Charles H. Stern Agency, Herb Tannen & Assoc. and UTA (United Talent Agency).

There Are So Many "Mixed Levels" Agencies

Most of the thus far unlisted agencies represent client rosters that in some cases include a few top stars, many established and continually in demand people, and a few new people with potential for rapid advancement.

All agencies hope to represent lists of known talents for whom there are constant calls for roles based on the broad industry knowledge of their talents. Those are the "bread and butter" clients who continually pay the agencies' office rents and operating costs with the constant flow of their commissions on acting employments.

The formula---if there is one that applies in most cases---is: (1) As many as possible "names" of whatever starring levels, to constantly elevate the agency's position; (2) As many as possible well established co-stars and well known top supporting actors, constantly in demand and constantly bringing the agency decent-sized commissions. (3) A large list of established and known "character actors and actresses" known and liked by directors, producers and casting people; and (4) Some (never too many) handsome and pretty young people whose talents can get roles in auditions and who have some history of working to insure that they're known to enough people already to have them called for again by the same people.

New people looking for agency representation must recognize, as those agents do who'd like to help them but know they can't afford to, that a new talent, so totally unknown in too many places, requires so much initial expenditure of the agent's time and effort that it's a too discouraging prospect in the minds of many of these agents.

A few of the "Mixed Levels" and "Mixed Categories and Types" agencies do specialize more than others. Even though a one man or one woman office, the agent may be a recognized "star maker", respected throughout the industry for his or her perception of what creates quick boxoffice stardom. Another may specialize in "character" types, male and female---those not pretty and unusual-looking types that work so often because of their unique looks and other qualities.

Some of those that specialize more than others include **Aimee Entertainment** (strong on character types), **Carlos Alvarado Agency** (represents mostly Hispanics), **Irvin Arthur Assoc.** (comedy, musical people), **J. Michael Bloom** (likes to develop new talents in whom he's interested), **Iris Burton** (specializes in top children, kids and teenagers), **CL Inc.** (voice overs), **Susan Crow** (children), **Lil Cumber Attractions Agency** (pioneered Black talent employment, still represents predominately Black clients), **Coralie Jr. Agency** (handles many Las Vegas Club acts and lounge performers, circus performers, variety people, twins, little people, etc.), **Devroe Agency** (variety people, club acts), **The Hollander Talent Group Inc.** (children and teens), **Jackman & Taussig** (comedy), **Kelman/Arletta & Assoc.** (mostly teenagers with excellent backgrounds), **Robert Light Agency** (mostly musicians and composers), **Ken Lindner & Assoc.** (news & anchor people), **Guy Lee Talent Agency** (a mostly Oriental list), **Ken Lindner & Assoc.** (broadcast people), **Omnipop** (comedians for motion pictures/television), **Pro-Sport & Entertainment Co.** (sports celebrities), **Sandie Schnarr** (voice overs), **Charles Stern Agency** (voice overs), **The Tisherman Agency Inc.** (voice overs), **Erica Wain** (characters), **World Class Sports** (mostly important athletes) and **Stella Zadeh & Assoc.** (game and talk show hosts, anchor people, TV reporters, etc.).

The "Mostly New People" Agencies

All agencies have to start somewhere. Those who come from previous sub-agenting with other agencies usually bring to their own newly formed agencies a pretty complete list of well established people who've left the prestigious agencies for which the new agents worked to be handled by that person whom they've been handled by and appreciate. An agent of this background and ideal position for starting out is usually hesitant to take on more than one or two new people without backgrounds at any given time.

It's all the other "mostly new people" agencies---usually single men or women who've rented a small office and been successful in persuading the State Licensing Div. and the Screen Actors Guild that they're qualified to be franchised---that we need to talk about, and at length. It's these "mostly new people" offices where actors may en - counter "scams" or ignorance of how to promote actors, lack of knowledge of contracts and procedures, haphazard handling of actors' checks, little or no visibility in casting offices, lack of industry friends, poor handling of actors' photos and résumés, etc.

Some of these eagerly take everyone, are honest and well-meaning, but are often less knowledgeable about the business than the actors they offer to represent. Actors visiting such offices should inquire as to what other agencies the new agents have worked for. If a new

67

agent has no prior experience as at least a sub-agent working for an established agency, chances are that agency couldn't be of any help whatsoever to actors for some time to come. It takes time for agents, whether they be sub-agents new to agency processes or new agents just starting out with no credentials, to even find out how casting is handled, how to use the Breakdown Service, where the hundreds of offices are, how to submit actors for roles, how to negotiate salary and billing, etc. And it takes longer to establish acquaintances and credibility with casting people for their taste and judgment.

What's worse, there are some "new people" agencies that open as exploitative, money-scrounging "fronts" and that, instead of really representing actors for employment, pay their office rents and build huge bank accounts by referring new people (usually non-SAG newcomers who have no recourse to the Guilds for abuse) to friend photographers who "kick back" to the agents part of the money paid by the actors. In the case of one such scam at an office on Ventura Blvd. in the Valley, SAG finally revoked its franchise after sufficient proof that the "agent" was the stepmother of the young woman to whom all "new people" were required to go for photographs and even acting classes!

Agents operating scams entice as many strictly "new people" to their doors as possible. They're careful in their interviews, usually dis - couraging any members of SAG or AFTRA, since what they're doing is against artist manager regulations and if reported by <u>union members</u> to their unions they'll have their franchises revoked quickly.

It's the <u>non-union</u> newcomer who's "fair game" for these charla - tans. That newcomer is less informed and not so quickly aware hat he or she is being taken. And non-union people's complaints to SAG or AFTRA must go unheeded. Neither guild has any purview for policing these abuses unless the complainants belong to the unions receiving the complaints.

There are, though, those recourses of which the newcomer can avail himself or herself that are mentioned earlier in the chapter about "Newcomer Scams". If photography by a specific photographer is re - quired, simply look elsewhere. If it's sexual coercion, call the Vice Officers of the City in which the office is located. If any payment is required for signing you, that's not a SAG-franchised agent in the first place. If you find yourself mistreated in an agency office in any way, don't just lick your wounds. <u>Do something about it</u>!

The "One Man" or "One Woman" Agency

Don't for a minute think that because an agency is operated by just one person, be it man or woman, it should be ignored. Some of those are the most diligent, dedicated nd productive agencies.

68

Although the film industry is so spread out and difficult for a single agent to cover ideally, those agents take the Breakdown Service (to know what's being cast, where, who's casting it, etc.) and budget their phoning and rounds to offices in a so organized manner that they often serve their clients more effectively than some of the larger offices that must operate on a less personal basis.

Most of these one-person offices are also careful to limit the number of new people they represent to a special few, then work their tails off for those few. They often represent a few stars, a large number of established co-stars, many constantly working character people and usually just one or two newer people, if any at all, that they've de-cided to push for because they have excellent potential, ideally developed talents and "star quality".

Some of these one-agent agencies come quickly to mind because they stand out as not only hardworking agents but also because they enjoy highest respect among casting people, directors, producers and others for the quality of those people whom they represent:

Barry Freed, Pamala Ellis (Ellis Talent Group), **Ilene Feldman** (IFA), **Michelle Gordon Assoc., Jacqueline LeWinter** (FPA), **Suzze Moore** (Moore Artists), **Steve Stevens, Stella Zadeh & Associates.**

There are of course other one-man and one-woman agencies, but in the foregoing list we're talking about the kind of one person agen-cies that enjoy highest respect for their small but prestigious offices.

Some Top Producer/Director/Writer Agencies

Many producers, directors and writers are handled almost ex-clusively by Business Managers, Entertainment Lawyers, Personal Ma-nagers, etc.---because their affairs are complicated and contracts and payment bases are varied, but many are also represented by a stellar group of top agencies along with performing talents. The following list is probably not complete, and will change, but it includes many of the top agencies that are known for expert handling of producing, direct-ing and writing talents on the West Coast:

The Agency, Agency For The Performing Arts, The Artists Agen-cy, Badgley • Connor, The Chasin Agency, Contemporary Artists Ltd., Creative Artists Agency, Endeavor Talent & Literary Agency, The Gersh Agency, Innovative Artists, Int'l Creative Mgt. (ICM), Paul Kohner, Major Talent Agency, Metropolitan Talent, The William Morris Agency, Paradigm Talent & Literary Agency, Renaissance Literary Agency, David Shapira & Assoc., Susan Smith & Assoc., UTA (United Talent Agency), Writers & Artists Agency and some others.

Top Writers' (Literary) Agencies

There are many agencies of strictly "literary" nature that repre-sent writers exclusively, don't handle performing talents, producers, directors or any other creative talents. Just writers. A current list of those, complete and constantly updated, should always be gotten by writers from the Writers Guild of America (WGA) West.

Some of The Top Commercial Agencies

The following list doesn't represent itself to be complete. It's simply offered as a list of those who in the writer's judgment stand out from the very large number of agencies that either involve exclusively with commercials or have commercials as one of their several other areas of representation and have departments devoted to commercials.

What the commercial actor should bear in mind is that the com-mercial field is an entirely separate entity from the film and television fields. Agents in the "commercial" category have more contact with advertising agencies' account executives and casting people, manufac-turers and sponsors. It's rare that an agency which handles acting ta-lent for film and television can as effectively cover commercials.

Those listed below certainly deserve to be listed in any "top ten" list of primarily "commercial" agencies:

Abrams-Rubaloff & Lawrence, CL Inc., Commercials Unlimited Inc., Cunningham/Escott/Dipene & Assoc., Kazarian-Spencer & Assoc., Susan Nathe & Assoc., Special Artists Agency, Charles H. Stern Agency, Sutton, Barth & Vennari, Talent Group, Herb Tannen & Assoc. and **Arlene Thornton & Associates.**

Some Top Modeling Agencies

Many agencies *include* Modeling as one of their many areas of representation. However, there are those which almost exclusively represent modeling talent or who, even if they represent some clients for commercials, etc., are best known as top models' agents. The fol-lowing list is perhaps not complete at the time when the reader sees it, but it includes a vast majority of those longest established and most specialized in the field:

Elite Model Management (John Casablancas' West Coast Office), **C' La Vie Model Agency, Colours Model & Talent Agency, It Model Mgt., L. A. Models, Mademoiselle Talent Agency, Dorothy Day Otis.**

Some Top Agencies in The Voice-Over Field

While some of the top commercial agencies have Voice-Over departments, following are some top agencies which are best known for their Voice-Over excellence and their agencies' emphasis on the field:

CL Inc., Sandie Schnarr, Charles H. Stern Agency, Sutton, Barth & Vennari and **Tisherman Agency Inc.**

Strictly "Theatre" Agencies Are In New York

In Hollywood, although most agencies are also franchised by Actors Equity Assn. for handling union-signatory theatre work, not too many Hollywood agencies handle clients for theatre exclusively. Some agencies actually prefer people with strong theatre backgrounds, but they prefer them to be available first and foremost, once signed, for film and television, knowing those fields will advance their clients' careers, billing, salaries and agency commissions much more rapidly.

Most theatre actors scout their own roles and production contracts anyhow. Just as in New York, where there's so much more of the *paying* kind of theatre, actors must do much of the job search themselves, even when they have agents for negotiating of contracts once they find their own opportunities. The agents in Hollywood know that when anyone but a top starring theatre actor is wanted for a theatre role here the production expects to pay no more than Equity scale salary and will fight to keep all supporting salaries at that level.

Most Hollywood agents are simply too busy rooting out film and television jobs for their clients to spend much time on the less paying theatre arena if any at all. Most who hold onto their Actors Equity franchises do so just in case one of their clients does get a long-run Broadway hit role and can be expected to pay the usual commissions on such a job over a period of time.

Some Top Agencies for Children and Teenagers

Of course there are over 150 talent agencies representing some children and teenagers along with predominately adult clients, but the following are some of those that represent kids and young folks almost exclusively (or exclusively) and rank among the best in the field:

The Benson Agency, Iris Burton, Susan Crow, The Hollander Talent Group Inc., Kelman/Arletta & Assoc., Stacey Lane, Patty Mitchell, The Savage Agency.

Agencies' operations change from time to time. Don't count on these listings remaining up to date for too long. To stay up to date, always get the current issue of **The Agencies---What The Actor Needs To Know!** Samuel French Bookstores (Sunset and Valley) always have it.

71

THE AGENT'S TYPICAL DAY

For those who don't understand how talent agents function, it may help to profile a typical day in the life of an agent, for example, who operates a one agent office. Although some of the activities vary in other offices where there are several agents, with each agent delegated to handle individual aspects of the agencies' operations, most of the details described here have to be handled by someone, and in a small one person office they're predictably all handled by that one person. So we'll follow a "one person office" agent for a typical day.

He gets up early so he'll have time to read the previous day's _Daily Variety_ and the _Hollywood Reporter_ over a hurried breakfast, then before leaving home probably has to make a couple of desperate calls to catch clients who haven't returned phone calls the night before about appointments for the coming day. Then he takes the fastest streets to his office to check the Breakdown Service casting sheets that have been delivered there in the early morning hours, to see what he can send clients out for that day or make calls about to request interviews for them if the casting people already know them.

Checking the roles available in the Breakdown, and deciding whom he should suggest from among his clients, either in written and photo submission form or by phone calls, takes time, along with gathering the photos and resumes into groups for submission. If he has nobody to do it for him he himself will want to personally deliver some submissions to several of the casting offices to be among the first on the casting directors' desks. He knows other agents will be there first if he isn't. For his office stops he has to lay out his "rounds" so he can cover the most territory as quickly as possible. This all has to be done by 9AM or so, so he can get out on his production office rounds and catch as many offices as possible during the morning hours.

Most Breakdown Service lists caution "No Phone Calls" so the majority of the agencies won't tie up the casting office telephones. With approximately 275 to 300 agencies at any time, that cautioning note is easy to understand. And the smaller agencies without clout know that they should respect the request. The larger agencies with clout and with perhaps a couple of series star clients on the studio lot know that they can get away with calling in spite of the warning request, and they do it all the time.

The small office agent we're watching this morning probably spends some time debating whether for one of his actors he should "go over the head" of a casting director who he knows doesn't like one of his clients who he thinks the director or producer should feel to be perfect for one of the good roles. The larger agents do this all the time--- "go over the casting director's head" on behalf of one of their clients, but the smaller agents consider it a bit risky. They know that some opinionated casting people may resent it and it might jeopardize future relations with that casting person. After much troubled thought at his desk this morning----balancing his client's rightness for this one job and his agency's relations with the casting director involved for all future jobs, he decides to simply submit the actor's name as a suggestion and not risk trouble by "going over somebody's head."

Most agents have beepers, and as the morning hours wear on and they're out of their office they frequently have to get to pay phones to get to their clients in response to interview calls or deal offers that need to be discussed immediately with their clients. They spend much gas money zipping from Univeral and Columbia in the Valley to MGM and Fox far out to the southwest, and the trips take a lot of their day too, since many miles lie between those production offices they must visit. And if they hope to see and talk with anyone in any of those offices there's usually some waiting time in an outer office at each stop. The agent we're watching has to wait twenty minutes at Universal before getting in for a three minute talk with one of the casting directors, then fifteen more minutes before getting in to talk briefly with another. The same happens at Columbia. He knows the same will happen at MGM and Fox or that the receptionist at one of those offices may even say the person he wants to talk with is "not available" or pehaps "in a meeting". The smaller agents are told this many times as they watch one of the large agency staff men or women sweep imperiously past them and walk right into the inner offices. There's a definite "pecking order" among the agents. The large agencies, with many stars in their client lists, are never told "Not available."

Being on the studio lots at noontime, agents like to have quick lunches in one of the studio commissaries or in a nearby restaurant frequented by producers and directors, just to accidentally run into, if not meet officially by appointment, those production people. Then it's off on more "rounds" in the afternoon, trying to cover all offices where there's potential and urgent action that day.

Around four o'clock in the afternoon agents start streaming back to their offices, to get the late afternoon deal-making and next-day-interview-setting calls from the studios and offices. By five o'clock most agents are back in their own offices, probably kicking themselves for failing at a lot of what they planned and hoped to get done that day; checking the mail and salary checks; deducting their commissions from their clients' salary checks and making out their own checks for the balances due their clients; perhaps calling some of those clients to tell them they can come in and pick up their checks the next day, etc.

This late afternoon time is the time when, if they're currently scheduling any interviews at all, they're most likely to have a few interviews set up, even though they're tired after their long day. It's the one time of day when they least mind calls from clients and sometimes feel inclined to call a few of their people just to encourage their spirits and reassure them that something will happen soon.

There are always some clients for whom interviews have been set for the next day who---when the agent tries to reach them---aren't anywhere to be found. This means that the agent, throughout the evening hours and sometimes late into the night, sits on hot coals wondering if they'll be found so the interviews can be kept. Often they have to wait and wonder, and keep calling their clients' numbers with no response, until one or two o'clock in the morning. Then the agent's bedside phone will probably wake him out of his desperately needed sleep. It happens all the time.

By bedtime most agents are totally exhausted. Many have urgent financial problems that pursue them into these bedtime hours and prevent their sleeping at all. The only agents actors are likely to meet in the stylish star-hangout night spots late at night are those with the larger agencies who have to be there because that's the only time they can meet with their stars. The little guys...the one person office agents...are trying to get to sleep somewhere while worrying about their clients, worrying about the office rent, and worrying about the day's failures to achieve results for some of their clients.

Agents' nighttimes often being the unhappy times they are, if you know your agent's home address it's those nights when he or she has come home from a busy office / studio day's work that, in checking the home mail, a card or letter of appreciation is nice, or some flowers waiting with a note letting them know they're loved and appreciated, or something else. They need spirit boosting just as the actor does. Thoughtful gestures by their clients during the daytimes at the office mean less, agents say. It's those night hours when the failures of the day assault them. You might bear this in mind as relationships continue and deepen over longer periods.

CONTINUING ACTOR-AGENT RELATIONS

It's important that actor-agent relations get off on the right foot to start with. A "game plan" should be talked immediately.

If you're a newcomer with few or no credits there's not much to talk. The agent will decide how you're to be handled and all you can do is accept that plan or change agents.

If you're somewhat established, salary setting is a touchy thing, but it needs to be done right away upon signing with a new agent (if not before signing, in fact). And from time to time it needs to be revised, whether officially or unofficially, between you and your agent. This means setting the amount of salary that the agent feels is practical to ask that you be paid when you work---whether on a daily, a three-day for television, or on a weekly or term contract of any kind. You should recognize that, except in a few cases, it's a round and approximate figure. The agent would normally check with you anyhow, any time an offer comes that is for less than you've previously accepted as your "established salary". In some cases the agent may advise that you take the lesser amount for some extenuating reason. Usually you're getting good advice based on the circumstances in any such particular case. Some production companies habitually pay less. Some television productions have what's called "Top of The Show"---a figure that's stated to be the top salary ever paid for a guest role.

Don't ever tell your agent to "Say no...but don't lose it!" In other words, don't tell your agent to try to get your customary salary, but if he or she can't, to go ahead and accept the job. This ties the hands of the agent on negotiation and it exasperates and disenchants agents. If you're worth the money level set with the agent and the agent feels the production can pay that salary, let them go for it...and if you lose the role you lose it. It's much better that way. Casting directors will almost always try for a special deal. Your agent knows that and also knows that if you're really wanted the difference can be taken away from some other role in the budget.

The agent also knows that every studio keeps either computerized or card-filed records of each salary you earn, both at that studio and, to the extent they can find out, at every other studio. The agent therefore knows that if you accept a job for less at one studio not only that studio but several others, following inquiry, will also know it in the future and keep trying to pare you down because you're that kind of patsy and available for less with a little persuasion. Even if the casting person promises it will be a "no quote", secret "special favor" deal, never reported to others....that's no assurance these days.

In a continuing relationship with an agent remember that the agent is part of your business staff. If you've done a poor job on a reading, tell the agent. Maybe some manner of fence-mending can be done with the casting person or producer immediately---by the agent. If you get a sensational comment from a casting person, a director or producer with whom you work...or from the film's editor following the dailies, tell the agent. Those comments can be quoted by the agent in other casting offices and results can be kindled by them quickly.

When you're invited to lunch or dinner by your agent, or especially when the agent agrees to have lunch or dinner with you at your request, you should offer to pick up the check. Yes, you should! Even though any agent is supposed to be wealthy from all the commissions you've brought to the office, some aren't. Remember, the busy agent is taking valuable time away from other business---and often from larger-commission-earning clients to spend the time focusing on your career. That's why you should offer. Nine times out of ten the agent will insist upon paying anyhow, just to save face with the client.

If you're an actor who likes to do theatre, it should be borne in mind that in Hollywood your agent may have some very good reason for asking you to not accept certain roles or even to not do theatre at all in the current period because of something in the works or possible, so at least make a phone call to the agent and check before saying yes to anything. The item uppermost in the agent's mind in such cases is the fact that you'll be in rehearsal or committed to perform for a given period during which any number of higher-paying offers or at least opportunities may come up for you and you'll be unavailable.

As for a more personal relationship and constant "crony-ism" between agent and client, most agents avoid this like the plaque. Time and again they state that they are part of your business team, not your private life. They don't really want to know it when you're behind in your rent....it

75

scares them with the need to help you pay it. It can cause them to fall into compromising you by seeking smaller roles or "just anything" to help you out of holes.

Only if an agent seeks a closer personal relationship (and hopefully with no strings attached) should there be one. They're usually too busy and have little time for close relationships with clients.

Normally it's death to the actor-agent relationship for you to even think of circulating your own photos and resumes to casting and production companies. It reduces the agent's negotiating position if and when roles do come up. Some agents won't quibble with you doing it when you're first starting out and nobody knows you yet, but once you've started working at all it's usually a definite no-no.

There's an exception to the foregoing, however. There are some very low budget productions which advertise their casting in _Drama-Logue_ or_Variety_ or elsewhere, seeking "Union or Non-Union" people for their upcoming roles. In such cases the agent probably isn't going to bother with them or would do so very perfunctorily, and if it's clearly understood out front with the agent that you'd like to circulate on your own to these productions, or at least send your photo to them, perhaps the agent won't mind. After all, agencies have to concentrate on the larger opportunities for the most good of the most clients at all times. They probably won't make the drive to that producer of a low-budgeter in Arcadia or Azusa who may never get his picture off the ground at all and if he does will probably be paying "scale" for all people and the agent can't even take his commission on "scale" salaries.

Sometimes, as you become more in demand and have worked with a good director or producer a few times, perhaps have even become a friend with him or her, the producer or director will probably call you direct and ask you to do a role in something coming up. Carelful! Don't accept or even talk salary in that phone call. It's far better to say you'd "certainly be interested," but you think your agent has "something coming up that might conflict," so the producer or director should check with your agent, or you can have your agent call them later the same day or tomorrow to discuss it. Don't accept or talk any negotation points on the phone. Get your agent into the picture instantly. As soon as the friend has hung up, get to your agent. Tell him or her all the details you've been able to get thus far and ask the agent to follow up on it, which of course he or she will want to, immediately.

Don't trust the producer or director friend to call the agency. It's better that the agency call them, since some don't really relish dealing with agencies anyhow and might not make the call....whereas, if the agent calls back right away they feel obliged to start honest negotiation. That way, the agent can stay on top of it as it develops so that you won't be taken for granted, important decisions about your participation won't be put off, salary won't be left vague, billing won't wind up being less than you've been initially promised, etc. Agents know how to protect these things. You may not know the steps.

Just for your own information and feelings of security with the agency, from time to time go into the Screen Actors Guild Agency Department and ask to see the Client List of your agent. You may find that there are several of your type currently represented by the agency...which might account for the paucity of calls for you. You may find that you're the only one with decent name or credits, and feel you're with the wrong agent. You may discover that the agency has lost a lot of clients recently and may want to find out why....or that the agency appears to be signing too many new clients and spreading itself too thin.

When you finish a role, call the agent the minute you're released from the set and tell him or her you're finished and "available". It helps them plan more interviews for other jobs immediately if they know this one is finished. Thank them for getting the role for you---even if they didn't get it in the first place and obviously hope you won't realize that the director or producr called for you with no work on their part. They like to believe that you will think they got it for you. Unless some problem came up during the filming, be sure to tell them you had a wonderful time.

Never bad-mouth your agent in casting offices. The casting director may be a friend of the agent and word may get back. It's death, as far as any further trying for you by that agent. The agent figures that you're preparing to leave the agency soon anyhow, and simply stops working for you. Besides, casting people like to work with happy actors, and you run the risk of sounding bitter.

LEAVING AND CHANGING AGENCIES

The time may come when you want to change agencies for some reason. It's a good idea to find the new agency before terminating the current one, for obvious reasons. Then go in and talk. Explain your reason and keep in mind the current agent's vulnerable ego. Why? You may find out later that you've made a mistake and want to come back. As mentioned earlier in this chapter, some will take a former client back and some won't. Some will do it only if the client's commission potential justifies the concession in *strictly money terms*, since the earlier excitement of building the actor isn't there anymore.

Larger agencies continually proselytize from smaller agencies. The smaller agencies resent it---and naturally resent their client leaving them just when they've become recognized and are bringing in higher commissions through the smaller agent's career building efforts. But if the client wants to make the move there's little the smaller agent can do to prevent it, and it's an awful reminder of the pecking order in the agency field. It makes the small agent feel smaller. Don't leap to change to that larger agency unless there's a damned good reason.

Some larger agencies (1) are far more impersonal, and may have only a fleeting interest in you for a specific project that may fall through; (2) may be taking you on because you're coming up and threatening one of their established clients (this has been done, with disastrous results to the inno-

77

cent and naive actor who immediately notes the stagnation of their blossoming career because the large agency is literally preventing their getting the roles being reserved for the agency's current star); or (3) you may simply be known to one or two of the agents in the larger agency (who persuaded the higher-ups there to let him or her take you on) and you may still remain a stranger---overlooked and ignored---to the other agents there. With those other agents (who aren't interested in you or perhaps don't even know you) handling the production company groups and studios where you've previously worked you'll probably be forgotten quickly in those offices because your name will no longer be brought up.

Hopefully in a good agency relationship your career will experience what are called upward "career moves". Larger roles, better billing, higher salaries. If after many roles, many times receiving the same or no real billing, and no salary raises when you work, there's little upward mobility observed, then it's probably time for a sitdown with the agent to find out the reason. If the reason given satisfies you, okay. If the agent feels it's impossible to do any better for you at the time then you might consider looking around among those agents who handle the next higher level of talents. One might recognize your worth and offer you representation.

Don't, though, tell the current agent that you're starting to look for a new agent. Again, the enthusiasm will evaporate in the same moment, and you'll be even worse off while still with the current agency. Simply look, go on interviews with new agents, and when you're satisfied you've found the right place sign with the new agent and the same day send the SAG-required termination notice to the agent you're dismissing. Or go in and handle the dismissal in person along with the official written termination.

Termination letters should be friendly notes, thanking the agents for their efforts in your behalf and explaining that you're going to give the other agency "a try". That way, you're leaving the door open with the agent you're leaving, in case you want to go back someday.

If the agent seems to be working for you, and seems qualified to conduct the appropriate level of negotiation and career-moving representation you want, stay where you are. If you seem to be moving beyond the capabilities and prestige of the agent perhaps you should consider changing. It's that simple. You'll rise or fall backward on that one decision as you move upward.

An agency realizes that it's only as good as the clients it represents and that's not a bad criterion for the actor to remember as well. If you know your agency represents some pretty fine people, gets them good roles, good salaries and good billing, chances are you're with a good agency. If on the other hand you get the impression that you're the only frequently working client and you aren't constantly moving upward in the kinds of roles called in to read for; if the salary levels for the roles you get aren't moving upward at least slowly; if the billing you get isn't becoming any better over a long period...those are signs that you should probably consider the desirability of changing agents. They're the best reasons we can think of. It could mean that you've outgrown the agent's negotiating abilities.

Chapter Eleven

Other Avenues
Newcomers Can Try

Sometimes actors can try and try over long periods and still be unsuccessful at obtaining agency representation. Don't despair. There are other things available, and other avenues for the getting of them.

While the "theatrical" agent (for motion pictures and television) is often tough to get, getting a _Commercial Agent_ is usually much easier. While purely "theatrical" agencies usually limit the number of talents they feel they can represent at any one time---to either very few or maybe fifty to seventy or so, "commercial" agencies usually represent from two to four hundred or more people, since when commercial agents send people out for the casting of commercials it's like shooting buckshot and when a young "Coke" type is called for they like to send several of that type out on the chance that just one of the several will have the face, body and personality that will strike the fancy of the commercial production group as being standout.

For a commercial it's impossible to know which of several very similar type actors will appeal to the large panel of decision-makers involved in the commercial's casting. It's usually some special uniqueness---a face, a smile, a manner or something else that determines which actors will get "call-backs" for second consideration of a smaller group, and it's usually still one of those same special uniquenesses, rather than acting talent, that determines who finally gets the job. That's why, on any commercial interview, an agency's client should expect to run into several of the same agency's other clients who are of the same age and general type. It's very common procedure for a commercial agency to send several "30 year old house-wives" or nine or ten "teenage Coca Cola types". And, upon arrival for first auditions, it's customary to find the outer office filled with from fifty to a hundred others of the actor's general age and type.

Commercial auditions are literally *"cattle calls"*, but for a newcomer such wide open casting is great, since in the early period of seeking work and in those first auditions you're on absolutely equal ground with hundreds of actors with extensive credits...and you may get lucky and be just what the commercial needs!

Also, you don't have to already be a SAG membr if a commercial agent wants to handle you or if a commercial producer wants to hire you. It's one of the quickest and easiest manners of obtaining SAG membership, being cast in a commercial. A commercial, being a selling tool of the advertiser, can hire a non-SAG actor for his or her very first job without being fined by the union, simply because he or she is considered by the commercial's production group to be the *only actor considered ideal for the role.*

So don't hesitate to really concentrate on trying to obtain a commercial agent as soon as you have your photos and résumés and a sheet of proofs ready. You need only a few 8x10's printed up, to indicate what you look like, before seeking commercial agents' interest. If the agent likes your "headshot" and calls you in and subsequently decides to handle you that agent will choose (from your proof sheets) the photos you're to have made up, and tell you where and how to have them done for your composite.

If you have only "headshots" on your proof sheets, the agent, upon deciding to take you on as a client, will probably require that you go to an experienced "commercial" photographer and have a "commercial photo shoot", coming away with many shots of you in separate wardrobes, handling props, in authentic-looking locations, doing things. Those are needed for your <u>Commercial Composite</u>. Bring the proof sheets to the agent for choosing of the shots to have printed and included on your composite.

By the way, if you've already gone to the expense of having complete composites of the type required by commercial agents made up ahead of time on your own, nine times out of ten the agent won't approve of them and you'll be required to have another composite of their design made up quickly. Trust them when this comes up. They know how they plan to sell you for commercials. They know far better than you what kinds of composite photos they'll need to do it right.

Once you have a commercial agent, plan to have daytimes free because interviews are in the daytime and come suddenly and without any warning.

You should also plan to check with your answering service almost every hour on the hour, or always leave your locations with the service if you don't carry a beeper, since commercial interview appointment calls are usually of the "Get over to....right away!" type.

Commercials will be gone into more thoroughly in a later chapter. Here, we're talking about _getting_ a commercial agent as one of the things you can do while you're marking time getting the other (theatrical) agent.

Another thing you can try for during this early period is _Low Budget Motion Pictures_. The advantage you have with these is that the top stars won't generally do them except when the industry is in a production slump. The money the low-budgeters can or will offer usually gets a flat "No!" from more established people's agents. The low budget folks know this out front and much of the time look for "new faces" with talent and ability. In fact, a lot of the low budget producers don't even want to have to deal with agents. They have their reasons, of course---mostly centered on money but also on the simpler negotiations of filming and working conditions when actors are negotiating for themselves.

There are good, meaty roles in these low budget pictures that the less established actors and even talented newcomers stand an excellent chance of getting if they get lucky in interviews and readings.

Many upcoming low budget motion pictures are listed, with their casting needs, in _Drama-Logue_ each week. To avoid the problems of dealing with agents, these productions are happy to list their roles in the paper and encourage actors to submit themselves direct.

If you're not yet a SAG member you can often obtain your SAG card in one of these low budget films. Many low budget productions are SAG signatory. That way, you'll at least be paid SAG minimum salary, with no agency commission to pay. If the production says it's going to be a SAG film, call SAG and confirm this so you'll know. If it's to be non-SAG (non-union), simply watch out for the working conditions, on time payment of salary and other things SAG would otherwise be assuring for you.

There are also _Industrial Films_ which are often open to newcomers and whose casting needs are also published in _Drama-Logue_. Try for those too. They're not for theatrical release, of course, because they're designed as training films and company sales and identity promotion films for convention showings, etc. But they pay, and some are SAG signatory, again offering the SAG membership opportunity which will put you in a better light with any agent you're still seeking.

The top universities and colleges in the Los Angeles area offer _Student Film_ opportunities for newcomers as well. Their graduate and post-graduate students make them as part of their course requirements. They usually shoot on weekends or at night. They're usually "shorts" (between twenty and thirty minutes long on the average), but for the newcomer they offer the opportunity to work in front of cameras, get used to actual filming conditions, hitting marks, doing take after take to get shots right, learning to match for editing purposes, etc.

81

There's no money involved in student film performances, but once in a blue moon some magic strikes and a student film which is outstanding lands a Universal contract for Steven Spielberg (as it did) and it's seen by many people, benefitting its cast members (including perhaps Amy Irving, as it did also). You can often persuade the student filmmaker to give you a copy of the film later---many offer this without being asked. Then you can use it or a clip from it for your personal audition tape purposes.

There are also the *"5 and Under Bit Roles"* in television sitcoms and soap operas that are taped under AFTRA jurisdiction. They're offered to newcomers almost exclusively. Litle more than "extra" roles, they nevertheless often turn into effective "getting acquainted" opportunities and top casting directors like Fran Bascom and others often become helpful forever after for the people willing to start in this manner.

A "5 and under" role is, after all, a speaking role---even though it has five or fewer lines. It's an effective manner of auditioning for better things. It also, as a speaking role, makes young AFTRA members eligible to join SAG.

We should discuss *Extra Work* also. There were many, many years when it was unthinkable for actors bent on important careers to even consider doing extra work when starting out. That's changed. Most industry people accept the change and don't hold it against you if you've done early extra work to get started. Whether it helps get started on imporant career stuff is up to you. Do it only for the money and access to film sets where you can learn so much from observing, also perhaps meet people who might like you and later try to help you.

But beware those *Ads in Daily Papers's Classifed Ad Sections* that offer "Extra Work", as mentioned in an earlier chapter. There's always some charge for being registered, and it's not the way to go.

To obtain your best chance at getting "extra" work in motion pictures, you must be accepted by one of the organizations that get the calls for lists of extras needed for next days' film sequences. Central Casting is the main one. If they can use your type currently you'll be registered with them. Once accepted and registered with Central Casting, you can then go to Screen Extras Guild offices and join the Extras Guild.

And there's plenty of *Theatre* production in the many small theatres in Hollywood and nearby cities close enough for industry attendance to make it meaningful, aside from the good practice for your craft that any theatre experience offers.

Of course none of these opportunities will fall to you without your having read for them with producers and directors. So the casting interviews and readings for roles need a lot of discussing in one of the next upcoming chapters.

But first---still as one of the other avenues open to actors for starting their careers rolling---let's talk about *Modeling!* For some of today's top stars *modeling* was the beginning, and for some still at the peaks of their careers it's an occasional multi-million-dollar day's work!

Chapter Twelve

Modeling...Many Important Film Careers Have Started That Way!

Count them...the top film and television stars whose <u>modeling</u> careers brought them their first recognition and eventually, sometimes quickly, led them to important starring careers in film and television. At least **Tom Selleck, Cybill Shepherd, Marilyn Monroe, Jennifer O'Neil, Maud Adams, Brooke Shields, Mark Harmon, Brigitte Bardot** and others spring to mind immediately. But there are many, many more than these few who began as models and rose to acting stardom without those early modeling pages of their history being widely publicized.

Most actors don't know that when some *soap opera*s are casting for beautiful or handsome young cast members it's often the <u>modeling</u> agencies that get the first calls, with the stipulation that the models "have some acting experience" as well. When handsome and beautiful people are needed...as they always are in soap opera casts...where better to look first? As a round figure, about 90% or more of the new young faces in soap operas are currently either represented solely by modeling agencies or have recently signed with "theatrical" (motion picture and television) agents for the "soaps"...while remaining with the modeling agencies for modeling and perhaps commercial print work.

And surely you've noticed that many of today's biggest stars, once long ago top models, still <u>combine</u> their two careers when the money's right...and when *they* return to modeling for a one day shoot those checks can be for up into seven figures!

Many actors fail to realize that there are modeling careers for not only the pretty people, whether male or female, but also for the very *un*-pretty, very plain or just very interesting-looking "character" folks. Of course they're not "fashion" or "runway" models...but they're often very much in demand as "commercial" models.

Whichever category you may fall into...pretty or handsome or just plain or interesting, here are the things you must consider and steps you must be prepared to take for a modeling career.

MODELING IS HARD WORK!

Rose hartman wrote a fantastic overview of modeling in an article entitled "Pretty Hard Work" that appeared in *Taxi* Magazine some years ago. I'll quote as closely as I can remember:

Beauty, good bones and the right height are important, but she or he must also be an <u>actor</u>! A good fashion or runway model understands what any piece of clothing can do. The sparkling smile or air of hauteur must be continually held in those turns, glides and vamps on runways, and in shoots for products of all kinds the attitude, poses and expressions that ideally present the products involved must be <u>good acting</u>. Advertisers appreciate the fact that it's the model's look that will sell their product. They happily pay $5,000 or more a day for the right model, after considering many, and those models who rise to the top through their ability to bloom like hot-house flowers in the frenzied, high-strung, elephantine-ego'd atmosphere of an important shoot can make as much as $350,000 or even more a year!

Bright-smiling, eager hopefuls waiting in the outer offices of Eileen Ford, Johnny Casablancas or Zoli in New York, or Elite Model Management (Johnny Casablancas's Hollywood branch), Mary Webb Davis or Nina Blanchard (also in Hollywood) have those top dreams. Some are accepted and signed for promotion; some are told "Your eyes are too close together, your lips are too thin, your shoulders aren't broad enough, your legs are too heavy" and other very straight-out critical and very personal comments that can dash all hopes for the most desperately hopeful. The modeling field is too fast to give anyone a break or waste time mincing words when someone should be quickly discouraged. The act of discouraging them is really a kindness in the long run.

Abigail Eaton-Germack, one of the heads of Eaton-Germack Agency, a Division of Eaton-Germack Productions, Inc., and one of the top talent and modeling agency heads representing some of the top and swiftly rising models working both coasts, agrees. She says:

"A model must have determination and gumption, a tough skin and a constantly maintained positive attitude. Models must be flawless, intelligent beings that can think on their feet and continue to shine throughout a long and demanding project. A good diet, a good skin care program and a good exercise regimen are main elements which contribute to the development and maintenance of a good model."

"Abby", as her clients and many of us know her, has laid out the following steps...steps that should begin as soon as someone decides to pursue a modeling career. Starting in the manner she suggests, the first steps can be stopped summarily if there's discouragement instead of encouragement by those who are willing to give candid, objective advice:

FIND A GOOD AGENT

The very first step is to find an agent who will be able to honestly and enthusiastically represent you.

An agent shouldn't charge a fee to _train_ you as a model. A good agent will be able to label your look as either "Fashion" or "Commercial" immediately and know whether he or she can sell you.

Interview with as many agents as possible. Find out about their backgrounds and histories; discern from talking with them what they may be able to do for you. Again, there should be absolutely _no financial investment_ required for representing you. Don't confuse modeling _schools_ with modeling _agencies_. There are no guarantees in the modeling field. Any investment on your part should be seriously considered. Recognize that every penny spent in the early period is strictly "venture capital" of a one man or one woman private enterprise, and may stay that for some time.

START A PORTFOLIO

Next, if there's enough encouragement to go for a career, compile some fantastic photographs with which to begin your _Portfolio_. Your newly found agent should be able to recommend a number of different photographers, some of whom may be interested in "testing" you. (More on testing later.)

Consult fashion magazines, American and European. Decide what kind of shots you want to start with. Headshots are probably the best to begin with. For a Fashion model, a photo similar to a cover shot for a fashion magazine would be good. For a Commercial model, something less glamourous is best. An honest, straight forward shot is good. For a "commercial" look, some product shots or "character" shots as banker, mother, blue collar worker, etc.

Line up appointments with a number of photographers to look at their books..._their_ portfolios...to find out what types of work they produce. It's also an opportunity to become acquainted with them and find out if you'd be comfortable working with them.

Find a _stylist_. A stylist will assist with hair and makeup and possibly even wardrobe suggestions; will prove to be very helpful on the set of a shoot, finessing the shot. Either your new agent or a photographer will be able to help you find the right stylist.

Start with black and white photography, because of the expense of full color shots. After the shoot you'll receive a contact sheet from which you may pick some photos to be enlarged to 8x10 size. Don't make your own decisions or selections. Consult your agent. Your agent should be looking for versatility and ease in front of the camera, as well as a look they feel they can market.

Work with as many photographers as possible. Each photographer will see and shoot a different look. For _fashion_ modeling, compile a wide variety of looks and shots, once again referring back to fashion magazines for helpful ideas for shots. Gather a variety of shots like lingerie, bathing suits, full figure, elegant, casual, location, studio, etc.

Next, prepare a _Composite Card_. Modeling agents call it a _Comp Card_.

YOUR COMPOSITE CARD

A composite card is a model's "calling card". Most are 5x8 standard, with up to four or more pictures with your statistics on the front or back. Once again, your agent should be asked to help you put together your composite card layout with shots that are sure to help get you bookings.

Every time you go on an audition a composite card should be left with the client, so they'll remember you after you leave. Your agent should always have an updated supply. Without a "comp card" it's impossible to market a model!

Composite cards are an investment. After the photography and the actual printing of the cards, it's not unheard of to spend $500 to $800 or more for those full color cards. As few as 100 cards may be printed at a time, but it proves to be more economical in the long run to print a larger quantity...500 or more.

Comp cards should also be updated about once a year, with the model's changing looks and maturing. If the model is being effectively marketed by the agent the supply should dwindle swiftly anyhow over this period of time and therefore need to be replaced.

A comp card should demonstrate as many different "looks" as possible. The front or cover shot should be the strongest shot on the card, as that will be the first impression picture. The more variety on the card, the more bookings it will produce.

MORE ON PHOTOGRAPHY FOR MODELS

We mentioned "Testing" earlier. A _Test Shoot_ is considered an opportunity for the photographer to "test" a model, a film, a lighting situation or a combination of all or more. There should generally be little or no expense involved for the model. In fact, often a test shoot is considered a "free photos" shoot for the model. Sometimes one or more prints are given to the model as payment for his or her time. Generally the atmosphere is very casual, however the model is still expected to be professional. Perhaps there'll be only a stylist, the photographer and the model present.

A *Fashion Shoot*, on the other hand, may have a number of people involved. An Art Director, the Client, a Stylist, Hair and Makeup Artists, one or more Models, a Photo Assistant (or "P.A.") and a Photographer. Often the same will prevail at a *Commercial Shoot*. In both cases, the product...be it clothing, cosmetics, deodorant or a screwdriver...is the focal point. The model is hired to sell the product by making it appeal to the public. Attitude sells. The model is expected to *act* the "happy Mom" who's just discovered a great laundry detergent, or the glamorous woman who "just became more glamorous" by using a particular hair-coloring product. Through lighting, location, the model's facial expressions and attitudes, the product will sell.

WHEN YOU'RE BOOKED

The phone rings. It's your agent. Your answering machine gets the message if you're not in, but if you're there get all the pertinent information regarding the booking.

CLIENT...for whom you're to work...

DATE...

TIME...A model's call is generally about 15 minutes early...

LOCATION...Get these details *exactly!*...

WARDROBE...Will there be a fitting, or will the model supply?...

MAKEUP AND HAIR...Will someone else do it, or you?...

RATE...If you have a set hourly fee will it be paid?...

A good model will have a *Weekly Appointment Book* next to the telephone, so all of the above information can be recorded, and the model will know immediately if there will be any conflicts with other scheduling. Read back to the booking agent all the information you've taken down for confirmation so you're sure everything is correct. Also, find out if an *Agency Fee* will be *added to* the rate or *deducted from* the rate. Get as much information about the booking as possible.

FITTINGS

If a *Fitting* is required of the model for the shoot or show, be sure to show up on time, with a complete *Tote Bag* in hand, looking great. (More on the "Tote Bag" later.) If it's a department store, for example, try to appeal to the store's look and project nothing but a professional, ready attitude. Be pleasant and outgoing.

You'll be given some outfits to try on. Never make negative comments. You may despise the outfit; they may love it. Or they may hate it too but know it'll sell. The client is always right. Smile and leave final decisions to the client.

After the clothes have been tried on, hang them back on the hangers they came off of, rack ready. Make notes as to anything...shoes, accessories...you may need to provide when you return for the shoot. Thank them for their time and leave. Don't stay and shop. If shopping is on your mind, drop your tote bag in your car and come back in as a customer, not a model.

You'll generally be paid for the fitting. However, this isn't always true. Make sure you've checked with your agent about this.

THE FASHION SHOW

Fashion Shows are a great opportunity for models to get into the "act" of things. When on a runway or ramp, the model is really *acting*...cute and fresh or bitchy and sophisticated...whatever the garment suggests. The clothes worn will determine the attitude that's right.

A *Runway Model* must be tall, slender and striking. Height is imperative, as most couturier designs are designed to fit a tall build. A runway model is a *quick change artist*, sometimes having only about 30 seconds to completely change from one outfit to the next and perhaps even changing hairstyle! She or he must return to the runway completely composed and relaxed, overflowing with confidence. The rewards aren't always great in "runway", compared to "print" work (the latter usually being display advertising for magazines, etc.), but a good "Show Girl" or "Show Fellow" will make as much as $4,000 per day in European design salons of world-famed couturiers. Note, though, the key word here is "good".

To be successful onstage in a show, a model must be successful backstage also. It's vital that he or she be fully prepared. Showing up a bit early allows a little extra time to get everything arranged for yourself and make sure everything about your person and your accessories is ready to go into action.

BEHIND THE SCENES

When a model arrives at a fashion show, the first thing to do is check in with the Coordinator. Pick up a lineup and check the clothing to be shown. Organize the items of clothing in the order in which they're to be worn. Unzip, unbutton any zippers or buttons for an easy, quick "on" for each item, in the right sequence, once the show begins.

Lay out all accessories and shoes, then introduce yourself to any models you may not know. Relax and get ready. Remember, never smoke, drink or eat around the clothes or in the dressing room. The model is ultimately responsible for the condition the clothes are returned in. Be as quiet as possible backstage, and listen to the Coordinator. Even if the show has been rehearsed, things might change at the last minute, so always do as you're told, even if this differs from a rehearsal.

After the show, take time to hang all the clothes back up, rack ready, and clean up the area where you were dressing. Remember to check out with the Coordinator before leaving.

TOOLS OF THE TRADE

A model doesn't need a lot to be successful...just determination, a positive attitude, and a great look. A pulled-together _Portfolio_ is of course a must, and a _Comp Card_ to leave with prospective clients.

But there's one more item which is considered a model's "survival kit"...the _Tote Bag_. The Tote Bag should be lightweight, durable, easy to care for and inexpensive. The model's name and also the agency's name, address and telephone number should be tagged to the bag. The bag should zipper or close and should be carried by the model to all fittings, shoots and shows. Never embarrass yourself or employers by showing up without this item!

TOTE BAG ITEMS FOR WOMEN

A roll of masking tape	Sewing Kit	Makeup Hood
Assorted Neutral Lingerie	Scissors	Assorted Shoes
Tweezers	Assorted Pantyhose	Deodorant
Accessories	Cotton Balls	Clothing Brush
Kleenex	Aspirin	Underarm Shields
Breath Spray	Anti-Static Spray	Appointment Book
Mirror	Pen or Pencil	Manicure Kit
Makeup Touchup Kit		

TOTE BAG ITEMS FOR MEN

Jockey Shorts (not Boxers)	Posing Strap	Athletic Supporter
Dress Shoes, Brown & Black	Socks, Over-the-Calf,	Shaving Equipment
Comb and Hair Brush	in Dark Colors	Socks, Athletic
Hairspray, if used	Shirt Collar Tabs	Cuff Links
Assorted Ties	Belts, Mixed	Deodorant
Kleenex	Anti-Static Spray	Hand Mirror
Lint Brush	Breath Spray	Safety Pins
Suspenders	Voucher Book	Pen or Pencil
Appointment Book		

In addition to the above standard items for all, anything else that the individual model's appearance suggests in terms of what kind of modeling he or she may be called upon for.

A MODEL SHOULD NEVER BE UNPREPARED

Modeling interviews of all kinds come quickly, without warning. From the moment of getting out of bed in the morning into fairly late night hours, a model must be bathed, hairstyled, made up, cleanly and neatly dressed and ready for inspection. The male model can't afford those days when he doesn't feel like shaving and wants to run around sloppy.

Because of the suddenness of some calls---especially for those "just a quick look-see" inspection interviews some clients demand, the model should never be without his or her Appointment Book, Portfolio and a supply of Comp Cards to leave in offices. A comb and hairspray if used should be handy at all times too.

AND MODELING IS ALWAYS *ACTING!*

If you're also a finely developed actor or actress when you're employed for a commercial or print shoot it will save much time and hourly fee cost for the many participants in those shoots, and your *acting* talents will excite the ad agency people who'll surely be there supervising the handling of the product you'll be beaming at. Remember, those same agency and sponsor people also produce television commercials....perhaps with you as a principal or even as the product's spokesperson if they've really appreciated your talents in a previous employment.

Modeling really has been a stepping stone in the early years of many film and television acting careers. It's decent money while you're waiting to be discovered in strictly acting talent terms, and you're more likely to meet all kinds of people who travel in important entertainment industry circles, when modeling, than you would be in a lot of other kinds of work.

It's also great in terms of how much you can learn about working for the camera! There aren't many professions that offer that so continually and so ideally.

Chapter Thirteen

Casting Interviews and Readings For Roles

There are two kinds of interviews: **_General Interviews_** (for casting people to simply meet and talk with you and obtain first impressions) and actual **_Readings For Roles_** (where scripts or sides are handed you and, following preparation, you read before a casting director, a director or producer or perhaps all three people).

GENERAL INTERVIEWS

General interviews in earlier years were held weekly, sometimes daily, by most casting people. The industry is faster paced now, though, and most casting people don't grant general interviews except in very special cases. A few grant them when activity slackens, but even then only on a sporadic basis. General interviews take too much time for the current rat race. When you get one, if you do want some, you're lucky....or so you think at the time.

It's difficult for casting people to correctly appraise your talents or even your theatrical personality in general interviews. After you're out of the office you're often out of their minds---at least to an extent. Maybe there has been some interest aroused by you and by what they could sense in the brief meeting, but what good does that do in an industry where a casting director's continuing employment depends on their supplying *dependable, experienced people* for all those upcoming roles?

Most casting directors are "independent" now, meaning that they're independent contractors and not studio employees assured of any longevity. The time for chance-taking on newcomers is past. The casting person who brings in too many new people who don't impress the producers and directors and waste hours of precious interview time are soon replaced by other casting directors.

Be sure to bring your photo and résumé to a general interview (also to reading interviews, by the way), even though you or your agent may have sent your material ahead of time. Casting people don't like to have to look for that picture and résumé they've accidentally thrown in the wastebasket or filed somewhere. Have one ready to hand them when you walk into their office.

In only a few cases will you be handed something to actually read at a general interview (for getting acquainted purposes) or even be asked to come back at a later time to do a scene. Again, it's the press of time. You have that one very limited chance to get acquainted with the person across the desk and for them to become even perfunctorily acquainted with who you are and what you are and what you may be able to do as an actor. This kind of meeting isn't likely to accomplish much, so don't delude yourself. The actor scheduled next after you is just as sure that he's "special" and that his talent and personality will "knock 'em dead". Chances are, he'll fare no better than you after walking out the door again.

Aside from its dubious worth in the eyes of most casting directors and agents---and in the eyes of actors who've been through many of them with little or no result---are the opportunities such interviews present to make unremediable mistakes that actually prolong career starts rather than quicken them.

A quick way to make yourself forgettable in those precious first meeting opportunities---so precious to you but to nobody else---is to proclaim how _versatile_ you are and then spend the meeting time finding ways to impress them with the fact that you can play _any_ role well. Chances are you'll be trying to show so many aspects of your talents that they'll be unable to categorize you in any niche that might come up for casting.

Stanislavski said it long ago: "It is important in our art for every actor and actress to know his or her type." Some may be disdainful of the type-casting practices so general in the acting world, but it exists, and for good reasons, and you're better off facing it---especially when you're at that early point where you're going on general interviews at all and hoping to be remembered. To be remembered, you must be remembered as _something_!

The "*Big Smiler*" loses opportunities just as often. Certainly you're glad to be there face to face with a casting person who hasn't previously known you exist. But imagine how many people sit where you're sitting with those same big smiles of gratitude on their faces for the same reason. You may be a very deep, interesting or unusually unique actor when you're *not smiling*.

A general interview is really an audition of personality. All the rest is talk. The casting person needs to know you in *casting* terms, not social gratitude terms. They can become very tired of the perpetual "*Please Like Me*" smiles on most of the faces they meet which tell them nothing about the true personalities. Unless your smile is your biggest asset don't overuse it and be forgotten because of it the minute you walk out the door.

Often, too, that "big smiler" in the inner office of the casting director may have erased his chances ahead of time in the outer office or waiting room by being one of the self-defeating *V.I.P. Actors*....the apparently self-important actors who strut into outer offices and treat receptionists in a manner which might be okay from a temperamental and impatient real VIP who is sooner forgiven for such behavior. Often the "VIP actor" is really so insecure underneath that facade that he feels he must compensate to cover his nervousness, so he falls into this trap in the outer office.

Unfortunately, the secretary or receptionist knows exactly why this actor is there and doesn't need to be impressed with his importance. His name is on a list of new people just barely fortunate enough to even have that interview at all and it's common knowledge that general interviews are for people just starting out. Treat the receptionist rudely or impatiently, and the minute you leave after the interview they'll go inside and effectively ruin any chance you may have created inside while behaving so differently in the presence of the casting director.

Another thing that the "VIP actor" should bear in mind is that in this money-saving era in the industry this year's secretary-receptionist will probably be next year's casting director in the same office. It happens all the time. And they do remember you. If they're in a casting office at all that's part of their job.

The *Résumé-Padder* gets into trouble also in general interviews. If a number of films are listed on your résumé when you aren't even a membr of the Screen Actors Guild this will certainly be noticed and questioned. If you mention being in something you weren't in, or something totally fictitious, chances are that's exactly the item you'll be asked to talk about. Bet on it. Casting directors aren't dumb. They can smell lies and pick them out quickly.

Al Onorato, head of casting at Columbia at the time, was quoted in an interview/article in *Drama-Logue* with the advice that when you're starting out everybody knows you don't have a lot of background and doesn't expect it of you. Mr. Onorato seemed to be assuring that you'll be judged more on potential and what can be discerned about your personality and readiness.

If you do decide to "pad" your résumé with some lies and some ficti-

93

tious credits and production companies that don't exist you're running the risk of getting caught and embarrassed in interviews. Remember, casting people know of or even know personally so many people from so many parts of the country and of the world. In fact, they cast pictures for some of those out-of-town and foreign production companies---often with exclusivity in American-based production. They are usually at least aware of what work is done by whom, even in outlying cities. Don't make them suspect you. Nobody appreciates being hoodwinked and the least suspicion that you're trying to fool them offends their intelligence and you're dead in your tracks with them.

Then there's the _College Drama Department Star_...fresh from rave reviews in college papers and the former favorite of the Drama Department head and starred in most of the Department's campus productions.

It's inconceivable to this luminary ego that there's any more to learn about acting. Most of his or her acting experience in college was on large theatre stages, and there is still training for film which has to be obtained here in Hollywood in most such cases. Casting people will generally ask with whom these folks are training or by whom they've been trained here already. They know the importance of continuing training under professional coaching here, whether these folks do or not. Frequently they offend these young egos by being so presumptious as to suggest they seek coaching. They're always suspicious that these folks haven't learned to reduce theatre projection to the "living presence" level demanded by film and to get rid of the "Speech Department" perfection and get back to ordinary, unaffected American talking style. Casting people know that some pretty bad habits can have been developed in college training if it hasn't been professionally oriented toward all performing mediums by someone with at least some professional, rather than only academic background.

Don't ever tell a casting director that you've _finished_ studying. You might in fact ask them for the names of some more outstanding coaches and teachers. Better yet, be _already studying_ with someone here before you start going in on such interviews.

The Actor, too, has made many mistakes in interviews. The perfect speech---so laboriously perfected to lose a regional accent; the very correct social manner---rather than a looser, more natural and casual manner which allows your personality its freedom; the statement that you got excellent reviews in those Shakespearean dramas---since there's not much Shakespeare being done in Hollywood; the "Noel Coward and Laurence Olivier", affected and polished English---that you thought would make you an "instant matinee idol" upon arrival in Hollywood......these and other carefully cultured and unnatural sophistications brought into casting offices by "the actor" are obviously wrong for most roles which the casting person is likely to be working on at the moment or at any foreseeable time in the future. "Actors" are seldom cast these days. _Interesting human beings_ work all the time! It's something more newly arrived actors should bear in mind.

Don't thrust your _portfolio of photos_ in front of the casting person unless it's asked for. Some prefer to only glance cursorily at your material if at all and then concentrate on back-and-forth, wandering subject matter in talking with you, feeling they can learn far more that they're interested in and be able to judge you better in that manner. However, as mentioned before, even if you know they've previously received your photo and résumé, take another with you to the interview anyhow. Just remembr that it's a "live" interview you're at, not a showing of a model's portfolio or an audition for your photographer's work.

Above all, _don't beg!_ Body communication and body language tell a lot about you. The casting person knows you're there because you're hoping to inspire them to call you for a chance to work. They know you're still on the bottom rung of the acting ladder and desperate to climb up through their help. But try to enjoy meeting them on a peer level. Of course it's difficult for you to think that way, because of their position and all it implies, but it's not impossible if you simply remember that you, the actor, are necessary in their daily business. Their finding of exciting talents---especially those that are available at low beginner salaries---is their bread and butter even if not their cake. Remember that you're bringing them an interesting personality with intelligence, confidence and self-respect---and hopefully something uniquely your own that nobody else has. Otherwise, you'll be forgotten in the lowest category of forgettables on the whole totem pole of variations..._The Beggar!_

SOME GOOD ADVICE

A few years ago, in one of the author's industry panel discussions, the head of a large casting department and one of the most candid and straight-talking lady executives in Hollywood made some comments about general interviews that this author will never forget. Having recorded them, and having her permission to reprint them as long as I don't give her name---although most who know her will recognize her in a minute---those comments are put down here verbatim for you:

"If your smile is all you have, turn it on! Brighten my office up with your sparkling personality and light up my day by apparently thinking I'm a turn-on too. None of that half-smile stuff, though, that tells me nothing but that you're happy to have the interview and want me to like you whether you like me or not. If I like you I might play poker with you in my Saturday night club sometime but it won't make me hire you for a role.

"But if you're really at heart a moody, serious actor, what the hell's wrong with letting me see that side of you more than anything else? Okay, sure, smile a little once in a while so we don't both sink into a downer and start crying, but mostly plan ahead to have something to talk about that'll let me see that moodiness...that ability to experience things deeply. That's what I want in my important acting roles. And yes, I said plan! If you don't plan ahead, and get your subject matter into the interview, you'll just fall into what I call my 'pattern' interview stuff....._Tell me about yourself_....._'Where are you from originally?'_....._'Who've you studied with?'_ and so on. Now, how can you get that nice moodiness and depth into that kind of discussion?

"Talk about Hollywood conditions...that can make any of us moody. Talk about an old bag lady that came up to you outside the gate begging when you arived...that's sad enough to give you an opportunity to evidence some feeling. Of course there won't actually have been any old bag lady, and Hollywood conditions aren't all that terrible, but the point I'm making is that you've planned ahead of time to introduce those things into our meeting so you can show me your serious, moody side...your sensitivity...and so you'll be entertaining me with something different from all those '*Ask me some questions so I can have something to say*' people. You'd be surprised how many of those we see when we're interviewing. Correction!...those people we actually don't even see. We ask our usual questions and probably don't even hear the answers!

"If you're a real crumb ...a bad-ass...and if you can realize that my seeing that side of you will get you roles almost immediately in one of our shows if you can also act the way you really are, then the same thing's true. You don't have to be mean to me personally...I'd throw you out fast! Once Eddie Foy had an interview with a Tim somebody for something, and the guy came into Eddie's office at Screen Gems and pulled out a gun and aimed it at Eddie! That was the last time he got onto the lot, I might add. The guy planned ahead, but he planned a little too crazily to do himself any good. Actually, bad-asses and crazies are what he's always played, but he may have pulled that little stunt in some other offices too, because to establish himself as a crazy bad-ass he finally had to produce his own picture to get his career going.

"Just plan ahead, no matter what. Plan ahead how to get into our talk something...anything that you can really take off on and vent your spleen on in front of me. It won't offend me. I'm just there seeing that side of you that I wouldn't be likely to see otherwise and never know you have available. I guarantee you you'll be called in to read for a role quicker than a lot of others. There's constant need for you real crumbs, you bad-asses. Don't miss out on letting me find out that you qualify to be thought of that way.

"Now, there's that other area too... If you think you're tomorrow's sex symbol you can keep me from laughing at you behind my polite smile and get your point across subtly, but don't be too ridiculous or I'll giggle and think you're stupid and throw your picture away as soon as you leave. Just think a little of how you're sitting, what quality you think enhances your sexiness, your charisma, your appeal, whatever it is....and remember that you can't borrow or mimic those qualities, those manners, from Tom Selleck or Marilyn Monroe. They have to be yours.

"We're back to that uniqueness that matters always. Low-cut bodices won't do it; neither will those macho, spread-leg positions for you fellows. Some things do offend me. Be a little subtle, for God's sake. If it's there I'll see it. If it isn't, even though your friends tell you you're hot suff, don't kill your other kinds of opportunities by aiming for just a heavy visceral response and looking ridiculous because you're not cut out for it.

96

"In your case, those of you who think you have a chance in the sex appeal area...which does get jobs sometimes, let's face it...I can't tell you what to do, because for that quality to come across it's an individual thing. If it's Tom Selleck stuff or Marilyn Monroe stuff I've seen those in the original and I can see them coming a mile off. You've got to have something new, something I've never seen before. I guess the best advice I can give you, if you're going in this direction, is that the sex thing isn't the whole thing anyway. When it's there it's just part of some other special quality. You can recognize that it's there, but I think it's more important to realize that it's a result of something else, another personality thing...and you'll have to develop ways of bringing out that other personality first. The sexiness or appeal will come with it.

"I see some older character people here. I guess some of those last comments could apply to one or two of you I see here that I know. At least I think you've kept every ounce of your appeal...but mostly you've got to recognize that when you get to your age and from then on, your look, your special casting niche in a strictly visual sense is just as important as your personality...at least in my office. If you're less attractive now...go for it! If you're fat now, or skinny now, or craggy now, or little-old-lady-from-Pasadena-ish or whatever now, that's what I want to remember about you more than a single personality thing that's not there now as much as it may have been at one time. The time for youthful attractiveness, handsomeness or beauty is past for you. Just be what you really are now...whatever that is...and don't try to cover up any of those interesting differences from the rest of the human race. Let your mole show. Those wrinkles may be just what we're looking for right at the moment. Even a few varicose veins can give you character. Don't ever try to be 'dressed-up pretty' or 'ex-leading-man handsome', even if you were in that category some years back. And especially don't try for it if you've never been in that category even when you were younger. We know who among the still pretty and still handsome real ex-stars of that kind will work for the money we have for a role and they're going to be first on the list, naturally, because they still have some name value in cast lists. Lots of people still remember them and enjoy seeing what they look like now. Get yourself out of trying to compete with them. You haven't a chance. Be what you are when you're not feeling dressed up. We'll hire you a lot sooner.

"Oh, yes...especially you younger guys...late teenagers. Bear in mind that there are more roles these days for disturbed teenagers than for nextdoor nice guys and girls. Don't smile too much in my office, and don't dress up for the interview as if you're applying for an office job. Hell, don't dress up at all. I don't mean come in dirty and smelly. Just wear something that looks like you don't care that much what you look like. If you come in looking selfconsciously neat that won't suggest a single, solitary role to me. Be sure you dress in some manner that lets me think you might be right for some of the kinds of roles that we have in so many films now.

"One more thing. I think it's my pet peeve. See? I follow the fashion magazines. I'm what they call an executive, so I do. But I don't particularly like these horrible things I've got on, and if you young women come into my office in these loose wraparounds and belts and things how am I going to know what kind of body you may have? Sorry, but that's still important. And I won't see your face, probably. I'll spend all the time wondering if all that fashionable goop came from Rodeo Drive, and how much it cost, or if it came from somebody's attic. Your dress...whether you're a man or a woman...should never distract from your face. There aren't that many close-ups of dresses or pleated pants. Don't make me focus on what you have on.

"When the interview's finished, the casting person usually has a standard way of letting you know it...maybe just something like getting up and picking up some papers and saying 'Thank you for coming' or something like that. When it's over, don't dawdle. Don't stand and look beseechingly into our eyes as a last-moment plea for a handout job. Keep your dignity and avoid any last-minute begging. Shake our hand or do whatever else feels right, or just thank us for seeing you and leave.

"When you're outside the office, check your watch. A standard, half-hearted interview with a casting person may take about ten or fifteen minutes. If you're on the button of that length of time you may as well figure nothing really happened. If you've gone twenty or maybe thirty or more minutes it's been a darned good interview and you can hope to at least be remembered. See, when we're interviewing people most of us schedule people that way...fifteen minutes is standard. We know how to wrap up an interview politely with those standard ways of ending it. We know the actors won't end these visits so we're ready to when the time's used up. If we choose to visit with you longer, when we know there's the next interview waiting, we're enjoying you and our mind's working on how to peg you for casting later. Your picture and résumé are probably already in a special drawer or pile even before you're off the lot. It may not produce any instant result, or even one in the next week or month, but sooner or later there'll probably be a call from that casting director to come in to read for something.

"Oh, yes...those other "general interviews" some actors who don't know any better try to sneak in...the ones where there's a casting person at a party or somewhere where there are actors who haven't met him or her. Casting director Rachelle Farberman, a very straight-on person, has a standard response, she says, for the actor who walks up to her somewhere away from her office and says "Hi, I'm so-and-so...I'm an actor." She says she usually responds with "I'm Rachelle Farberman...I'm a human being, and I'm not in my office." Don't make those kinds of mistakes."

ROLE INTERVIEWS AND READINGS

When there's a role to be cast, along with the other roles in a production---whether it be television or motion picture, there may be _no readings at all_ for that particular role. It may be cast by inquiring about an actor the director has requested and, after finding out from the agent that the actor is not only available when needed but is also available at the salary and billing that's been budgeted for the role out front, the actor will have been "firmed" immediately.

Roles which require readings and interviews of a number of actor candidates usually signal the calling in of from five to eight actors (or fewer if the casting director is tops in knowledge of people and also in understanding the director's preferences).

Appointments are set up by the casting director's secretary calling the agents of those selected for call-in. The agents are told that their clients may come to the casting office and pick up the "sides" (a few pages of dialogue and action) that they can take home and study to prepare for the readings. These "sides" are required by the Screen Actors Guild to be made available to the actors twenty-four hours prior to their appointment times.

Arriving and Preparing To Read

When you arrive there may well be one, two or more other actors of your type there in the outer office who'll be reading for the same role you're there for. They'll be preparing in the outer office to do a better job than you do. Don't be dismayed if the casting person behaves as though they're close personal friends, giving them a peck on the cheek by way of greeting. It won't help them with the director and producer in the inner office who'll choose the best one for the role in spite of the casting director's best persuasions in the conference after all the readings are finished.

Arrive ahead of time, so you'll have enough time to look over the script (if a copy can be looked at) and prepare to read. Get there about a half-hour ahead of time. When the casting director has the list of names and their appointment times ready and gives it to the director and/or producer it usually says "10:30 - James Hallowell", "10:40 - William Jennings", etc. And James Hallowell's agent will have told the actor it's a 10:30 appointment...but 10:30 is the time when the actor's expected to be <u>ushered into the inner office</u>, not just arrive for the appointment. Get there a bit early.

If the receptionist can be persuaded to let you look at the whole script in the outer office there are some quick ways to find out more of what you'd like to know about your character than what you can learn from just those few pages of dialogue and action on the "sides". Check the first entrance of your character. In film and television scripts that's where you'll find the large, wordy description of your character. Check throughout the script quickly to see how important the role may be. Notice what other characters say about you...those often give you a clear picture of your character. "Sides" tell you so little. At least try to find out more.

Even if that description of your character at its first entrance in the script should be nothing like you as to age or description or even gender, don't start worrying. Calling you in at all simply means that they've decided to "go a different way" with the character and that you're definitely a possible for their new concept. The script changes, reflecting the new concept, simply don't yet appear in the script or sides given you for preparing to read. This happens often.

Your Reading Styles Determine What You're Cast For

It takes some actors a long time to find out---if they ever do---that there are good reasons for their failing to get certain roles (if not most) that they read for.

They may be good "dialogue" readers; they may have a goodly amount of access to their feelings and emotions; but they may be employing the precisely wrong---or at least less than effective---styles of reading for particular roles.

As soon as actors begin reading in those inner offices with casting directors, directors and producers it becomes apparent that they either do or don't understand the different styles of reading which make them ideal for the different levels of roles.

Some actors lucky enough to read for leading roles don't notice---as they give those "excellent line readings" full of intelligent insight, dramatic expressiveness, speech-coach-cultured inflections and perfect grammar, over and above a respectable degree of blievability and (too often) a lot of eye-to-eye working with the person reading opposite them---that the producer and director soon turn away surreptitiously and look at production schedules or something. Interest in the actor for that leading role has paled quickly. The actor is simply reading in a manner which makes him ideal for one of the "bit" roles. But most of the time an often-hired favorite who's worked for the director many times in those "bit" roles has probably already been set for that "bit" role even if the actor in to read for the larger role or his agent would consider accepting it.

If on the other hand it's a role of enough lines that the actor can at least accept the stepdown from the top role originally read for, and the direcor's friend may not have been set and is subsequently discovered to not be available when needed, the actor may be offered that smaller role and, on the set later, cuss his luck for not rising above those tiny roles. The actor wonders why. So does his agent. Neither realizes for a long time that he's simply a "pretty good actor" who gives "excellent line readings" which make him perfect for small roles but don't bring much else beyond the dialogue. The screenwriter has already been paid for the dialogue. The actor should bring what the writer can't supply. While this "pretty good actor" who gives "excellent line readings" usually brings the clarity (supplied by the writer) and brief moments of believable communication and interaction with other characters (supplied by the writer), he fails to bring the life of the character....the personal experience of the character that lies behind the dialogue and action.

Perfect dialogue delivery can quickly mark the actor with the "bit player" and "day player" labels in those very first moments of reading for roles. It makes him suitable for that quick-cut shot saying "They went that-away!", perhaps, but not much more. It's simple duplication of what the screenwriter has already contributed. Often it even falls short of that because if the script is any good the writer has probably at least created a whole human being...and the actor hasn't.

Leading Players Are Easily Spotted

Watch the leading players in films and on television more closely. Notice---even if for the first time---that the top stars' dialogue sounds original; that they seem to search for their words and phrases---which they of course know, but their characters shouldn't; that they don't speak sentences in a capital-letter-to-period rush or even observe punctuation like a high school grammar teacher; that they hesitate and struggle a little more with the obstructions to dialogue ease which result from their characters' fragmented inner thought and feeling processes; that there isn't nearly as much eye-to-eye communication as was taught you in your early acting classes; that they take their time and allow more experiencing time to intrude into their dialogue so that their personalities, the characters' moods and feelings and their own identifying with what they say and do can be brought into their performances.

Starring actors and actresses have usually cultivated he art of duplicating human processes more faithfully and at some point in their careers have become courageous enough in readings for roles to bring those processes into their readings. Perhaps at some point when they were called in to read for a somewhat smaller role they were sent back out into the outer office and told to come back in to read for a very important role---their very first starring role! If this happened it was probably because they were brave enough to make themselves less than ideal for the smaller role and at the same time impressed the producer and director with their "leading role" potential by bringing a total human being rather than an expert "reading" which would have denied them that unexpected opportuniy. So few actors realize this basic principle. Some, realizing it, aren't brave enough to observe it when reading for roles.

Film used to be called "talking pictures." The actors talked very well. Observe how easily some of those earlier performances might just as well have been transferred to radio without losing a thing. The same art, now, is called "_motion_" pictures. Screenwriters seldom write melodramatic dialogue anymore and the actor must not attempt to bring any total human being through _dialogue dramatics alone_!

Whether they're doing it consciously or not when listening to actors read, producers and directors almost automatically categorize the actor in one of about three different levels of employment during the very first moments:

"The Bit Player"

This actor is probably destined to be that all his life. He gives "excellent line readings" for all those small roles from Joe The Doorman on up.

He's ideal for a walk-on role because the simpler his delivery of the dialogue he's given the less likely he is to attract attention from the leading player he's in a scene with through any exhibiting of an interesting personality. The star will be watched more exclusively, while the bit player can be heard but almost ignored in the scene. The perfectly right dialogue reading will require less time on film in a short scene, making it possible for more "minutes on film" to be devoted to the more important leading roles.

Eye-to-eye acting is appropriate for this level of role at all times because, with its constant focus on the player opposite him the bit player working eye-to-eye is suggesting that that opposite player deserves being kept so continually in focus by the viewer as well. It definitely suggests that the bit player, working eye-to-eye so uninterruptedly, has nothing important of its own at the moment on which we should concentrate.

Directors often call these folks back for more tiny bit roles time after time because they "can do the job", say their few lines acceptably and quickly...and go home. But the perennial bit player had better have some distinctive quality or look to go along with those expert dialogue deliveries that are his total contribution, because there are so many, many other bit players who can also "do the job"...in the same exact manner...with the same obvious, trite line readings...who may be _more interesting_!

"The Supporting Player"

This actor probably makes a decent living as an actor, usually playing short but fairly decent scenes which run longer on film but still don't dominate to any degree. It's a regrettable fact that an actor may spend most of his life in this "middle but no higher" level even though he may _understand_ the importance of bringing total human beings and their inner experiences rather than just dialogue. The "supporting player" probably could do what the "leading player" does in readings, but may be too much in awe of the director's and producer's rushed timespan for readings to actually _bring_ those more universally human characteristics of behavior and their internal causes into play in his readings.

This actor often misses, time after time, the meatier, more interesting and more important role opportunities for which he's qualified. His dialogue sounds a little more---but not sufficiently---real and spontaneous. His body becomes somewhat more involved and more interesting therefore---but not sufficiently. His personality has at least enough opportunity in his reading to be detected. But he simply needs _more bravery_ and _less concern that his readings must be rushed_. Speed kills...in readings for roles as well as on the highway!

And it's such a miscalculation in the first place. After all, out of all the actors in Hollywood, the actor has been selected to come in and be one of the few given the opportunity to read. The producer and director hope that every precious minute they've set aside for actors' readings will be ideally productive. If the actor, worrying about the producer's and director's busy schedule, rushes his reading instead of being brave enough to bring all the colors he knows belong in the role, he has essentially _wasted_ some of those precious minutes and, worse, wasted yet another opportunity to advance his career beyond the "middle level" in which he's stagnated.

"The Leading Player"

A leading player is often discovered in a reading for a lesser role. This actor is _interesting to watch_ as he struggles with feelings and emotions _behind the lines_ rather than trying to "show and tell" them through line readings presented dramatically. This actor seems to not know what's coming; not know what he's going to do or say next. He passes periods and commas just as we all do in real life. After starting next phrases with confidence sometimes he becomes hung up after a few little words (rather than at those commas and periods)---just as we all do in real life.

His _personality and uniquenesses_ have more opportunities to involve themselves organically. Even his moments of listening to other characters reading opposite him are more interesting because he's brave enough to enjoy those tiny, closeup-inviting reactions as he listens---unlike the worried actor who, because he's focused on how to deliver his next lines instead of the character's natural experience behind them, is nervously preparing the next lines' perfect readings. The leading player knows that the upcoming lines will be there organically---still flowing out of the base feeling or mood which is the dominant thing he's concerned with. He never rushes, therefore doesn't _feel_ rushed or nervous. He's far more convincing and interesting because he's placing more value on _the experience of the character_ that lies _behind the dialogue and action descriptives._

This actor, in preparing ahead of time to read, experiences far less nervousness about the upcoming reading. While the other actor across the room may be breaking out in a cold sweat because of concern with getting line readings fixed and ready, the leading actor, preparing the _experience of the character_ first and foremost, is looking forward to his own experience of going through the character's moments with belief, with as much "illusion of the first time" for both himself and the character as is possible, and with the struggle and insecurity that that "illusion of the first time" can bring for him.

The foregoing are the three approximate cateories which detemine the sizes of roles actors will play most often. The reading styles outlined could be determining whether you, too, are employing the most appropriate reading manners for the particular levels of roles for which you're currently reading and those for which you want to read as soon as possible. It's too bad that so many actors never learn these differences!

A Few Items To Bear In Mind

Often before you start to read the producer or director will ask a few questions to listen to your _non-acting_ sound and observe your _non-acting_ personality when you're not trying to adapt your naturalnesses into the role you're trying for. Often that's one of the most important moments in the whole interview. They figure that if you appear right for the role and you---the person, not the reading coming up---can assure them that everything will be alright if you don't "act" the role, then on the set the director can use the "you" who was called in and keep you from whatever wrong thing you might do or plan to do.

If you're asked how you like the role---which is not an uncommon question if from the start they think you're perfect for it, discuss it in _first person always_. From the moment you walked into the room they've been hoping to continually see the actual character you're in for...not an inept, too obvious characterization...the real character! If you say "he" in talking about the role instead of "I" _as_ the character it will break their picture and stop the film that's been running of your performance. The minute you say "_He's_ a nice guy" or something like that you'll be handing the role over to another "he" waiting in the outer office. Sounds simplistic? It is. But do it!

Remember, too, that the producer, the director, the casting director and even the outer office receptionist are all desperate to have you get the role. They feel that way about each person brought in. They've set aside a time period for casting, and the sky falls in if they have to schedule another period the following day because you and the others seen in the session failed to get the role. They're desperate for you to persuade them that the role is yours. They're not there to waste time auditioning talent or giving you a test for simple get-acquainted purposes. They're there to _meet the characters in the script_ and watch them come to life in the readings. Then they can go back to arguing with the star over the latest outrageous demand, to scouting ten more locations before sunset, to alibi-ing production delays to the studio and a million other things that are pressuring these people during the exact timespan in which casting must be completed so they can get on to all the rest that's imvolved.

Some Things To Watch Out For

There are a few things that some actors do when reading for roles that can kill any hopes for their readings producing anything but a quick "Thank you. We'll be in touch with your agent." That's the signal for you to leave...and it often comes quickly, before you've gotten more than three or four sentences of your reading out!

If you're a "head bobber"---continually shaking your head just to talk, very apparently emphasizing every syllable with a shake of the head with no confidence that the words will speak for themselves quite easily, you'll suggest nothing except a pert bobbysoxer carhop at a drive-up hamburger stand...certainly not an adult. Some actors carry this habit into adulthood. The film camera magnifies this habit and it's so distracting that directors are always careful to avoid these actors in casting sessions. Watch top actors. There's not a single one who brings this habit to their film work!

"Hands-talkers" are just as carefully avoided by directors. Many actors---especially actors trained in the "action, intention, objective" methodologies---can't help talking with their hands. It's too bad. Talking with one's hands should be reserved for only such roles as Professional Communicators of one type or another---Teachers, Lecturers, Demonstrators, Vacuum Cleaner Salesmen, etc. Most acting roles involve characters for whom communication is not the main experience of the character. No character for whom there's any kind of personal experience in its moments should be caught talking with its hands. It violates the "incoming", "being done to", "being impacted upon" nature of personal experience. Worse, for the camera it's awful! If there's any closeup potential for the character's moments the head is what's in the camera's shot, but if the perpetual hands-talker is hands-talking the head jiggles and in a closeup there's nothing to indicate why the head is jiggling and bouncing around, since the hands are not in the shot.

One top actor ---one of the few who've become and remained stars in spite of this habit, is joked about by cameramen and the directors they work with. They know ahead of time that they have to watch him....usually shooting his scenes in medium shots (including the talking hands) or suggesting to him, when they want closeups that involve any talking to other characters, that he do something with his hands around his own face, etc. He remains a star, but for people at the point where they're reading for roles in offices it's death. Again, when observed to be a habit of an actor reading for a role, it signals a quick "Thank you" dismissal.

New actors who don't know any better sometimes look down at the script too much. Especially when someone like a casting director is reading opposite them, these folks are busy checking their next speeches and mentally preparing them. Wrong! Terribly wrong! Film is more <u>reacting</u> than acting, and when other people are talking and your character should be listening it should also be reacting. Notice in many film sequences that there are moments when the character who's speaking isn't even the one whose face appears on film. It's the listener....the character who's "being done to" by what the other person is saying.

The best manner of knowing what's coming....perhaps your character's next speech....while listening and reacting to what the other character is saying, is to glance down briefly (if you have to) when the other person *starts speaking*, check your next speech (at least the beginning), then look up while the other person is talking and take in what's being said, with whatever reactions are evoked by the other person's speech. In that manner there's not only an interesting "listening" experience for you but, knowing at least the beginning of your next speech, there's the opportunity to use the brief moment at the end of the other person's speech to form your response as you would have to do in real life.

Some actors hold their scripts in one hand to read. Of course if you're told to stand to read you may need to. But usually if the role has some speeches you'll be seated. There'll almost always be a table or desk so that the casting person or director reading opposite you can have their script in front of them. If there is something to lay your script on, do it. If you hold the scipt in one hand that's what the director sees....<u>an actor holding a script</u> rather than the upper half of a character with its body free to experience the kind of movement and use that gives the director a much more complete version of what you'll do, bodywise, on film if you're cast.

READING FOR SITCOM AND OTHER COMEDY ROLES

For Sitcom and Comedy role interviews much of what is written in the previous paragraphs must be forgotten or shoved aside! What they're looking for in sitcom interviews especially is what they often find at the Comedy Store or The Improvisation in Hollywood, at comedy improv theatres or on standup comics' stages in Las Vegas. But they also sometimes hold interviews for some good comic roles---in spite of the almost exclusively "regular cast only" formats used in sitcoms to avoid expensive guest star salaries.

Most often, interviews for comedy and sitcom roles are more prevalent during "pilot season" time. When pilots are being prepared for showing to networks for pickup and first season tryouts the productions try hard to find new, exciting comedy talents that appear able to "carry a series" with their talents, and usually do this in Hollywood. If they have to settle in the end for a "name" or already established comedy star it will cost them much more than the "first season with options" contract they can negotiate with the agent of a brand new talent.

One nice thing about interviewing for comedy roles of any kind is that there's no real "level" or "category" difference---no "Bit Player", "Supporting Player" or "Leading Player" concern. A "Sitcom Player" is a sitcom player, whether for top role or bottom role consideration. If a good dramatic actor can be also a good sitcom player it's a refreshing change for that actor to experience this absence of any pecking order.

Like any comedy, sitcoms require a few standard technique items, no matter what else you bring, and these need to be brought to the reading interview, so the director can know they'll be there aplenty later:

<u>TAKES!</u>...They're number one! If you can't do "takes" that will give the camera good reaction closeups...then give up, or start learning to do them if you want to do comedy. Takes are a prime ingredient in any comedy. They, more than most other things, underline the comedy and create comic timing at the same time. They make the things done or said by <u>*other characters*</u> even more comic because of their enlarged reaction qualities. They give the viewer not only the moment to laugh but even remind the viewer that something that just happened was worth laughing at, in case such a reminder is needed. They make the viewer laugh even more than he would otherwise, simply because an already ridiculous character opposite ours is being made even more ridiculous by the "take" we do on them. Takes also help to make our own ridiculous attitudes more specific and more comic.

For anyone who enjoys doing comedy and who's confident with it, they're a helluva lot of fun, too! They're really not complicated. They're just one very definite look, expression or reaction (usually of a comment nature) which tells us all. They're a "mugger's paradise", because that's just what they are quite often...big "mugging" reactions. Throw away your caution and your disdain for "showing and telling" if you're a dramatic actor. A take is precisely that. Show and tell the whole thing with a look that is provoked suddenly by another character, as if by reflex, stays along enough to register with the viewer, then perhaps goes away just as quickly.

FACING FRONT!...for film, toward the camera...for theatre, toward the audience...for all sorts of things, especially reactions and takes; even for thinking and sometimes talking about something. This is something looked for in those interviews too. It's a habit that's sometimes difficult for strictly dramatic actors to either accept or form, but you'll need this ability and need to be able to bring it comfortably into sitcom readings and other comedy roles' tryouts if you expect to get them.

ATTITUDE...1,000 PERCENT!... To be a comic character with any value for a script you must bring a definite attitude for your character. Throw away your judgmental subtlety and go all the way! The script won't often provide you with enough bare situation to make you funny. Much of it has to come from your character's own self-conviction that it's sane, or right, or intelligent or something else---1,000 percent!---while other characters are crazy or dumb, or vulgar, or snooty, or whatever seems to be most opposite of your own character.

So much of the comedy collision depends on this one thing---this "juxtaposition of the incongruous". The audience enjoys knowing ahead of time that your character is going to shocked, or outraged, or scared stiff or something else as you enter a scene...and the reason they know this ahead of time is that you've previously brought and maintained a nice, clean and definite, 1,000 percent atitude.

NICE, CLEAN, CONFIDENT LINE DELIVERY!...is another big plus in sitcom readings. Comedy has to be easy to see and hear. No mumbling allowed...except in a moment when the mumbling itself is what's comic. Light, bright, inflected dialogue is the norm, unless your character must go a different direction entirely because it's one of the weird ones. The "searching for words and phrases" recommended for dramatic character reading and performance, if used at all in sitcom readings or in comic performances, must be turned to a comic form. The dialogue in sitcoms needs to be fully prepared and delivered "just right"...the exact opposite of dramatic dialogue delivery!

Of course for _character_ comedy there's no special rule of this kind, because character comedy depends more on the character itself, in whatever unique manner it's to be brought. At the moment we've been discussing "_Sitcom_" playing and reading. The differences between the two types of comedy work aren't that vast, but they're important to understand.

Here are some examples of the differences: In the old "_Mary Tyler Moore Show_", Ted Knight was certainly a comic _character_, as were Cloris

107

Leachman and Ted's dumb girlfriend and one or two more. The other characters of that series---Mary, Ed Asner, Valerie Harper and Gavin McLeod---were essentially "sitcom" players (at least as their characters for that series were formatted). In *"The Jeffersons"*, Sherman Hemsley was a comic *character*, as were Marla Gibbs as Florence the Maid and the English neighbor from upstairs. The others were primarily *sitcom* characters. In *"Happy Days"* Henry Winkler played a definite comic *character*, while most of the others were *sitcom* roles. In *"Alice"* , another of the genre during the same timespan, the comic *characters* were Flo (until she left the show), the drinking-straw-exploding Vera, and a few others in smaller roles, while Alice herself and the owner of the diner were primarily *sitcom* roles.

More recently, in *"The Golden Girls"*, Estelle Getty as Mama, Betty White as a dum-dum, and to a degree Rue McClanahjan as an over-the-hill sexpot are comic *characters*, while Bea Arthur's droll style is more of the *sitcom* category, with most of her comedy coming from her very clear and very effective comic takes.

The main difference is that a *comic character* can usually make us laugh just walking through the door and continually throughout a role with its unusual and amusing manner and quirks of all kinds...while the *sitcom* role is one which usually relies more on the script for comic situations and comic results. But the sitcom player still requires those items listed above----the ability to do "takes", "face front", bring "1,000 percent" attitudes, etc., to help those comic situations achieve the most result possible. We're not comparing talents here...simply the two different kinds of roles usually found in sitcoms...all of which, though, require those rudiments first mentioned above. If you're aware that they're necesary for getting any kind of sitcom work and know how to bring them easily you'll get these roles!

For Sitcoms You Get One Shot Only...The Interview!

For sitcom interviews, by all means *Dress For The Roles!*.....Yes, that's what I and any other sitcom casting director would advise you. Don't go to a sitcom interview wearing anything but what can help visualize your idea of the character. Comic characters should be immediately recognizable as what they are. Wardrobe can make the difference. If it helps your own comfort in the interview of course you can go ahead and ridicule the thing you found to wear. The interviewer will appreciate the effort and thinking you've gone to to prepare and bring your idea. Remember, anyone involved in sitcoms, from executive producer on down, is always looking for fresh ideas. You may be bringing them an idea, whether they use it with another actor later or hire you simply because of that idea.

You can get more sitcom roles by using the foregoing ideas, but for comic *leads* in television series or movies you should also get in some practice with constucting *comic characters* in the hope that, along the way somewhere, in one of those sitcom interviews, you'll get the opportunity to impress someone who'll later want to write a series around you or have one written for you.

The fact that you're discovered to *know how to do* comic character work (not just sitcom) could even help you get some sitcom role that can start you moving into top comedy. Character comedy is actually more desirable than pure sitcom ability, since a good comic *character* in any sitcom stands on its own, requiring little from the writers to make it comic in individual episodes or throughout a motion picture. Those "characters"...not simply the sitcom situations...are usually the main drawing card of sitcom series, causing viewers to return every week to watch them because they know ahead of time that the "character" lead will be funny whether the script is funny or not.

To suggest a manner of coming to really enjoy comic character work I'm going to give you here the *"Comic Character Checklist"* that Chico Marx wrote out for me when I directed him once. This is the list that Chico implied to me was used by each of the Marx Brothers in constructing those zany (and highly successful) comic characters:

THE MARX BROTHERS COMIC CHARACTER CHECKLIST

(1)   A turned-up, ridiculous attitude---the "1,000 percent" mentioned earlier;

(2)   A special walk...one that either fits the character ideally and makes it more ridiculous or may be so out of place for it that it's ridiculous on its own:

(3)   A special speech or dialect---again, that's either perfect for the character or else ridiculously out of place;

(4)   A special piece of wardrobe;

(5)   A special hairstyle;

(6)   A recurring body "thing" of some kind that comes and goes at odd times, and

(7)   Maybe one prop of some kind.

If you think about each of the Marx Brothers' characters one after another for a moment you'll observe how this list probably helped inspire so many of those zany character ideas.....or, some of Carol Burnett's brilliant comic characters, Red Skelton's lovable gallery of characters, Johnny Carson's zoo of Mighty Carson Art Players, etc.   Consider also how this list---apparently known to and used by many comic players, may have contributed to the building of some of those comic characters mentioned in the series talked about in the early "sitcom" vs. "character" comedy paragaphs.

Of course you shouldn't be expected to bring all these things to a sitcom interview, and probably shouldn't try to, but they're worth considering one by one while you're looking over the script in the outer office or at home, just in case one or two of these items might suggest something that will help you get the job.   Try to bear in mind that any sitcom interview is really a comic *performance*.

In the end, for sitcom readings, I'm reminded of something Lucille Ball said before a comedy workshop group once..."Comedy is something which if you ain't got you ain't gonna get!" For the most part this can be true. But if you can come to enjoy some of the few things listed above, and get some practice with them, you'll stand a better chance at getting some of the roles you're at least a borderline possibility for...roles you'd cerainly miss out on if you _don't_ bring at least _some_ of these things into the interviews.

YOU WANT LEADING ROLES?....START LEADING YOUR INTERVIEWS!

Whatever the interview is for...dramatic or comic role; motion picture or television; sitcom or character comedy; theatre....whatever...it will always help if you do some "leading" in the discussion period. You have a limited amount of time allotted to you. You should try to lead the disussion into areas that can be productive for you personally. Certainly shift the conversation to areas that will allow you best opportunity to display your strongest points. Actually, those interviewing you will be supremely grateful that they don't have to continually spark new talking points only to see them die and require some more new starts.

Really, they'll appreciate your leading the talk a little. If you don't the interview will probably be "fomatted" to proceed in a usual manner which the interviewer has had to endure too many times, and little will result.

The one who stands out after all people have been seen has created his or her own opportunities to bring areas of talk that were a little different from all the rest and he or she has led some of the discussion into different waters from the never-ending river of dull sameness which some directors report experiencing when there isn't any initiative taken by the actor being interviewed. It can really matter. Ty it.

Psychology majors understand this. Watch groups of people in conversation. The one who is leading the talk is usually serious and struggling, because the mind is having to work swiftly to keep details coming out, and that struggle to keep up with the story makes that person interesting...but look at all those other faces around the talker. See how they smile with appreciation, real or feigned understanding and relaxation because they're not having to talk? It's the same with any industry people when they're interviewing you. Help them relax and enjoy you. Let them enjoy listening and observing, more than having to continually invent things to talk about with you just to get you to talk.

TELEVISION SERIES STARRING ROLES....THE INTERVIEW STEPS

Interviews and readings for television series pilots are like stairsteps with no guardrails. You can keep climbing toward that coveted role at the top of the stairs...or you can fall off at any step. It helps to know what's happening at each step, and why.

You must expect *several* interviews and perhaps two or three actual readings on a callback basis.

First comes the initial interview---probably with the Head of Casting for the studio or production company only...to check out his or her first thoughts for the role, even while the calls are going out to agents about a bunch of "names" and "semi-names" the producer and director or somebody at the network has said to check out for availability for the series. The lists of those are gone over ahead of time among network, production and casting people and early decisions are made as to what's to be looked for.

Some of those people in whom the network representatives or producers are interested may be available, which narrows the initial field somewhat. But where pilots are concerned there are usually only about two name stars on those "Call for availability" lists that the production company will be able to afford in the end---within the cast budgets they've set with the network ahead of time. The other roles, in the end, are probably going to go to people in lower salary brackets, just to fit the budget. So, you see, even newcomers have a chance, and a fairly good one, at series starring roles in television series pilots.

The casting person who's expected to come up with the new, unknown candidates for those lower-salaried roles is on the hot seat. The choices that are even brought in will be judged by not only the producer and director. The network bigwigs delegated to shepherd the project through its pilot preparation are watching and checking too. They're not concerned with the money...yet...as the producers are, so they're still checking TVQ rating lists and making their often quite unrealistic (money-wise) suggestions and in the early period will be almost totally ignoring the casting director's new people until the last ditch of decision is reached, with the budget tentatively set and starting to pinch.

So...first comes the meeting (perhaps a checking-out reading too) for the Head of Casting. If he or she knows you well it's mostly to talk, and to check on how you look at this particular time. If you're not well known to this woman or man you may be asked to do a preliminary reading for them.

At this very first point, don't be careless about what you wear to the meeting. You're up for a series. You're possibly going to become a public figure overnight if you get the role. Dress with two things in mind...a little leaning toward the kind of role you're up for, and mix with that some thinking of some street clothes that suggest you'll look good in public. The network people especially watch for this, and if you consider it in the first interviews the casting person---firmly on your side because you're one of his or her proud suggestions---can check what you have on and say it's great, tell you to wear the same thing for callbacks, or suggest something else. For the later interviews and readings wardrobe can be *supremely important*.

Next, if you're still on the casting director's list to be called back after that first checking-out meeting, will come the readings and lengthy talking interviews with the producer and director. Sometimes, to save time, a network representative will be at even the first readings of potential people, but not too often. Usually the producer and director are allowed at least (but not much more than) those first "elimination and zeroing in on the few that seem like prime possibilities" interviews.

In that first "reading and talking" interview with the producer and director be prepared for all kinds of personal questions. There's a long term relationship being considered, and it's like an employment interview for a major corporation's executive post. That informal-seeming chat that goes with this reading interview may even be taped, but in most cases not yet.

Keep a cheerful demeanor even if it kills you! Personality problems are subtly looked for, and eliminations follow when they're detected or even suspected. Producers know that enough problems are bound to come up later if the series gets off the ground and goes a few seasons, and the fewer the personality problems out front the better. They start making sure at the earliest possible moment---in these first interviews and readings---that there isn't something there already in your personality and attitude that spells trouble down the road.

What you wear to these producer-director preliminary readings and talk-meeting sessions is doubly important. The casting director will have counselled you, of course, but the point is that you may be in line for "grooming" for presentation to the network people---if you get past this first big hurdle. Things are being polished. You're one of those "things" if they think they may want you for the role. Do anything you have to to make sure your wardrobe doesn't dominate and distract, but be sure that it looks moderately expensive, because you're on the "store shelf" in these meetings, and there is a "buyer" looking you over who will have to "sell" you and your "packaging" to a "customer" (the network). Stay casual...so you won't look selfconsciously dressed up and too eager, even though they'll know by then that you're anxious for the role.

Be aware of what colors set your hair and your eyes and your personality off best. You're being interviewed for a medium that involves _color!_ One casting director friend of this author confided that, with all this in mind, she even advised a handsome young man whom the producer and director were meeting at her suggestion to put light blond highlight rinse on his hair before meeting them to make it more _color television_ attractive. He did it, and much farther down the line---after many more interviews and the film test---came away with the series. The young fellow still uses the blond highlight rinse on his hair now, in the third season of the series.

This may sound like a lot of hogwash, but it isn't. Because in this kind of interview it's _you_...because you're a prospect for a "_you_" role in the series, that's on display. This isn't your run-of-the-mill "character role" in a single episode that lies within your grasp at this point...it's the series version of something very close to your own personality or at least something which falls nicely within the category of roles that you're most apt to be considered for.

112

If you "pass go" with this first big step, next expect an immediate callback (in either a few days or about a week) to read and perhaps be taped in another callback...this time with the network rep or reps there. Again you'll either be counselled as to what to wear or asked to wear the same outfit that's gotten you that far. It must be working for you.

In that meeting, remember that the producer and director have, in effect, now become your "agents". That's right. They're trying to sell you to the network folks. You don't have to focus too much on the producer and director by that time...and shouldn't. It can more beneficially appear that they and you already constitute "a great team". It's now the network man, woman or group sitting there with veto power in their pockets who need to be impressed. You'll have all the help and support your new "agents" (the producer and director) can give you, because if you've gotten that far you're certainly one of the leaders of the pack for the role...at least in their estimation. But some of it is still up to you.

The network man or woman is probably (usually) not in your corner yet for the role. He or she is still getting "inspirations" every hour on the hour...for your role!...and phoning the producer or director every hour on the hour to ask that some more "star name" and "high TVQ" people be checked out for their ratings-enhancing abilities if the series is picked up after the pilot. Often they're even cynically considering the advantage of *loading* the pilot with TVQ-rated people, just in case the series *isn't* picked up and has to be slotted as a "Movie Of The Week" or special of some kind in the Spring to recoup its production costs! They want as few "no public name" people in their pilots as possible.

If you sense some reserve or even hostility on the part of these "intruders" from the network, handle it in a warm, understanding manner. After all, you know that they're not meeting you because they want to. If you're not a star yet they definitely *don't* want you. They're still hoping that one of those stars they've suggested can be persuaded to take the role. They're simply accommodating the producer's attempt to hold down the going-in budget by not signing too many top-heavy stars out front. Simply understand the arguments between these two decision seats at this point--- the network rep and the producer-director team. Some may even be carried on right in front of you in the meeting. Just be happy that you've made it to this important checking-out meeting. Breathe easy when you walk out of the big office. You'll have done your best, and the next move is up to the fates and the all-determining Budget Departments involved.

The next thing you'll hear, if it's still positive, will proably be that there's interest in "testing you", and that a "deal memo" is coming down to your agent. The details will be explained to you by your agent (or should be), including the first year salary offer per episode, the numbr of episodes you're promised out of all committed to be made, the second and five more seasons' salary amounts (with what the production company considers their best bid as to upward escalation that you and your agent are likely to accept) and many, many more clauses that bind you to the series and how you'll be expected to relate to it if you get the role.

You'll be surprised at the amount being paid you for the pilot itself---if you do it after being tested for it. That's because of a SAG regulation in the contract which requires that you get at least double the individual episode salary for the pilot, in return for which the production company has the options it needs during the "waiting for network pickup" period. Complicated stuff in those "deal memos" will have your head spinning---if it's your first such series chance, but your agent is surely on top of them.

Even with the deal memo in hand, you don't have the series or even the pilot yet. Next will come the <u>Screen Tests</u> of the leading contenders...of which you're now one!

Your series contract details will already have been set before you're allowed to do the tests. There's no negotiation left. Once you get to the tests your salary and all working (contract) conditions, your billing and everything else for the next seven years, are on the books and you're locked in if they want you after the tests. Bear in mind, still, that it will all mean next to nothing if, after the screen test, you don't get the role. However, if after the test you're chosen to do the pilot....that's it. They, as well as you, are locked in...unless they later decide to cut you out after the pilot and pay off your contract because your role may have been written out as the series gets set to go or because they've decided to replace you for the series run with another actor---probably with one of those "network rep inspirations" of a name or semi-name actor who had turned down the pilot but later decides he or she wants the series because something else has fallen through.

But we're still talking "Interviews and Readings" essentially here. And for television series pilots the next upcoming "reading" will be the on-camera test.

You'll be in wardrobe bought or supplied by the studio (in most cases). You'll be made up to look your best; you'll be filmed on a sound stage at the studio or network, with a partner who's trying for his or her own series role...and there'll be five or six other contending "teams" trying for those same two roles (yours and your partner's). They're made up and in pretty much the same wardrobe, standing by the set watching your test or off in the corner to make sure they *don't* watch you while they're waiting their turns to test.

You may even find out upon arrival at the set that you're sharing a dressingroom with another of the contenders for your role. Bear in mind, just to keep yourself from hoping too much, that that other person has also signed a contract for the series which will go into effect...instead of yours...if that other person is chosen after the tests.

Since the film testing is the last step, your interviewings and readings for the role in the series are finished. It's then in the hands of the Gods. Good luck!

INTERVIEWING FOR COMMERCIALS

Ah, those sometimes "cattle call", two-minute experiences where there may be close to a hundred people seen for the same brief roles! If the big and continuing income from a good "Class A" (national, network prime-time) commercial didn't offer such wonderful enticement it wouldn't be worth the hassle. But there's big money when you get one of those, so...some paragraphs at least about this excrutiatingly competitive, sometimes rather insulting, rush-rush kind of interviewing and on-camera "reading for roles".

The aspect of being always prepared for quick and unexpected calls is impressed upon you by all commercial agents. Interviews often come up quite suddenly. Some agents even tell you to have a bag in your car at all times with things in it like toothbrushes, glasses, a cup, a towel, an apron, certainly a comb and hairbrush and various kinds of makeup for the ladies, etc., in case something is called for in an interview storyboard (we'll get to that item) and in case it might help if you have such an item with you. Certainly, if you have a hairstyle that has to be just so, carry with you always whatever it takes to get it in that condition without much time or warning.

Most agents will also want you to always have at your fingertips (in your car trunk or...?) several pieces of wardrobe of the right kinds for interviews in case you get a rush call and can't go home to change.

For men, most commercial agents recommend beiges, blues, plaid shirts and slacks (not blue jeans), unless you're an older character actor for whom other clothes are wiser. Character people should in fact have handy all sorts of special wardrobe in their car trunks!

For women, whatever colors really set off your visual assets. And dresses, ladies...not slack suits. No gold, red, orange or glossy fabrics. No small checks or houndstooth fabrics that create crazy line-blend when on camera. Some of you know what those colors and fabrics do on film, but they're mentioned here for those of you who don't. By all means, a sweater or two that you can do things with---maybe on occasion the draped-around-the-shoulder effect, tied in front loosely if you like; maybe just worn if it feels right for the character. Lightweight, though...not heavy.

On all these recommendations, listen closely to your agent's advice and make notes when they're telling you what they'd like you to wear or have handy in your car at all times. They know how they want you to present yourself because they know what they'll be putting you up for. When they call you for an interview they'll probably in fact tell you which way to dress to go in. Some even have you supply them ahead of time with snap-shots or at least desriptions of your available interview wardrobe so they can choose and tell you which to wear when they call you to go in.

As to makeup...even fellows should have in their carry bags some kind of powder or pancake...to kill the shine on their faces when they're taped in interviews (as they'll usually be). There's nothing that turns a commercial "buyer" off more than a face that shines on tape. Ladies are usually warned by their agents against trying for a "glamour" look at any commercial interviews except those for beauty or couturier products. For women what the agents recommend most regularly is versatility and believability within their categories for casting in standard roles.

For those who don't know, there are very standard categories into which commercial actors must fall. There are *"Coke and MacDonalds"* teenagers---attractive and full of energy; there are *"Housewife"* women who don't stand a chance in *"Catalog"* or *"High Fashion"* areas; there are *"Business"* and *"Executive Suite"* men and women; there are *"Brat Pack"* kids with freckles and outdoor wholesomeness; there are *"Grandpas"* and *"Grandmas"*; and so on and so on. Your category will determine what kind of wardrobe and props your agent will recommend you keep handy.

By all means be prepared to get some of the commercials you try for by having watched many, many commercials on networks ahead of time to become familiar with the kinds of clothes generally worn by people in your category; watch for the kind and level of commercial acting---face and body aspects especially. Those brief expressions on faces need to be clean and definite. Note that the bodies are usually moving, doing something. Commercials usually require some kind of constant "business" or movement to keep the footage "alive and interesting and attention-holding."

When called to audition, be sure to carry a head shot or your standard composite (or both) and of course your résumé attached to each photo or composite that you plan to hand in when requested to do so. It's always asked of you if you don't look for the table where a lot of other photos have already been deposited.

Upon Arrival, the Clock is Ticking!

Immediatly inside the reception office or area, get the *Copy Sheet* from the receptionist or from the shelf where a pile of the same copy sheets will be waiting, identified with the product name at the top. *Sign in.* On the *Sign-In Sheet* (required by the union) are blank spaces for your name, your social security number, your agency, the time of arrival, the actual time for which you were called, and a blank for you to sign out and indicate the time you're released. Leave the last columns blank, of course, until you can fill them out when leaving.

At those check-in shelves or desks you may find that there are more than one commercial being cast at the same time, with separate copy sheets and separate sign-in sheets for each. Be sure to sign in for the one you've been called for, and be sure you pick up the right copy sheet to be looked over and prepared before going inside for the taped audition.

One frequently working commercial actress we know has told us that there's a little trick she has used that has accidentally gotten her two "Class A" commercials. On a first occasion she was of course called for just one particular commercial. But upon arrival she saw that another commercial was being cast in the same office that day and that it had a character of her type being seen for it. She hadn't been called for that second commercial, but she signed in on *both* sheets and got ready with the copy for both, putting down a fictitious time as the time for which she had supposedly been called for the second one. Whether the casting person caught it or not upon seeing her name---and certainly knowing her because she had worked for the lady before, she did get both interviews, being essentially right for both. And in the end...while also getting the commercial for which she'd originally been called, she was the one chosen for the second commercial as well, and later earned over thirty thousand dollars from its lengthy, market-saturated run!

There may also be some cards there on a table or elsewhere on which actors are asked to note other details about themselves...sizes of all clothing items, etc., so the commercial producers can have most of what they need for the final narrowing down toward choices of actors and to get those items to the wardrobe people quickly or even to pair them up with other actors.

Preparing To Be Taped

Once signed in, bear in mind that you may be called almost immediately for some reason. Commercial interviews are fast. If there's a _Storyboard_ (an artist's rendering of the kind of separate, progressive film frames to be shot, indicating action and props involved), look it over. It will usually resemble a giant comic strip on a stand-up board. Then get to preparing for your audition.

Maybe step outside to go over the lines aloud for yourself, to get used to and also tailor the sound and inflections you think will best serve the copy. Commercial copy is _"advertising"_, remember. You can't be all that subtle and point-losing in your delivery if you want the advertising agency and sponsor people to fall in love with you and hire you because of the way you present their very expensive message.

Some experienced commercial actors advise to memorize the copy. Some, equally experienced, say you should not; that you should just read it when you're being taped. Make your own choice as to what works best for you. But bear in mind that once the tape is running inside and you've identified yourself for the tape with your name and your agency, what goes onto the tape should suggest the best possible version of which you're capable in terms of continuing paricipation in the action. Having to constantly look down at the copy in your hand is probably going to distract fom the "reality" which they'll want along with the special contribuion to the effectiveness of the copy delivery. Also, your eyes are important, and if you're constantly looking down at the copy when you're being taped nobody's going to see too much of your eyes.

For the latter reason, often there'll be a _"Cue Card"_ or " _Copy Board"_ set up beside the camera, so that you can actually look directly at the Copy Board and read your lines. Some readers may not realize that although you're looking directly at the Copy Board the camera lens makes it appear that you're looking directly into the lens.

In the outer office while you're waiting your turn there'll probably be quite a cluster of people who look much like you, because that's the particular look the sponsor and the ad agency account executives have called for.

Those other folks are of course up for the same role. There'll undoubtedly be some very recognizable faces there...people you've seen in a lot of commercials. You may feel your own hopes deflating rapidly as you look around at those faces competing with you. You'll probably feel that they...so obviously experienced...stand a far btter chance of getting the role. Not so! Some have in fact been "over-exposed" in commercials already and don't stand a chance, simply because a viewer seeing that very recognizable face in a Boston Baked Beans commercial would automatically think "Toyota" or "Home Federal Savings" or "Clairol" instead!

Some of those very experienced folks in the outer office---veterans with years and years of tough competing for commercials under their belts---may even try to discourage the competition and cause the field of prospects to thin out, with people leaving feeling they haven't a chance and needn't waste their time trying out. A few of these "old commercial pros" may come sauntering out of the inner office saying (just loudly enough for all to hear) "I guess I got it," or something equally discouraging to those already dubious of their own chances. Those folks know that if they can send some people out without their even trying out the field will narrow down considerably. Your agent would kill you if you fall for this kind of obvious and sometimes used ploy and leave without auditioning.

The Taping of Your Audition

When you're called, go in smiling. If you know the casting director very well you might call him or her by name to make yourself look like you're one of his or her well-liked favorites and therefore must be very good. Some casting people, however, say you shouldn't even speak to them, rather look for the ad agency people who don't yet know you and stay focused on them. Make your own decision about this.

Once inside, step up to the camera confidently without even being told what to do. There will usually be "chalks" or "marks" on the floor indicating where they want you to stand for the camera. If you still need to check the copy (and if there's no Copy Board) hold it in front of you but well below chin level so the camera can see your face at all times. Also, with the copy held just high enough it will keep your head from having to dip down or back and forth to check your lines. If you're asked to also hold the product in such a taping, hold it at approximately chin level, beside your head and quite close, so it gets into the shot with your face on the tape. Sponsors, to whom their products are holy, like to see you and their product side by side in those closeups.

Remember, if there is a *Cue Card* or *Copy Board*, look at it rather than into the camera lens. The camera---on television newscasts, weather map reporting and soap operas and any other televised works where the actor hasn't had time to learn lines or copy securely---make it appear that, even though the actor is actually looking a little to one side of the lens he is looking directly into camera. Talk directly to the cue card as you read, as if you're talking directly to the viewer through the lens. It will appear convincingly as if you are!

Don't be the least bit stiff and static with your copy delivery. Remember how much movement there usually is in commercials that reach the networks and run for long times. Commercials are not "still life".

At the end of the taping, after your last copy word, somebody will probably thank you as your signal to leave. Thank them in return. Smile or say something that may help them consider you or at least remember you. One much used commercial actor I know says he always freezes a rather kooky expression on his face in that last moment, just in case the camera is still rolling and will catch those final moments...and it obviously works for him, indicating as it does much flexiblity and malleability in case they come up with more ideas later for the actual commercial shoot.

Callbacks...And The Long Waits

If you're among the callback people later, with just a few others who remain contenders for the same role, wear the same clothes as the ones you wore before...unless somebody has asked you to wear something different. Don't surprise them with something different unless they've asked you to do so. Watch out. They liked you earlier, just the way you were...and sometimes what you had on will have helped leave the right impression.

You'll seldom have too much of an idea of what the final commercial is going to look like or include. You'll spend weeks after shooting it wondering if and when it will ever start running. You won't know for some time whether you've been "upgraded", "downgraded" or "outgraded". The just over $300 or so you'll have received as the "session fee" may be the total you'll ever receive from the commercial you hoped would make you rich. People are often cast, shot, and then as the commercial is prepared "downgraded" from "Principal" (whose face can be identified in a finished commercial, insuring a flow of residuals) to the degree that there won't be any residuals because the face isn't recognizable in the final cut version...or even totally "outgraded" (cut completely out in the final cut)!

There are so many things that can happen in terms of how the commercial is decided to eventually be used, or tested regionally in a number of markets, or first run as a dealer co-op (paid for by the product's sponsor but provided to dealers for their own time buys), etc. Even if eventually it goes "national", as you should cerainly hope it will, to bring you a lot of money, you might receive another check along the way at some point (for much less than you've been expecting) and you may give up hope for greater exposure and the big money...being convinced that it isn't going to "go national" after all. Don't lose hope. It happens often that national (Class A) commercials are simply trial-run in certain markets in "tryout" or "flagship" runs to compare their results with other commercials which are also ready in case they prove better response-evokers. National runs may still be planned and eventually happen. All you can do is hope.

For commercials, go in, do your best, and from then on it's a roll of so many pairs of dice in ad agency offices back east on Madison Avenue.

119

IN ANY INTERVIEW, CONSIDER YOUR BODY COMMUNICATION!

There are a few more pointers that apply to *all* types of interviews. Don't forget *Body Communication*...what your body, sitting positions, the way you talk, etc., imply to the more perceptive and insighted people "auditioning" you. This area applies to actors to double the extent that it applies to the business sector interview.

The person who hunches his or her chair forward toward the interviewer is often judged to be less sure of his or her ability to communicate ideally, or else it's a come-on-strong, self-selling device, or perhaps even an argumentative human being!

Those who continually talk with their hands too much probably lack confidence that they can get their points across easily.

Those who social-smile all the time may lack depth and may be "Please like me!" folks, desperate for acceptance and having less than ideal self worth.

All of these and many more points are written about in some excellent books on the subject.

A producer and director, some yeas ago, were casting the role of a genie for a television series. Many, many stunning actresses were being interviewed. Finally one of the most beautiful walked in smartly and, rather than sitting in the interview chair like all the others had done, climbed on top of the back of the interview chair with her feet on the cushion, looking so much like a real genie that she was cast instantly! Unlike those who had preceded her---all sitting forward in the chair hopefully and looking more like self-sellers of the previously described type, she seemed completely in command of whatever might come without any need for self-selling. Her name was Barbara Eden and before she even walked out the door she was "Jeannie".

You, as an actor, should in fact consider *intentional and calculated* body communication.

For instance, a top executive (role) needs no self-selling. His or her position is secure enough without it. On the other hand, a "snitch" in a detective series needs to sell himself and what he knows. A "grand dame" wouldn't demean herself by self-selling under any conditions, but her niece with the voracious appetite for the grand dame's largesse would probably do it every moment. You can always tie the two together to a degree in interviews---your own image as a confident actor and some concept of the appropriate body manner of the character.

Since casting directors are usually the people who schedule most interviews, select the actors to be called in, handle the casting interviews and negotiate employment contracts with actors' agents, the next chapter is devoted to helping readers understand the casting director's processes.

Chapter Fourteen

The Hollywood Casting Directors

Most actors and actresses, when they're just starting out, think casting directors are some kind of gods or something. Not so. They're not magic wand-wavers at all. They've simply been hired to use their mental reminder files, the <u>*Academy Players Directory*</u>, the *Breakdown Service*, calls to and from agents and their own developed knowledge of who would be right for a role, then bring in the most exciting possibilities who are available for the budgeted salaries and billing levels for producers and directors to look at and select from for casting in roles.

Casting directors themselves don't really decide anything in the end, and have no say in final decisions as to who will be cast, but in the early steps of casting discussions, over and above the people the director and producer direct them to check out for availability head of time, they're expected to make their own suggestions---from the sea of actors' faces in Hollywood---of people they feel the director and producer should meet and read for some roles if they don't yet know them.

Often entire casts are handpicked by the producer and/or the director ahead of time. In such cases, in the very first casting meeting with them the casting person is directed to "Check on John Wilson for Harry, Sue Pangborn for Marge, Helen Waters for Mom Cassidy and Andy Converse for Bo. If they're available, set 'em!" If those people are discovered to be available (at the salary the budget allows, the billing that can be offered or quickly negotiated with the agent, and for the numbr of days or weeks the production will need them), the show is all cast within a few hours of phoning, without any readings at all for the roles. Most casting of top starring roles is done in exactly this manner, with the producer and the director having very clear ideas from first readings of their scipts as to which stars they'd like in the roles.

The exceptions are those times when, even though they know whom they'd like in those top roles, knowing they may not be able to satisfy those stars' salaries and billing demands, even though asking the casting director to still check with those stars' and co-stars' agents just in case, they ask the casting director to also "Find out who else is available."

At that point the casting director consults the list of suggestions he or she has already prepared ahead of time and brought to that first meeting, and suggests some alternates. If the producer and director like some of the names, the casting director will leave and check with the agents of those people for their availabiliy at the desired time and at the money and billing levels that are available. As the first choices of the production people are found to be "unavailable" for whatever reasons (money, billing, other commitments) some of the casting person's suggestions, found to be "available" and willing to accept the offered billing and money, may be quickly "set" for the roles after quick phone calls to the producer or director for approval. There'd still be no actors called in to read for roles.

However, a standard practice is to release a copy of the script ahead of time to the organization formed years ago by Gary Marsh called "Breakdown Services, Ltd." The Breakdown Service goes to work "breaking down" the script's roles, role by role, and listing all the cast characters' names, full descriptions of each as taken directly from the script (or described by the casting director), information as to what kind of billing will be offered, how long employment is expected or guaranteed to last, etc. This information is then distributed the next morning to all agents who subscribe to the Service (most do) so they'll know what's being cast, where and by whom, and all other pertinent information. In those cases where certain roles are already cast "the Breakdown" indicates it.

Agencies get on the phone quickly to either the casting director or to the producer or director (whoever is most likely to be quickly responsive to their suggestions) to suggest their clients for the available roles. Sometimes the well established and well known role candidates so quickly obtained in this manner allow the production to quickly cast all or almost all roles the same day, because the players are all known to the production people, from stars down to the smallest bit role candidates. So again, in this case, no actors are called in to read.

If you think your agent isn't doing his or her job if they can't get you in for many opportunities to read, perhaps the foregoing will help you understand what they're up against. Even when you or your agent may be close with a casting director, it takes great perseverance, persuasion and determination on the part of the casting person to talk the production people into seeing you if there's somebody they already know who's found to be available. It's also a bit dangerous for the casting person to attempt to persuade them to set aside some valuable time away from other production details to let you come in. The casting person's job is on the line in such cases. Don't bank on this happening too much of the time. Your agent understands all this, and you should too.

There used to be many casting directors on *permanent staff* at studios and major production companies. There still are a few, but not many. Logistics have taken their toll with respect to casting directors' employments too. Only the "studio" ones are continually on the studios' payrolls if they're under contracts, whether the studios have productions to cast all the time or not. That's the reason. Nowadays, they're more than likely whisked off the payroll and off the lot at the end of each picture's casting or sent off on lengthy "vacations" or "layoffs" (without pay, of course) for the periods before next productions are due to start casting.

Remember, there aren't many major studio lot pictures made anymore. Unless the studio itself, rather than an independent company renting space on its turf, is producing a continuing television series or two or might be continually producing major motion pictures on its own money, because it's managed to have a few recent boxoffice smashes, any casting directors with offices on its lot are now "independents".

It's the current face of the industry, in fact. The casting director who sits behind that big desk---to whom you look for employment---may be out in the street, or worrying about this month's rent, tomorrow. Casting directors nowadays spend more time scouting up next assignments and fighting other casting directors' money bids to get them than they do in the actual casting of either television or motion pictures. The getting of their next assignments often depends on the prices they quote to get the jobs. If nobody's bid is low enough, often the producer's secretary or the production company's former casting secretary will get the job for less money, whether eminently qualified for it or not. It happens more and more these days.

THE CASTING DIRECTOR'S JOB

The casting director's job usually consists of (1) being hired to cast the project; (2) being given a budget beakdown of how much is planned to be spent on each individual role in the script; (3) making up a preliminary list of suggestions of people to be considered and checked out in case the production people will consider them; (4) meeting with the producer and/or director to compare lists and discuss the people on them; (5) having little voice in which roles are to be cast by simply making offers out front for many top roles that are pre-cast in the director's or producer's mind; (6) checking on the "availability" of those people for the periods for

123

which they'll be required, after being provided with what's called a "Day out of days" list which tells how long, and when, a player is expected to be needed; (7) more meetings to discard the ones who can't be gotten at the right times or at the right prices or the right billings; (8) more frantic searching of inspirations and lists for still those top roles; (9) finding out whom the producer or director will allow them to bring in for reading interviews...in which meetings some names must be struck off quickly because the producer or director doesn't like their work or their look or is paying alimony to them; (10) calling the agents to set interviews for a list of people to read; (11) holding the reading interviews---usually in the producer's or director's office; (12) having a long discussion or a very short one with the producer and director immediately after the readings to find out which roles can then be set from the people seen and which roles sill need some more interviews because nobody's felt to be right yet; (13) doing determined negotiation on the phone with agents to make satisfacory deals on the people that have been okayed by then, perhaps not being able to get some at the salary or billing planned and having to report back to the producer that they can't be gotten, necessitating still more additional reading interviews in some cases if the producer won't steal some money fom another role or two to add to the deals of the ones being turned down by the agents; (14) calling in more people for the remaining roles still open; (15) finally getting the last remaining roles cast; (16) finalizing those deals; (17) with the total cast list in hand, calling "Station 12" at Screen Actors Guild to check for their okay on everybody; (18) if some SAG member is delinquent in dues and required to pay up to the Guild before working or else have their agent "guarantee" that they'll pay up immediately after working, notifying the agent to quickly call to give SAG the guarantee, or if the actor is a "must join" (not yet a member), making sure the actor goes in immediately to pay SAG and join, or if it's found that he can't, quickly recasting his role with an actor who was previously runner-up in consideration; (19) after SAG has okayed everybody, publishing the Cast List, showing the players' names, agencies, telephones, home addresses, social security numbers, salaries, expected work dates, etc., and having it distributed to all production people and departments involved in any way with the cast; (20) having all actors cast come in to pick up their scripts or having them delivered (for top players especially) to their homes; (21) coordinating their "wardrobe" situations---either having them talk by phone to wardrobe people (to save the production a "fitting fee") or having them go to a sudio wardrobe department person or elsewhere for a fitting if it's necssay; (22) having all actors' contracts typed up, also usually the studio or company's employment forms so that both sets of papers can be signed ahead of time by some actors or agents while others are to be delivered to the Second Asst. Director for signing when the day players report on the set for work; (23) eventually, the late afternoon before shooting in each cast member's case issuing their "morning call" to either them personally or to their agent, to let them know what time and where to report the next morning.

And some actors wonder why casting direcors don't seem to have time to meet them for little sitdown chats!

In addition to the foregoing, there are other details! They also need to keep their own careful records of how much all actors have worked for in their last and all previous jobs at the studio or through their own independent office, so they have a better knowledge of what the right amount will be to offer them when their agent is on the phone to make future deals or for consulting before even making those inquiry phone calls about availability and salary offers to their agents.

They must also keep their own voluminous files of thousands of photos and résumés, often referring to them for smaller roles or for desperate searching; even for top roles on occasion when nobody's available who's initially wanted by the producer, allowing a lesser known actor to be considered for a good, juicy top role for which there isn't much money in the budget. Those are the occasions that casting people really enjoy, but they're rare.

They spend a lot of their daytime hours between (and during) the above details talking with the agents who swarm in and out of their outer offices wanting to see them or on the telephone with other agents trying to sell them on certain clients for certain roles.

If they're one of the few who also set aside some time to meet new people in any general interviews these days, it's that much more detail and time. At the end of the day they're tired, beaten, and probably brooding over the day's mistakes, embarrassments and failures of too many of the people they've suggested and brought in for readings. Too many embarrassments of the latter kind can cause loss of their assignments in very short time because they've literally wasted the producers' and directors' precious time with their poor judgment of talents or appropriateness for roles.

Still brooding and also hungry, but knowing that they won't have time to eat a relaxing dinner, they may be one of those who constantly go out to appear at _Cold Reading Showcases_ and listen to readings of many actors who shouldn't even be there because they're not ready for such showcasing. At least the fees they receive for making such appearances go into the bank and help during those "rainy day" periods when there's no casting assignment. Some who make a big business out of appearing at such Cold Reading Showcases almost every night probably swallow a couple of Nodozes, grab hamburgers on the run and zip to the required places.

But others---even including some of those who continually appear at those Cold Reading Showcases---still have more details to handle between leaving their studio offices and meeting the new horde of eager actors that night.

Those who are temporaily officed in a distant, across town studio production office for a production they're curently casting must also check their secretary back in their own independent casting offices, or at least their answering machines there, and maybe even make hurried crosstown trips there to read their mail. They probably won't feel like looking through the big stack of photos and resumes received that day from thousands of actors and agents. Such things must wait till the current picture is over. But at least they probably have to return some urgent phone calls that have come in to their own offices before leaving, whether they're leaving to hurry to that Cold Reading Showcase and make another $300 or so, or to get home, finally---often around eleven o'clock or midnight---for a few hours of fitful rest.

For a casting director, at the end of his or her busy day, to go out to see people in a small theatre production, appear on a discussion panel, or even make that $300 at a showcase, is something just this side of Hell if they're also working on a production. Many do these things, summoning up the energy to do them, even though they know that later they'll wish they hadn't. Try to bear in mind how much kindness a casting director is showing when he or she comes to see your performance in a play or sit on a panel before you giving you inside information on the industry and what you can do to help yourself advance in your career. These aren't small kindnesses!

RELATING WITH CASTING PEOPLE

They're generally a likeable lot, and most are willing and happy to stretch themselves to help a lot of people when conditions are right.

In the first place, they *like* actors or they wouldn't be good casting directors. They don't generally mind getting occasional reminder notes from people they've met or have seen work and have evidenced interest in. But don't overdo it.

If you're appearing in something on television---at least in some role worth watching, let them know. If you're in a production or showcase somewhere, let them know. A brief, one paragraph note, perhaps on a card, saying you hope they'll be able to see whatever it is, is best. Even if they don't see the performance, you've used a perfectly legitimate opportunity for reminding them in a businesslike manner that you're still alive.

Send them brief thank-you's after you've worked through them, whether they're the ones who brought you in or not. Again, it's another legitimate opportunity to call yourself to their attention without begging...even if you know your friend, the director, was the one who obviously thought of you and called you in for the producer to meet.

But don't continually bug them by wastepapering their desk weekly with reminders or beggings. The most you'll likely ever get that way is perhaps a few very tiny roles---the kind handed out to beggars---but more probably they'll simply block you out of their memory bank as a nuisance and throw all those reminders in the round file without a second thought if they see your face on their desk too often. You'll be a beggar and, worse, a botherer.

Simply use your taste and judgment always. They're using theirs every day, and they expect the same from anyone in whom they're likely to have the slightest interest.

Chapter Fifteen

Audition Scenes And
AuditionTapes

Some Years ago casting directors and agents as well, if interested in an actor, would frequently offer the opportunity to do a scene in the casting or agency office, either for just one person or for several in the casting department or agency office at the same time. Actors used to scurry to find the right scenes for themselves, persuaded partners to work the scenes up to readiness with them, and eventually took the pieces into the casting or agency offices and, in their particular scenes' assigned timeslots among a number of other scenes of other actors being seen the same afternoons, presented the scenes to show their talents.

The office phones rang incessantly in both types of offices while the actors were doing their scenes. In casting offices producers often stuck their heads in the door and the casting directors had to interrupt the scenes to step out for hurried conferences on urgent matters. When the casting persons returned, nervous from the hallway conferences' emergencies, the scenes were either started afresh or because of the press of the emergencies simply picked up where they were interrupted. In agency offices too, the phones were always ringing with casting inquiries about clients or other urgent matters. It certainly wasn't the best condition for either the doing of the scenes by the actors or the judging of the talents involved by the people seeing the scenes. But it was about the only way in which new people with no film to show could have their talents judged at that early point in their careers.

With the arrival of videotape cassettes this all changed. Seldom now does a casting person or agent ask an actor to bring in a scene to be done in the office. Now most casting people and most agents offer to look at audition tapes if the actors have them. If they don't have either half-inch or three-quarter-inch audition tapes which can be left to be viewed at the convenience of the office then the general meeting is probably all there's going to be.

The cost of preparing a good audition tape, if it's to be productive to any degree at all, is usually beyond the pocketbook of most actors, and to have the master tape then reproduced for both sizes of VCR's and copied so that the actor has perhaps four copies...two of each...adds more expense!

Yet in most offices these days tapes are asked for. Having a tape of the actor's work allows the interested party to amass a number of such tapes and, if and when a spare moment comes, quickly view one after another looking for outstanding talents or considering the actors for specific roles currently being cast.

At least this manner of becoming acquainted with actors' talents has vast advantages over the old scene-watchings. When scenes were done in offices it was improbable that more than one scene per actor could be seen, limiting the actor to his best choice of material for that single opportunity to display only part of his talent and, under the conditions described above, probably fall far short of even that.

There are still a few offices where---there being no videotape cassette viewing equipment---a few scenes are viewed occasionally. Because there are still those few, we'll discuss scene-doing in offices first. From the standpoint of choice of material, many of the same considerations apply anyhow.

CHOOSING AUDITION MATERIAL

New people's biggest mistake in choosing scenes to do for agency or casting people is the choosing of heavy, melodramatic material full of violent confrontation and peak emotion. The actor, after all, usually feels this kind of material will best show his strong dramatic talents

The errors of this thinking are that even if that big, loud, violent scene shows the actor's ability to be big, loud and violent, the actor who's still doing scenes in offices isn't going to be hired for those big, loud and violent sequences or roles at that early point in his career and there's little a casting or agency person can find out about the other areas of the actor's talents in such a piece.

128

When actors are ranting and raving it's primarily the *situation* that's being featured...the *event* more than the participant. The *personality* of the actor is submerged in those peak dramatics and has little opportunity to be either experienced by the actor or judged by the viewer. Even the role category for which such a scene would be ideal auditioning is wrong, since the new player isn't going to get those roles for a long time into the future.

Casting directors *unanimously* warn against such big, melodramatic shouting matches as office scene-showing material. They all agree that it's not only wrong as a choice for auditioning and usually embarrassing, but also annoying in the cramped-together office spaces of casting departments.

The material chosen may be brilliant, but the writer doesn't need the audition. The dynamic shouting confrontation may be one of the best scenes from the total work. It may have gotten an Academy Award or Tony Award for the actor who originated the role. But its shouting nature gives no opportunity for the participant to bring his own personality and uniquenesses to such work. Those would be far more impressive in casting terms and more quickly productive of acting roles.

The actor seeking a scene to do in an office should bear in mind that in most roles, whether for theatre or film, there are only a few if any of those big shouting matches. Most of a theatrepiece or film role is instead constucted in such a manner that throughout the script the actor must bring far less pyrotechnical scenes to life in a quieter, more psychological and actually more demanding use of his talents. A deluge of rapid-fire shouting too often obscures both the actor's personality and his more interesting qualities for various kinds of casting in roles. The latter points are what casting directors hope to learn from viewing scenes. Speed kills! When you're zipping through frenetic dialogue there isn't much if any opportunity to bring much more than just that.

Don't choose a scene that takes too long getting to the meat of it. Casting directors state that they can judge your talents in the first few moments, and they indeed can to the extent that they may find out what they want to find out.

Definitely have some movement, although not big or fast or violent. The film art, once called "talking" pictures (here's that comparison again because it applies in auditioning as well) is now "motion" pictures. People need to see how you move. You may move interestingly, with your own unique manner, and people want to know whether you can keep film frames interesting with your manner of handling your body or may be just too dull to the observing eye to do so.

Don't pick that popular scene! Everybody has seen it a thousand times. That advice is repeated over and over by the people who suffer through so many scene presentations of Starbuck's "*Rainmaker*" scene or Biff and Hap's scene from "*Death Of A Salesman*". They cringe, they say, when those titles and similar ones are announced. Naturally also, those people are sure ahead of time that they'll have seen those scenes done much better and may even have seen the originals.

Don't do a scene associated with the brilliant and award-winning performance of a top star, for the same reason. Stanley Kowalski in "_A Streetcar Named Desire_", for example, has long been stamped with the indelible mark of a single star and chances are you'd fall short of that mark.

Don't involve a lot of props! They take time to set up; they're a distraction from your performance; and no casting person or agent likes to see their office being cluttered up prior to the start of a scene and know ahead of time that clearing up the mess afterward will keep the scene participants there far longer than the time allotted to them.

Once, when the author was casting, two actors scheduled to do a scene brought in a picnic basket full of real food and a blanket and began strewing dead leaves over my office floor! They told me "It's in the park." Another time a young lady started moving things on my desk aside and laying out a tablecloth and dishes! "It's in a little Italian restaurant," she told me! Try to not appear stupid and thoughtless.

Don't plan to use their telephone as a prop. It might ring, and they'll resent it and probably stop you anyhow. Don't start moving their furniture around. Most casting offices can be expected to be fairly small and will probably have one sofa and one chair or maybe just a chair somewhere opposite the casting director's or agent's desk. Don't expect much if any more. Plan for that amount of space and that amount and type of furniture.

And don't ask for a couple of moments to "prepare" or to "get into the mood." It's a mark of the amateur. Film requires that you simply "push the button" of feeling (as Marlon Brando has been quoted as recommending for film) and start when it's time for a take. If you aren't "prepared" ahead of time to do that with ease you're not sufficiently prepared to the point where you should be doing scenes in offices either.

Don't take up their time describing what has taken place leading up to the scene you're doing. The scene must stand on its own feet, and if it's a piece out of the established repertoire the people waiting for you to start know the story anyhow.

Don't bring extreme characterizations...types of personalities you probably can't be cast to play in film or television. The role should be your own age and offer opportunity to display your own personality and talents rather than the opportunity to show how well you can play roles quite unlike you in too many respects. That's not how film and television are cast.

If you can, choose the scene with consideration of what the casting person is currently casting. If it's television, watch an episode or two of the series. If it's a motion picture, find out something about it from your agent or someone else. Pick a scene which shows you in the general area which might produce an immediate casting opportunity, since as time goes by and they see more people your chances diminish considerably.

Most people who still do see scenes won't take time to critique your work afterward. Generally, they'll simply say "Thank you" and that's it. If one of them should discuss your work with you afterward it probably means they find you interesting enough to take that additional time with you. If they don't, they'll end the meeting rather quickly because their mind is full of notes about your work and you that they're anxious to write on your résumé somewhere to remember how you impressed them in casting terms.

Certainly don't ask to repeat the scene because "It didn't work as well that time as it should have." If it didn't work, rehearse further before doing it in any more offices...and scratch that particular doing of it off as a dismal failure without any hope that it will have left any positive impression on the casting or agency person's memory. Also, in such a case, how do you know that the casting director or agency person hasn't thought it excellent, then when you criticize it yourself may feel that his or her and your tastes and judgments don't agree?

It's good to prepare some scenes in your acting classes, under the supervision of a qualified teacher or coach who understands the film industry, before you present them in offices. A common mistake is to have actor friends watch and critique them. Most friends would do them differently, and your results in terms of your own uniquenesses will be reduced through adjusting to those friends' own preferred manners of working.

When you have the appointment to do the scene, if you feel you're not ideally ready, most industry people will accept that honest reason for postponing, although they may be a little impatient with someone who offers to do a scene, sets up an appointment and then, quite late toward appointment time, finally starts to prepare one, doesn't have enough time or rehearsal, and calls, perhaps the morning when the scene is scheduled, to ask for a postponement and another appointment. Generally the person scheduled to see the scene will be happy to have that breather in their busy schedule anyhow for the making of some urgent phone calls. In any event, doing a scene poorly is far worse than not doing one at all.

In blocking the scene with your partner, bear in mind that casting offices are usually small spaces. For that reason, and also because for film and television you'd be working more closely together with other characters (for the sake of closer "two shots") and casting directors become accustomed to such closeness, it's a small point but an important one to think ahead and block your scene so that you do work in close proximity to the other character most of the time. Maybe the casting person wouldn't notice if you don't, and if you work across a room from your partner...but maybe on the other hand he or she would notice, even if half-consciously...and feel something is wrong from a film camera standpoint. It's best to observe this subtle point, just in case.

There are more subtle points. They have to do with film technique. If you've studied film camera technique under a well qualified coach or teacher, or worked on a few film sets, you've been taught or you've observed that you should most of the time hold your head fairly erect and maintain to a degree that three-quartersing direction of facing----which for film is approximately three feet to one side of the camera lens, at lens level----for thinking, etc., so the viewer (who in effect should replace the camera lens in an office scene showing) can see most of both your eyes. Again, the scene viewer may know film technique and would be happy to find that you do too.

Don't look at the floor. Your face isn't visible when you do. Don't look at the ceiling, either, and give the viewer too many "jaw shots" as a result, while violating a human, quite automatic truth-experiencing position for the face as in real life it unconsciously looks to the horizon, not the floor or ceiling, for thoughts and image-imagining of places, people, things, etc. In film this is *always expected* and *always instructed* by directors when they get somebody on their sets who doesn't know this basic. The casting directors, if they know a few of these things, certainly know this item from watching directors work with people on sets.

Don't do a scene requiring you to hit something forcibly. In film if a character appears to hit a desktop or a wall it's skillfully faked and the sound is dubbed in a dubbing session. Also, no casting director wants his or her Queen Anne table hit or his or her Ming Dynasty vase knocked or jarred to the floor. This kind of violence suggests that the scene may be one of those too big, melodramatic scenes in the first place and is best avoided in the planning.

Dn't throw yourself around too much in an office audition scene. Movements should suggest that you know film movement, which is of a type which allows the camera to follow you comfortably. One of our director friends has said that moving before a camera should be like "walking under water." Under water, remember if you've done it, is more difficult as you push the weight of the water before you. What the director meant, of course, is that you simply slow those otherwise sudden or fast movements a little for the sake of good camera work. Too frequently those sudden, big movements some actors like suggest overacting anyhow, since in real life even those moments are less big and less sudden because in real life we're not as secure in such moments as actors forget and allow themselves to be.

Additionally, if your partner is willing to work with their back more or less to the casting director much of the time, so you can be featured throughout the scene, good. At least you can try to persuade them to. The result looks very much like a good "over-the-shoulder" shot to the viewer and approximates the way your own performance in such a scene might be played in one take on film. If the scene is fairly divided in the amount of dialogue, when the partner is doing the scene at his or her own appointments (not yours), you can even reverse positions easily for the same resulting effect.

Be sure that you both take with you to the office your photos and résumés. You're expected to do this. The previous photo and résumé will no doubt have been lost under a big pile of others and the casting or agency person mustn't be expected to hunt for it or to ask if you have another. Just offer the new one. They'll probably make some notes on it...and that's precisely where such notes will do you the most good later if they've liked your work. Offer the photo and résumé as soon as you come into their office. As mentioned before, the person viewing the scene can probably tell whether they like your work within a very few moments after the scene is begun and they'll want to start making brief notes on your material at that point.

132

Don't choose scenes that are dialogue and dialogue only. Dialogue offers so little of what the people seeing scenes are looking for. Make sure the scenes offer "living" and "experiencing" moments for the characters involved---between the lines. Those moments are the main opportunities for the actors' "special qualities" to be observed....far more than a dialogue-heavy scene will afford you.

Try to find a scene---either in a not often heard of work or even of your own writing---that nobody will have seen before.

You know yourself, and you know what you want people to see that you possess in terms of special talents, special personality and special manner. Those and other aspects, afforded opportunities in moments to be observed, are precisely what casting and agency people need to know about you. For this reason some very wise people write their own scenes if they feel they can....to exploit their own uniquely special things. Write something that exploits as many of those assets as possible. You might search forever in the standard repertoire on library shelves and never find anything as close to what you want as something you could write for yourself.

Be careful about being too considerate of the other character in the scene. The appointment is yours. Don't do a scene that affords the other person too much. It's your special time and your opportunity that's been given by the person seeing the scene, not the other person's.

Choosing another unknown person to do the scene with you is fine if you can't find among your acquaintances someone who is fairly known around Hollywood. Another new person may distract, though, without even trying to do so. The person viewing the scene will also be curious about your partner, since they too are new to the viewer.

On the other hand, someone whose work the casting or agency person already knows won't distract from you. And there's the additional advantage that if the casting or agency person is a friend or constant hirer of that other person then the fact that that other person whom they respect is there solely to help you will give you the unspoken recommendation that is implied: Someone who's worthwhile thinks you're worth their taking their valuable time to help prepare your scene and take the time to bring it in with you!

In a case such as the latter one---when someone's there with you whom the casting or agency person knows, don't be upset that a personal chitchat period between them will probably come. Don't feel that because the two take some moments to discuss other things you're being neglected or ignored. The scene is what matters in these showings, and your friend being there to help....not the talk. And no doubt your friend will turn the conversation to discussing you at most opportunities anyhow. If this doesn't happen...and it might not...at least you're there in the company of someone who matters to the viewer.

One of the most important things, when you hook up with someone who's willing to do a scene with you, is to remember that a "great" scene is not what you're looking for. It should be a "you" scene. The partner may know some fantastic scenes which as scenes are out of this world. But in all probability they won't be right for the things you want to display in your single scene-presenting opportunity in one or more offices where you'll have just that one shot at making a uniquely personal impression so you'll be remembered. Don't automatically go along with first suggestions of the partner just for the sake of expediting the start of working on a piece. Look for as long as it takes to find the right one.

As mentioned earlier, if you can't find what you know you must have, write your own. Have in mind at the typewriter all those special things that you are and that you can do and work out something which allows you to bring them into play logically and effectively. It's been done with great success by some of today's top people who got their starts most rapidly in this manner. The material was fresh. It was extremely personal...far beyond what might have been taken down off a shelf. It seemed "ideal type casting" for the person presenting it. It certainly should. It was written by someone quite close to the performer....himself!

If you write your own scene, of course you might try it out in front of workshop peers and a coach or teacher, in front of friends and relatives who know you well, etc. Get all the reactions you can. Ideas will probably be contributed, since others often notice things about us that we don't ourselves observe. Some of those comments may be great contributions. If you like some of their ideas, plagiarize like the devil. They won't mind. If they even know that you've used one or two of their suggestions they'll be proud to have helped and proud that their ideas appealed to you. But, again, watch out for those suggestions that come from your scene partner. The reasons are obvious.

Additionally, pick a scene that doesn't require a too dressy look. The scene-showing isn't a social event. It's a workday event, and it's acting rather than a corporation employment interview. Wardrobe can distract, because it involves the casting or agency person's own taste and fashion consciousness if it's dressy. Do you want the person watching your scene to wonder while you're doing your scene where you got your suit or dress or that crazy outfit that is currently faddish but that doesn't even look good on you? The dress for your character should be casual and un-dressy, so a wider spectrum of role categories can flit through the viewer's mind. Even workday or plain wardrobe is much better. You want absolutely no distraction from you, the actor. Avoid bright colors, too, and loud checks or designs that keep catching the eye whether the viewer wants them to or not.

Similarly, don't wear chains or necklaces or bracelets or anything else that will constantly rattle and enter the awareness of the viewer. It might not only distract if such noises keep occuring; it also limits the casting spectrum again. Such items tend to define the personality of the wearer into a too narrow area.

Some years ago the author coached a beautiful young black actress who, although she was a fine dramatic actress, couldn't quite rise past the good co-starring roles that fell so easily to women of her beauty. She was ideally ready for stardom. After insisting, even at her advanced career point, on doing a scene in some casting offices---to force people to see her in stronger roles---and giving outstanding performances each time the scene was done, per comments that came back to me, one casting person finally gave me the key to what was wrong. Every time she did the scene, just as every time she worked in my classes, she wore several bracelets and I had often called her "Bracelet Jangler". She was doing the same thing in all those offices too, distracting from her performance and still categorizing herself for "fashion" and "glamour" roles. Told of the comment, she discarded her bracelets...and has become one of today's most exciting black actresses in the dramatic roles that finally started coming her way.

Pick a scene, whatever you do, that doesn't require a lot of eye-to-eye, nose-to-nose acting! In one of those scenes you'd find yourself working in profile so much of the time, totally ignoring the consideration that if you want larger roles early in your career you'll have to learn to three-quarters and play "foreground" for the camera to get all that many closeups. The casting or agency person wants to se your face, not your ear and hairstyle, which are about all your profile can offer them. Block the scene so that you can "work foreground", with your face visible all the time, or even if for moments you "work background" (farthest from the camera) make sure your face will be turned forward (in that case toward the other person) rather than ever letting your face be turned away too much. You have to become comfortable working in those positions so often in film roles, and being seen to be aware of that fact makes you look more experienced in what film is all about.

Try to have some sitting time in the scene. The actor appears far more interesting when using furniture in some interesting manner than he does when he's hung up out in the air in those standing positions some actors associate with strong feeling moments. How many times have you personally remained standing in the middle of a room in very upset moments? Didn't you, in real life, attempt to find a place to relax and ease your tensions? It's a fact of life, as well as an important thought when preparing a scene, that sitting is more effective and more true to life in such coping-with-problems moments.

Some last, obvious no-no's: If you're an incurable "hands-talker", don't let the casting director---much less a director!---catch you doing it all the time to help yourself talk. It doesn't work on film, and even casting people know that. If you have to toss your head to communicate strongly, again you're doing something that film actors have to eradicate in the communication process. Some actors, not knowing any better, shake their heads to say every syllable. They're not ideal film actors until they stop that.

And don't be a "bouncer", bouncing up and down as you talk. Again, that's a no-no for working before the camera. So is "weaving" from side to side unconsciously, whether standing or walking. It causes interrupted takes on film sets when the cameraman can't hold you steadily in the frame he wants. Again, some casting people and agents are sufficiently aware of these seemingly harmless habits that cause actors, if they even make it to a film set, to lose their chances for second jobs or, if it's observed in offices,

135

keep them from ever getting to a set at all.

Enough about doing scenes in offices...especially since there aren't that many allowed to be done in offices anymore. Something else has replaced them...*Audition Tapes!*

AUDITION TAPES

Audition tapes can be costly, time-taking in their preparation, often mishandled as to choices of material, often poorly taped and edited, with poor sound track and poor lighting and sometimes with quite inadequate direction. But more and more they're the going thing for actors who want their talents to be judged by those who don't yet know their work.

For those who don't know precisely what an Audition Tape is, it's a cassette of half-inch or three-quarter-inch videotaped acting performance, about five minutes long at the most, which presents the actor in (ideally) several short sequences of different uses of his talents. It's for leaving with an agent or a casting person or a director to be viewed privately by them (usually not in the actor's presence), to enable them to become acquainted with his work.

The cassette should have on it somewhere the name of the actor, accompanied by the words "For Pickup, Call (the actor's number)." Too many tapes can be lost or even thrown away after sitting for some time if they don't have this information on both the cassette itself and on any cassette case or box in which it's left at an office. Agents frequently forget, or find themselves too busy, to pick up tapes of their clients at offices where they've been left for viewing, primarily because they don't want to rush the casting person with whom it's been left, so time passes and it's forgotten.

The actor should always have *his or her* name and phone number on the tape rather than the agent's. Many agents will be grateful to have the actor client do the picking up anyhow. Tapes are lost or mislaid in agency offices too! Some agents won't even accept the responsibility of having actors' expensive tapes sitting in their offices. They prefer to notify you, the actor, to deliver your tape to some office and be responsible for picking it up later...after they've persuaded the casting director to accept it for viewing. That's the agent's main responsibility, and it's good to have the actor take over from that point. You should offer to be responsible for your own tapes at all times. How do you know that you'll even still be with the same agent by the time the casting person or production executive is finished with your tape?

You should have a master of the total edited tape, in safekeeping somewhere. It's expensive, and there's only one such original master. However, you should also take the master to a tape-editing company and have about two half-inch copies and two three-quarter-inch copies made, so you have enough to have them in more than one office at a time. There are also Betamax and VCR considerations. You should have at least one or two of each type.

The original material can be recorded on either size tape, because all tape-editing companies can transfer from one size tape to the other so you can have both.

As to the material that's most desirable on an audition tape that has any hope of being viewed beyond its first 30 seconds or so...this is where actors make so many miscalculations either out of ignorance that quality is necessary or thinking that one long scene will be viewed for a sufficient timespan for someone to judge the actor's different feeling areas and levels, his versatily and his unique qualities. Remember, in many cases there won't even be an interiew...your tape is all that person is going to know about you. You must make it count and hopefully leave an indelible memory.

WHAT A GOOD AUDITION TAPE SHOULD CONTAIN...PREPARING IT

One long scene is a big questionmark. Two, three, four or five short clips (30-40 seconds each) of different kinds of work and different subject matters are much more effective.

An audition tape can be worthless if it's "homemade" by actors with friends handling a camera ineptly, with inadequate lighting, with poor sound, and with little or no direction for the camera. There may have been some saving of money, but such a tape is a waste of time and won't be viewed for more than the first ten seconds. The quality of your tape reflects upon you.

I've always recommended against going to one of those companies that advertise in trade papers to tape single scenes for actors for perhaps $250-$300. For many years some companies produced lazy and perfunctory tapings of single scenes, without any direction for the camera, even sometimes poor lighting and sound, with simply occasional tightening of shots to afford a few closeups. Actors unfamiliar with acting for the camera in many cases prepared those single, long scenes, with movement blocked as if for proscenium stages...and they were taped that way. Such tapes were totally worthless!

However, in recent years we've seen rave comments of our casting friends for the tapings of Alen Fawcett Sound Stage, located in Studio City. That particular organization produces excellent audition tapes, usually of the kind I so strongly recommend—a number of short, 30-40 second clips that afford the viewer the opportunity to judge actors' different talents and ranges. I understand from Mr. Fawcett that only in special instances—when casting or production people need demonstration of an actor's ability in comedy or intense drama—would he recommend a single, longer taped scene. I certainly agree.

And I've been told that some companies, including Mr . Fawcett's, are in the process of developing video-faxing capability to transmit high quality tapes directly into casting directors', agents', managers' and producers' offices, with tapes produced and transmitted electronically by the taping company, in response to requests from those offices, as part of actors' self-marketing tools.

Another fairly inexpensive manner of audition tape preparing is to be in a class or workshop where there's top quality color videotaping and a director directing the scenes or monologues for their tapings who has a good knowledge of film and television cameras, so the material won't just be stage-style scenes with occasional zoom-ins for closeups.

In such a workshop, when you're confident you have a number of excellent scenes or monologues (or a combination of both) on tape, ask to view the tapes, mark the cues where you want to cut in and out of each tape, and get permission to take the tapes to a tape-editing facility. There are many such companies, one of which we know of doing top grade work and charging approximately $50 for an hour of editing done in this manner, plus a charge for the cassettes of course, at decent prices also. You will come away from this kind of professional editing session with a quite satisfactory audition tape for your use...*if* the lighting, direction, sound, camera work and your own perormances when taping were as good as you think they were.

If possible---and if the workshop affords this special flexibility which is so desirable, have each scene or monologue done before a different setting, in different wardrobe, displaying a different facet of your talent in varying pieces, with as much closeup time as possible. This is not always available in workshop facilities where there are often two people equally featured in each scene and neither is sufficiently favored in closeups to make the tape ideally serviceable as an audition tape.

Scenes involving two people are a problem and a disadvantage. Two participants in a scene on tape means that somewhat wider shots are necessary in the taping, since the tape in all probability won't be edited afterward to cut from closeup of one, for instance, to a closeup of the other. The characters will probably have to be moved from the foreground position to the background, back and forth as is allowable within the context of the scene, to allow closeups within a "master" shot of this kind. It requires a good director to work out these movements (which you see so continually in soap operas but also increasingly in other dramatic film as well) and to handle the framing as each move is completed.

The disadvantage for the individual player by whom the tape is intended to be used is that the other person will be equally featured in much of the taped version of the scene. That's the main disadvantage, but there are more too:

Few workshop directors are either qualified or inclined to bother with the constant focal depth shifts of such filming if it's to be top quality in its end result. The usual result is what's called "split focus", so that both foreground and background player wind up slightly out of focus (or moreso, depending on the depth variances in the blocking). The problems of these two-person scenes are so numerous that the best efforts of all involved are sometimes met with faulty result and the whole is wasted.

AN IDEAL TAPING APPROACH....OVER THE SHOULDER SHOTS!

Some of us have conceived of a different kind of material-taping approach that ideally serves audition tape preparation. It is the use of what really are *monologues*. The manner of taping each is to place the featured player for whom the tape is being prepared---the actor who's delivering what really is a monologue---at least for the main part of the taping in fairly tight closeup, with just the side of the head and perhaps a shoulder of another player silhouetted (or lit, if preferred) in the side of the frame's foregound. A classic "over-the-shoulder" shot results, and it appears to be cut from a two-person scene. It's still actually a monologue, but it offers so many advantages.

Only one person is featured...the one paying for the tape. One person only has to know his lines perfectly, insuring that a second player isn't going to use up the tape and time by forgetting lines or messing up a piece of business. The face of the one single actor can be in perfect preset focus down to the tiniest hair. And no time is wasted on a second player's performance when the one person presenting the tape for viewing is the one the viewer wants to see.

Of course in some of these monologue tapings we open wide enough at the start to establish the other character in the foreground and an attractive set with good lighting and good sound. Hopefully also, good direction of the tiniest details will be easier with just one person featured. Then, after a few moments of the wide (usually called "establishing shot") framing the camera can tighten the shot into that previously mentioned quite close shot of just the one actor for the rest of the piece's taping. It works ideally, and casting people have praised this manner of presenting individuals' talents.

The author recommends that any workshop head who hopes for the optimum tape for class members obtain a number of backdrops or settings (to vary the settings according to the varied material)....perhaps an office set, a living room set, a restaurant corner, a bedroom, perhaps even a clearing in the woods or a convincing lakeside boat landing. The same thing applies if you've decided to tape material at home for yourself with the help of a couple of friends to handle the camera, lighting setups, sound checks, etc. You'll still want those several setting backgrounds for the sake of varying your material. And don't fail to provide authentic-looking furniture, set dressing such as anything called for in the script or just "set dressing" because it's a living room or kitchen or some other location. Do anything you can, in other words, to achieve a very professional-appearing result.

I personally recommend that actors get with a qualified advisor (whether their workshop head or someone else) and, viewing all the taped material in those varied roles and settings and types of work, pick the best parts and plan so they wind up with a total tape, composed of a number of effective but brief cuts from several pieces, of approximately five minutes total. No more.

In choosing the sequence in which the pieces of material should appear on the final audition tape, a word to the wise: Put one of the very best up front as #1; then a quite different piece second; again something different as the third; and so on...bearing in mind that---whether the viewer likes or dislikes your work----because of the press of time usually experienced by busy casting people it's improbable that the total tape will be viewed by all to whom it's delivered. Often a very positive or very negative opinion is formed swiftly.

There's another advantage, by the way, to these monologues done as "over-the-shoulder" shots: Even if you do think one of the $250-$350 places will give good quality and decide to try under their advertised "soundstage" conditions, hoping for best results, then at least these kinds of tapings, one after another in the same studio time and fee stucture, will give you closeups galore; a single lighting setup which can be more conscientiously prepared; better sound quality because the mike boom can be fixed and remain in the same location; "set changes" time will be less consuming; and in the end a better group of tapings can result, plus some saving of studio and crew charges as well.

Under any of the above situations, bear in mind some sound principles involved in filming: After a couple of rehearsals there will probably be some perspiration shine on your face...perhaps a shiny nose or glistening forehead. Powder down! Better, since it's tape and artificial lighting, have a makeup base on under the powderings so your skin will appear healthier. If the hands are to come into the shot (and they certainly should, from time to time, whether with props in them or not), have them made up to an exent also, just as is done in top filming, so they won't bring white skin up against a makeup covered face with the resulting distraction because of the obvious oversight. Comb your hair or muss it in exactly the right manner. These details are always carefully prepared for filming. You should do no less for a so important thing as your audition tape. Don't wear strident colors that will distract the viewer's attention, and don't showcase a faddish designer's wardrobe to the detriment of your own performance's impression.

Be careful and check the sound before starting a take on tape. If there's a slight hum underlying the sound test before a shot, find the cause and get rid of it. The workshop head, if that's who's taping you, may not care enough to correct it, even if he or she notices it. You should, for your own sake. And on color cameras there is adjustment of color to be concerned with also. Make sure that you look lifelike as to color of skin, etc., so you won't wind up with an orange face or a blue one. It sometimes happens.

If you're taping in a workshop, observe (as mentioned before) the appearance of the setting or settings available to lend variety to backgrounds for the different pieces. A wrong or amateurish set, or something that's an obvious nonsequitur in an otherwise right setting, can be distracting to the viewer.

If the workshop doesn't have such varied backgrounds for use as sets in tapings (all of them should but many don't), offer to provide some. There are many ideal wall murals available in wall covering outlets for around $29-$49. Usually they come in sections of four or six pieces. For a good office background, a lakeside background or a waterfall to backgound your closeup or over-the-shoulder shot you'd probably only need one of the pieces of such a mural---two at the most---taped to the wall behind you, unwrinkled and carefully checked as to lighing, for a thoroughly convincing background that will surprise and please the tape viewers later. Such a setting can be changed in three or four minutes...another advantage.

One of the author's favorite settings----used for many different "over-the-shoulder" tapings of various scenes---consists of just one panel from a Manhattan skyline nighttime mural, fixed to a wall, with a rich velour drapery framing one edge of the city skyline, with an elegantly set "penthouse dinner lounge" table before it. The featured actor is seated facing across the table toward the side of a "foreground-framing" actor's head and shoulder with whom he or she is talking. Still closer to camera, in tight foreground, are a few fronds of fern or elegant floral arrangement, slightly out of focus. With the expensive-looking setting and fine silver and crystal, plus the impressive night view of the Manhattan skyline outside "the window" in the background, a very attractive piece of tape is produced for the actor.

These easily available wall murals offer endless possibilities if you shop around a little among them. There are country farm outbuildings and fields, shaded dells with waterfalls, huge flower-strewn mountain meadows, marinas filled with sport vessels and sailboats, clearings in woods, offices, factories and just about anything you could want to appear to be outside a draperied window to establish an attractive location. Go looking around in those wall covering stores...especially in the discount or closeout places where you can get them more cheaply.

A cassette tape will probably cost about $4-$6. It will hold many tapings. The wall mural backgrounds, if you buy maybe three or four, should cost perhaps $80 to $100. Then all you need is the equipment, and a friend may have either a good color video camera or even a good camcorder. As to the costs, perhaps a friend will want to share even those and make up a tape of his or her own in the same sessions!

You neen't concern yourself too much with whether to use the fade-in, fade-out technique (this is available on most video cameras and camcorders), since later you'll be using only parts of most takes anyhow in the final edited version of your tape. But chances are that one or two of such tapings may be ideal from the start or at the end of the take, in which cases you could certainly use fade-ins to good advantage. So you should at least consider the nice effect of having fade-ins and fade-outs on all takes if the equipment has this capacity.

If you do use fade-ins, you'd better also have the cameraman do the standard film-take calls just before each take, so you'll know precisely when to start your dialogue and action.

When cueing up on the VCR or camcorder the cameraman should quiet anybody in the room or studio with "Quiet!".....then call out "Roll 'em!" just like a gnarled old First Assistant does, to signal you that the fade-in button is being pressed and the fade-out which precedes the fade-back-in is begun. This crossover process doesn't usually take more than ten seconds or thereabouts, so you know to be ready. During the fade-out, fade-in process of the camera he or she should call out the identification of the shot...for instance, "Johnny Valentine, Scene One, Take One!"....then, with

141

the crossover process completing and the picture continuing to fade in, just before the picture is at its brightest, the cameraman can call out *"Action!"* It makes a better fade-in if you're doing some action---sipping coffee, laying down a paper or something else as you start your dialogue.

If the word *"Action!"* needs to be removed in editing that's certainly no problem and the perfect timing it's made possible during the taping will be worth it.

In fading out at the end of the take, the cameraman should hold off calling out *"Cut!"* until the fade-out is completed and the camera has mechanically "gone to black". Holding off till then will obviate taking a moment to delete the call in editing. The actor should of course keep the character alive and the scene continuing in some manner after the end of the dialogue, until he hears the *"Cut!"* call.

Again regarding the possibility of these taping segments being manufactured in a workshop facility, you should make sure by asking ahead of time that tapes are maintained for a certain period to be available to you for any copying you may desire at a later time when you can afford to have your tape composite (the "master") edited and made up.

Back to the material to include in your tapings: It's good to have several short pieces that display all the different types of work you can do. If you can cry, have a crying piece. Have an angry one. Have (certainly) a warm, casual one that displays more facets of your personality itself without the distraction of any heavy drama. Another could be self-kicking, frustrated, mean and threatening....whatever, depending on what you feel your most important areas of talent may be. Run the gamut in your selections for taping. Then prepare them with your best performances. You may just come out with a tape that will boost your career swiftly if enough people see it and take the time to notice your different areas for casting.

When you have the tape in the shape you want it and have a number of half-inch and three-quarter-inch versions ready, somewhere at the botom of your résumé, in bold type, enter this kind of note: "Audition Tape Available For Viewing -- Half-Inch or Three-Quarter-Inch". Maybe underline it so it stands out to be noticed when somebody's looking at your résumé and perhaps finding your face interesting.

When you think about it, at least the *Audition Tape*, except for its cost, is a far better means by which casting and agency people can "audition" talent. The old "one scene done in a busy office with telephones ringing and other continuous interruptions" way was pretty awful, compared to having several varied pieces on a good audition tape that can be viewed at some quiet time when the telephones aren't likely to ring. And for those actors who do understand how to work in front of a camera it's an effective auditioning of that ability too.

Here's to audition tapes!

Chapter Sixteen

You'll Have To Join
Some Of The Unions!

You can't work in union films or union television, or even union theatre for that matter---and the professional ones of each are "union" exclusively---without becoming a dues-paying union actor yourself in the applicable unions.

The *Screen Actors Guild (SAG)* is the film (and most of television) actors' union. It has jurisdiction of all television, as well as film, that is done on film rather than being performed live or taped. The *American Federation of Television And Radio Artists (AFTRA)* covers all live and taped television and radio. *Actors Equity Association (Equity)* governs professional theatre of all nature.

Furthermore, you can't become a member of most of these unions until you've been offered a job in a union production. Some new folks consider this latter fact a "vicious circle" and spend years looking forward to getting that first union card.

There are two exceptions worth noting, though: You may do your first film role under the _Taft-Hartley Law_, which allows you to do a first film role in a SAG-signatory film without joining the Screen Actors Guild, after which you're called by the Guild a _SAG Eligible_ or "_Must Join_" and must join the Guild prior to reporting for work on your second role.

In the case of AFTRA, you may simply go in anytime and join by paying your initiation fee (we won't quote it here because it'll probably have been raised by the time this is read) and your first six months membership dues (which we also won't quote for the same reason).

The advantage of going in and joining AFTRA early is that if you're a paid-up member of AFTRA or Equity for a year and have worked as a principal performer in that union's jurisdiction at least once during that year's period you may then just go in to SAG and join without any SAG job offer. A lot have gotten their tough-to-get-otherwise SAG membership in that manner.

The sooner you have a SAG card, or at least an AFTRA card, the sooner industry people will begin to take you seriously. It's that simple. They know, then, that you're "a Hollywood actor".

The manner of joining SAG with your first film job is for you to obtain a letter from a SAG-signatory production's producer stating that you're desired for a principal (speaking) role in a specific film or commercial. Otherwise you must wait out that year as a member of AFTRA or Equity and work once during that time for a union signatory production of that union, then simply go in to SAG and join.

Until 1987-1988, whatever SAG's initiation fee and membership dues were at the time that you joined, if you had either Equity or AFTRA membership already that other union was called your "parent" (first) union and your initiation fee and membership dues for SAG, as your second union, were discounted by half. As long as you remained a dues-paying member in good standing (paid up continually), you'd continue to pay SAG only half of what it would cost you otherwise. This "parent union" basis applied in the reverse situations, also. If SAG was your first union then the other union memberships cost only half of what they would have otherwise for as long as SAG was always fully paid up to date.

This is no longer true, though. Also, SAG's and the other unions' membership dues escalate as your employment income rises. That escalation rate is also something we hesitate to quote here because it is often raised. You can always check when your situation starts changing to the point where escalation will probably apply in your case.

The _Screen Actors Guild_ offices are located at 7065 Hollywood Boulevard, just east of LaBrea Avenue. There's usually a Bulletin Board full of information of all kinds, including casting notices of upcoming film and television productions, in the outdoor patio at the entrance, available to all comers whether members of the union or not. Take a pad with you and jot down all the information you can.

The offices of the _American Federation of Television and Radio Artists_ are now across Hollywood Boulevard, at 6922 Hollywood Boulevard.

Remember that AFTRA covers all work in radio, recordings, live and taped TV commercials, announcers, soap operas, talk shows, voice-over narrations for film strips and slide shows if that work is to be made under union conditions.

The _Actors Equity Association_ offices are located at 6430 Sunset Boulevard, next to the corner of Wilcox Avenue, in Suite 616. It has jurisdiction over all professional live theatre, both musical and dramatic, including dinner theatre and cabaret productions, in the United States. To join, you must be offered an Equity contract. An exception is for registered Equity Membership Candidates who've worked in this apprenticeship-type program for 50 weeks at one or more accredited theatres in the United States. These folks may join without a current offer of Equity employment contract in hand.

Membership in Equity, as in the other unions, requires an initial membership initiation fee plus the first six months' dues. As with the other unions, even if SAG or AFTRA should be your "parent union" you now pay full dues to Equity too, the earlier "discounts" having been abolished in recent years.

There are two other unions you might need to join, depending on how you go about your career and whether it involves any "club act" work such as standup comedy or some other form of "club" work such as backup singer for a star attraction, etc., or whether you plan to do "extra" work for a few years in motion pictures to get started.

The "club" performer will need to join the _American Guild of Variety Artists (AGVA)_, which has union jurisdiction over "variety" performances in nightclubs, theatres, hotels, industrial shows, etc., of most kinds except full-scale musicals---the latter being governed by Equity.

AGVA's office is at 4741 Laurel Canyon Blvd., Suite 208, in North Hollywood, but think "Studio City" rather than North Hollywood when you're looking for it. It's on the boundary between the two.

That union's joining is simple. There's no employment offer or contract requirement. Simpy go in, fill out an application form and pay the approximately $300 initiation fee. Like the other unions, even if you already have a "parent" union there's no half-off discount anymore. At last word its dues run from $24 every four months or $72 yearly, up to $795 if you're earning more than $35,000 yearly.

The other union you might want to join is the _Screen Extras Guild_. To play non-speaking roles in union films under the Screen Extras Guild (SEG) jurisdiction you must join SEG within 30 days from the first work day of any employment. To get your first extra-ing job you must first register with a union casting office of SEG. Most of those offices won't register you unless they feel confident of your ability to work within the categories generally called for as extras. In the past those most generally called for categories were usually "ordinary people" of all kinds--- "business men", "business women", "housewives", "blue collar husbands", etc., preferably nondescript so their appearances wouldn't be likely to distract attention from the

145

foreground (principal) players.   And there were the "dress extras"---actors who could truthfully state that they had tuxedos, dinner jackets, dinner and cocktail gowns of all descriptions, etc. There were always nightclub scenes in most movies of the time. This has changed somewhat in recent times, though, and there aren't the limited number of categories for extras anymore.

Once a member of the *Screen Extras Guild* you can get lucky and be "upgraded" right on the set of a picture at any time into a speaking role, automatically qualifying you to join the *Screen Actors Guild* immediately upon notification to the Guild by the producer of the unexpected, unplanned "upgrading" on the set.

Again the author hesitates to quote the membership initiation fee for SEG, since it has been changing regularly. At least there's no escalation later resulting from increased income brackets as there is with the other unions mentioned. Many people work continually as extras without graduating into speaking roles...and many make very decent livings at it.

To succeed at working often enough as an extra the player should religiously call the extras casting office at the end of the day or at the end of one job to ask if there's anything for them "tomorrow" or "right away". It's expected, since the lists in those offices are so huge that people are easily overlooked, and the old-timers among extras do this all the time.

The *Screen Extras Guild*---although you don't go there first---is located at 3629 Cahuenga Boulevard West, at the top of Cahuenga Pass, near Barham Boulevard. You'd want to go first to *Central Casting*, at 9200 Sunset Boulevard, Suite 224, to register if they'll accept you, as mentioned above.

So....there you have it. You're not considered a professional until you have union cards in your pocket, and you can't join too many of the unions until you have your first job! But don't overlook the AFTRA "open shop" opportunity for new people which allows you to join that union *without* that first job and have at least one union membership card in your pocket.

However you manage to get your Screen Actors Guild card and membership...get it. As quickly as possible. Why? Because many casting people are hesitant to even consider you for anything until you have that card that says you've at least worked on somebody else's film set already and *just may* know what you're doing.

Many talent agencies, too, won't consider seeing you regarding representation unles you're already a member of SAG or AFTRA, preferably both. They know that if they took you on for representation without a SAG or AFTRA card they'd run into too many roadblocks in their efforts to get you your first job and your SAG card.

No matter how you have to do it---through joining AFTRA and getting one job in live or taped television during a year's period; by doing extra work and persuading a director to "bump" or "upgrade" you with a few lines not in the script, or however else, by hook or by crook, get that SAG card! It's the "starting out point" that many new actors spend a lot of their early period in Hollywood chasing down. The sooner you have it the better.

Chapter Seventeen

The Film Job, Step by Step

In so many of the seminars conducted by the author for film actors, some who've been working for years have come up to me afterward to say "I never knew that!" and other similar comments about some of the items which are included in this book. Often they've been actors whose work I've known and enjoyed in a number of films.

When I've gotten those comments from them I've had the thought that if they *didn't* know those things when they worked some Editor must have cussed in his cutting room and lost precious minutes over his Movieola because the actor wasn't "matching". Before that, a First Assistant Director must have cussed under his breath the sixth time he had to yell *"Quiet!"* for another take. The Director must have cussed and sweated when the Producer yelled at him that he was running over schedule on the film---because an actor required ten takes of a simple scene. The Second Assistant's

147

ulcer must have kicked up when the actor was late for morning call because he couldn't find Stage 8 and was too proud to ask at the gate. And the Wardrobe people must have had to hurriedly try to match a green tie that the actor had worn in the shot at the end of the previous day and inadvertently worn home and forgotten to bring back in the morning. The actor's friend probably cussed when, arriving at the actor's invitation to have lunch at the studio commissary, the gate hadn't been given the friend's okay. And certainly the Casting Director must have cussed when called by the Producer to inform him he was being fired for hiring another amateur.

Exaggerations? Perhaps...but maybe not. Actors make so many mistakes through ignorance...both on and off of film sets...when they have roles. Of course nine times out of ten they never know about their mistakes...but others do. And not only mistakes. Oversights, omissions, opportunities missed, people offended, busy technical people forced to become nursemaids, directors frustrated at having to teach instead of direct, etc. If inexperienced and sometimes even experienced actors were told of the many problems they've inadvertently caused for production staff members on films they've just completed---almost always without their even knowing they've caused them, they'd be ashamed of themselves.

If armed with enough foreknowledge about _what to do each step along the way_---from getting a role through to getting more roles because of the manner in which each is carried out, an actor can appear to be a seasoned "pro" on a film set the very first time he works. If _ignorant_, on the other hand, of the many, many things that should be known, checklisted to be done and systematically and professionally taken care of---before, during and after the job---the actor will suffer many indignities on the set, will probably never work with the director again, will have his role reduced to shreds on the cutting room floor, and will probably retire to a farm after enough such experiences.

So, here we go...into the many things that _can_ be done, _should_ be done, and in some cases _must_ be done to make each film role---whether the first or the hundred and first---a stepping stone to more and better roles and rapid upward mobility in a film acting career.

It all starts, of course, with being hired!

WHEN YOU'RE TOLD YOU HAVE THE ROLE

Your agent, or the casting office direct if you don't have an agent, has called. You got the role!

If it's your first job you won't care about the salary or billing. If it's another in a building list of credits you'll want to know the salary and the billing your agent has gotten for you in negotiation.

If you're not yet a member of the Screen Actors Guild the production company will have found it out by the time you're called or they couldn't have called to "set" you for the role. Station 12 at SAG has informed them that you're not a member, perhaps that you're a "Must Join" because you've done a role under the _Taft-Hartley Law_ and can't do that again. The casting office or your agent will want to make sure that you're financially able to join in time to play the role. If you aren't, you'll have to lose the role. If you are, you'll have to scoot over to the SAG office immediately, plunk down your membership initiation fee and your first quarter's dues, get your card and call the casting office to tell them you're now a member. (SAG will have called them too, of course.) No matter where you have to get the money, get to the SAG offices quickly and join, so the production company won't begin to worry that you may not be able to join and begin making calls to cast the actor who was considered runner-up for your role.

Next, you'll be called in to _pick up your script_ and, while in the casting office, probably be asked to _talk to Wardrobe_ by phone. It it's a role that doesn't require specially provided wardrobe that's how it will be handled. If on the other hand you have to go to the Studio Wardrobe Department or somewhere else for a _fitting_ because special wardrobe is required, a _fitting fee_ will be added to your paycheck automatically.

If you're a _day player_...working for only one day or perhaps two or so, and are hired at a "daily" salary rate, you won't be expected to sign your contract in the casting office. That will be done, along with other employment papers of the studio, when you arrive for your first day's work.

If it's a larger contract---perhaps a three-day contract (for television) or a weekly contract for film _or_ television, it will probably have been mailed or messengered out to your agent already, in which case your agent will probably have signed it for you, as your Power of Attorney, and sent it back or taken it in personally.

Sometimes the script is delivered at your door by courier. The script you receive first---either in the casting office or at your home---will be "_the whites_"...that's what the final shooting script is called. Sometimes there are _revision pages_ delivered along with the white pages, in which case you're expected to insert the revision pages, substituting them for their similarly numbered white pages. Revision pages are most often blue for first revisions, yellow or pink for second, green for third, etc.

Naturally, study the new lines each time a set of revision pages is stuffed under your door. This can happen any time up to and including minutes before filming a particular scene, right on the set. You must get used to these last-minute changes and take them in stride comfortably.

Women will be told to _talk to the Hairdresser_ and will be instructed as to what to do. Usually they're told to set their own hair in their accustomed manner the night before but _not comb out_. The Hairdresser must do the comb-out the next morning just before filming.

If you have a Public Relations person working for you, notify them of getting the role. They will "plant" squibs in _Daily Variety_ and _The Hollywood Reporter_. At least they'll attempt to, and will stand a better chance of getting them into print than you would. Even if you have no PR person so early in your working career, you yourself can send simple postcards to "Film Casting" or "Television Casting" at both of the two trade papers. *Daily Variety* is at 5700 Wilshire Blvd., Ste. 120, Los Angeles, CA 90036. *The Hollywood Reporter* is at 6715 Sunset Boulevard, Hollywood, CA 90028.

On the card, say simply "John Doe signed for (or cast in, or set to co-star in, or...?) the "Go Easy on Harold" episode of "Bears And Bulls"...or "John Doe signed for "Walk Softly But Carry A Bomb", Lorimar Productions motion picture starting Nov. 28th, starring Jamie Gleason in script by Helmut Schroeder, Andy Jackson producing, Henry Pearson directing." Later, look for your item in "Film Castings" or "TV Casting" columns in both papers. Keep checking each day for perhaps two weeks, since you have no control over when the item will appear, if it does at all. Casting people do often check these columns to see who's working and considered to be worth mentioning in the trade papers' eyes.

If it's a large role you have, ask the agent to get you a *Shooting Schedule*. It indicates which scenes are expected to be shot on which days, and where. This helps you prepare for and bone up on the next days' work the nights before. Also, you may want to invite a friend or your agent to visit you on the set. With a Shooting Schedule in hand you'll know where you will probably be, when---although these schedules must be totally changed sometimes along the way. Agents of course know to call the Production Office of the particular picture before leaving to visit you on that Malibu location shown on the Shooting Schedule for that day, to check and make sure that the shooting is actually there as planned.

For friends, of course, if you know they're coming, tell them to do the same before they come...simply call the picture's Production Office to check before making the trip and finding you not there. Even you may not know ahead of time how long you'll acutally be at a certain location or where you'll be shooting next, due to unforeseen circumstances.

Learn your lines cold! No actor should ever arrive on a film set in less than totally secure condition with lines. Too many things are going to happen on any film set that will be disrupting your concentration, so if you're less than secure on lines it will be found out immediately---as will be explained later under *Dialogue Director*---and you'll be in very hot water and cause shooting delays and retakes.

Some years ago there was a diminutive "Little Caesar" type producer of a situation comedy series at Fox. An insert page in the front of all guest actors' scripts stated "Know your lines securely. If you don't, there are other actors available to do your role."

THE NIGHT BEFORE YOU WORK

Don't party the night before you're scheduled to shoot! Be by your phone to get your *Morning Call* or *Work Call*, telling you where and what time to report, and to whom, the next morning. It will sound something like "Seven o'clock Wardrobe (or Makeup), ready Stage 8 at seven-thirty." To a newcomer it's gobbledygook! Find out *where* Wardrobe will be---in the Studio Wardrobe Department or on Stage at setside...or where Makeup will be---in the Studio Makeup Department or setside. "Ready" means in makeup and wardrobe, on the set of the stage indicated, at the exact time set...ready for filming!

Sometimes actors don't think or don't know---in these last-minute excitements---to _ask whether there'll be a "Drive-On"_. This means that if there's a drive-on your name will be marked on the list at the studio gate to allow you to drive your car onto the lot and park close to the sound stage or somewhere convenient, rather than having to park outside the lot and have a long walk to the gate even before the longer walk through the lot to the particular sound stage. Some lots are huge. If you can get a drive-on you'll save a lot of time and walking. In any event, allow plenty of time for arrival, just in case you do have some trouble parking and then have a long walk. (More about drive-ons later.)

If your role is a fair-sized one and you've been hired to work more than one day your call will also include the _scene numbers_ you'll be in the next day, so you can concentrate more specifically on the next day's filming, perfecting the lines involved and reminding yourself of ideas you have for different moments in the scenes involved.

Be sure to _set your alarm clock_ before you accidentally nod off and sleep through after studying your lines late into the night. If you're late for your morning call arrival all hell breaks loose and it can start your day off miserably. Sound stage and union crews cost big money. An actor who holds up the first shot of the day by lateness is too expensive to risk ever using again. And lay the script out for taking with you in the morning also. Changes are frequently given to you right on the set, due to any number of problems, decisions, stars' demands, the weather, or an unavailable location or change of location in those last minutes. Also set out a pencil to make those changes that may be given to you hastily on the set, just in case.

Speaking of the script...from the first telephone call or meeting with Wardrobe, Makeup or Hairdresser people, _start jotting down their names_ somewhere...just inside the front of the script is a good place. They like to be called by name and it's a "grace note" that can bring extra consideration. They're artists, just as you are. When you get to the set, continue this name-jotting, filling in names you haven't already gotten...Director, First Assistant Director, Second Assistant Director, Script Supervisor, Dialogue Director, Makeup, Props, etc. You probably won't have talked with some of these people prior to coming to the set. It also helps to start calling the Camera Crew folks---the Cameraman, Assistant and Slates---by first names. If your job is for several days you'll feel more like, and act more like, a member of "the family".

You probably won't need to take any _Blistex_ or _Lip Ice_ unless you want to. Some actors do, to protect their lips from lights-parching when nervous. Makeup will customarily have these at the edge of the set if you need them. Similarly, for people who wear glasses in roles, Makeup or Props people will also have some _De-Fog_ because they're used to the cold sweat on actors' faces fogging their glasses as they're warmed on the outside by hot lighting. Ask for either of these aids if you need them.

The *clothing from your own personal wardrobe* which you've been asked to bring for the role must not be what you wear to and from the studio. Sometimes several articles will have to be carried to the set by you for last-minute choosing from among several articles, and what you're to wear in the role is expected to be *left in your dressing room* at the end of the day so it can be cleaned or laundered during the night hours for next days' shooting and assuredly not forgotten at home on those next mornings. The latter mistake would be a disaster!

Don't take a lot of junk or valuables that you'd have to leave in your dressing room when you're on the set filming. Sometimes things disappear, since dressing room doors are usually required to remain unlocked--- for fire and insurance reasons of the studio---throughout the day. Leave those expensive things especially---jewelry, etc.---at home.

When your work call comes for the next day, women shuld specifically *ask whether the Hairdresser will be on the set*, as is usual, rather than in the Makeup Department. They will probably always be setside on the sound stage, but ask to make sure, to avoid confusion the next morning. It should be noted that women's calls are generally an hour or more prior to "ready" time on the set, rather than the usual half-hour (rarely an hour) for men, for obvious reasons of the added amount of preparation on makeup, hair, etc., for women.

Also, women...*don't wear any street makeup to the set!* For that drive through the chilly morning air to the studio or to a location, if you don't like being seen without makeup simply cover yourself with a scarf or something, like those old fan magazine candid shots of stars wearing low-flopping, wide-brimmed hats tied with scarves around their chins in those top-down Rolls Royces. Any makeup you might otherwise have on---out of ignorance of this standard procedure---would have to be taken off before Makeup can "give you your face" before shooting. You're expected to know this. Street makeup is not film makeup. It must be done---from start to finish---by the expert who's paid good money to make you look good or look whatever way you're supposed to look for your roles.

One of the experiences new actors go through when they're filming, whether on a sound stage or out on a distant location somewhere, is the feeling that their home details, laid aside hurriedly to report for filming, haven't been sufficiently organized before reporting on the set. A sound stage or location, despite the pleasure of being there and working, can feel somewhat like an "isolation tank"...as if the actor is "cut off from the outside world" and every other aspect of his life. It's almost as if everything but the film role has been turned off suddenly...as it probably has.

The best advice one can give to prevent this worry is that the day before reporting for a role is a day for cleaning up such details, doing the things that need doing, making all the phone calls needed to postpone urgent things and generally getting oneself into a state of calm and "togetherness" before reporting on the set for work.

Don't ever plan to make some phone calls from a film set's very busy telephone, because crew members and staff people (who've been on the film continually and haven't had any "previous day" cleanup opportunities for perhaps very long periods) will be fairly monopolizing those few telephones that connect a sound stage or location with the outside world.

AT THE STUDIO GATE

Arriving at the studio gate by car, unless you've been specifically advised to park off the lot, simply drive up to the guard shack at the gate and give your name and the title of the production you're working on to the guard. The guard will check his list, especially if it's your first day and he doesn't recognize your face, to make sure you're in the cast mentioned and not a gate-crashing attempt. Then if you need directions he'll direct you to wherever you're to report. Don't be ashamed to ask him or her "Where's the Makeup Department?" or "Where's Stage 8?" Don't plan to search on your own for your reporting-in location just to save face. Unless you're very familiar with the lot it might take you much longer than anticipated to find where you need to go and make you late reporting in. Even a few minutes lateness on the part of a cast member expected first thing in the morning will set off shock waves that are reported to the set immediately, and within a few minutes your home, your agent, the casting office and the production offices will all have been called trying to find you.

If you've been told there's a _"drive-on"_ arranged for you the guard will probably tell you where to park inside the lot and wave you in. On the other hand, even if you've specifically been told ahead of time that there _won't_ be a drive-on for you, you might still tell the guard offhandedly "I think there's a drive-on," upon which he'll check his list, not find one marked for you but perhaps think somebody has goofed and let you through _because you know the right words_ and perhaps are accustomed to getting one whenever you work. People who don't customarily rate drive-ons usually don't even know about them.

At the gate it's a good idea, if you have someone coming to join you for lunch at the commissary during your lunch break, to give their name to the Gate Security Guard who lets you in that morning. He needs to make a note that they're coming as your guest. If you fail to do this they might be inconveniencd and have to wait until the guard can check with the stage where you're working so they can enter the lot....and if you're in the middle of a shot when they try to contact you, or the phone on the set is continually busy as it often is, your friend might have to give up and go away.

Don't be upset if on a second or third day the Guard still needs to be told who you are and what film or show you're doing, because the Security people change from day to day sometimes and, even if it's the same man or woman at those later times the checking-in process is so procedured and brief that your face may not even be looked at. They hear your name and the production title, check it, and wave you in while they're visually checking out the next car behind you. You're not a star till you're a star.

153

INSIDE THE LOT

If there's a red light lit, flashing or waving anywhere in the street ahead of you, of if you hear _one long whistle or buzzer blast_ suddenly, it means there's some studio street filming going on right then, perhaps just around the corner of that building next to you. _Stop your car and shut off your motor_ until the light goes off, stops flashing or whatever, and you hear the _two short, quick whistle or buzzer blasts_ that signal the "all clear" again. Then, not before, start your car and proceed, or if on foot walk on. Of course if you were walking when you heard the first (long) whistle or buzzer you can walk softly on cement or gravel and continue on your way, but it's a little chancey so it's better not to. And don't ever whistle or yell hello to anyone on a studio lot. You're liable to ruin somebody's exterior shot and look like an amateur to people around you who'll all know better.

When you get to the door of the sound stage, if there's a red light lit or flashing beside the door it means there's a shot or important rehearsal in progress inside. Don't open that door until the light goes off.

The door itself will seem to be locked when you give the handle a pull. Don't panic. Sound stages must be soundproof, as their name implies. Doors have to be hard to open as a result. Just give it a good, hefty yank.

A friend of the author's, a top new York actress in Hollywood to do her first film, encountered one of those apparently locked sound stage doors just a few minutes before she was expected to report in on the set inside. Frantic, she ran all the way back to the gate and told the guard the sound stage was locked. After he explained about the hefty yank being necessary and she ran back to the sound stage and got in quite easily she found herself approximately a half-hour late for reporting in. Her agent had been called. Her hotel had been called. A production assistant was wandering around the lot looking for her after the gate guard had told the Second Assistant that she was somewhere on the lot. And her first filming day was a nervous shambles from the word go.

PEOPLE ON THE SET....WORKING WITH THEM

The minute you enter the sound stage or arrive at the exterior location, _report in at once to the Second Assistant_. Until you've done that you haven't reported in. Since you won't have met him or her, and won't know what he or she looks like, ask the first person you can "Who's the Second, and where is he?" Someone will point out the man or woman.

This man or woman, the "Second", is in charge of the actors. If you're leaving the set at any time, for any reason whatsoever, tell the Second. You'll be getting your next day's call from him or her at the end of the day. To use the sound stage telephone for an urgent call, ask the Second. Look to him or her for practically everything.

After noting your arrival time on his Timesheet and having you sign it, the Second will show you where your _dressing room_ is. You'll find your _wardrobe_, with your name pinned to it, neatly hung in the dressing room closet. Or if you've brought your own street wardrobe at Wardrobe's request you should ask where the Wardrobe person is and show to them the articles you've brought for their choice of what they think the Director will prefer. If you're doing a small role, or sometimes even if it's a co-starring role, you'll probably be sharing a dressing room with another player. It's pretty customary.

The Second will have you _sign your contracts_ if you're a one-day role player, also a W-4 and some studio employment forms. If you're a 3-day player or on a weekly contract it's improbable that you'll be handed a contract for signature by the Second because, as previously explained, your agent will have signed it and gotten it back to the studio quickly. If you do get your contract and other papers from the Second upon reporting in, sign and get all the papers back to him or her immediately, since nothing goes to the Payroll Department till the contract and other papers are signed, and the quicker the Payroll Department has your papers and knows you're working the sooner you'll get your first paycheck.

If you're a "day player", however, and first seeing your contract, it's probable that your agent hasn't even seen it for checking, so it's a good idea to check it over yourself quickly in case your billing or salary or any other item isn't as your agent told you it would be. There's usually an entry on these Day Player contracts for "_Conversion Rate_", meaning that should your role accidentally be extended to a week or more your daily salary _won't_ be what you get throughout the engagement....instead you'll be "converted" automatically to either a "3-day" (if television) or a "weekly". Sometimes the weekly conversion rate is calculatedly very low, compared to what you'd be getting if on your daily rate throughout the job, and you might want to have your agent call the casting director to see if this can't be bettered.

But, whatever question you might have, if any, or whatever error you think there may be in the typed contract, ask the Second to let you call your agent immediately to get whatever it is straightned out. The agent takes over at that point, and he'll tell you whether to go ahead and sign the contract and hand it in or not. You should certainly hope that everything can be straightened out easily and quickly so that your contract can indeed be handed back quickly to the Second so it can be enroute to Payroll.

The Second will usually introduce you to the _Makeup_ person...of course making sure from his check-in sheet that you've been taken to whichever person---Makeup or Wardrobe---you've been instructed to go to first.

Because of the unlocked dressing room you'll be leaving to go to Makeup or have coffee while waiting to film, or while out of your dressing room on the set somewhere, if you can't carry your walletful or purseful of credit cards, ID's and cash on your person at all times, leave them with the _Props_ person, to be picked up at the end of the day or when you leave for lunch.

Even in the _makeup chair_ you can look like either an amateur or a "pro". First comes the makeup base---to keep your face from looking white or shiny. The Makeup man or woman will smoothe on the base. Next comes the blush and other colorings for women and probably a bit for men too. The next step is the telltale one for fellows...the eyelining pencil...the "ouch pick" that men aren't used to if they're not on the set frequently. It helps the Makeup person if you close your eyes and actually look down with them closed while the top lid is being lined, then have them open and looking far upward while the bottom lining is being applied. Of course the same is true for women, but they're used to the "ouch pick" from daily use.

Powdering you down presents no problem. But then comes another telltale operation when the Makeup person says he or she wants to "give you your hands." Certainly don't ask what he means. Just make sure your sleeves are rolled up past the wrist and hold out your hands palms down. Makeup will dawb some base onto the backs of your hands. It's your job to spread the makeup evenly over your hands and up onto the wrists or even onto the arms as far as needed to meet your wardrobe. Then wipe off the palms of your hands on tissue from the box in front of you so you won't get makeup all over your wardrobe. Powdering down of the hands and wrists after makeup is usually done for you also, after you've spread the base evenly. This hands makeup is necessary so that in shots your face won't be one color and your hands stark white as they'd appear by contrast if not also made up.

The facial tissue that's been put inside your collar or dress bodice by Makeup should remain there until just before the actual filming of a shot in which you're involved. It's to protect your wardrobe. Then, when a shot is finished, if there's to be some time between it and the next shot you're in, put another tissue in its place. They're always available on the Makeup table. Don't worry, they won't forget and film you with the tissue sticking out of your collar. It's customary for actors to keep the tissues in place through a rehearsal or two before filming, then remove them.

The next person you're likely to meet is the _Dialogue Director_, if the production has one. Many---especially motion pictures---do.

The Dialogue Director---think of him or her as "The Spy"---is normally a good friend of the Director and normally knows the Director's tastes and ways of working, since the Dialogue Director's function is to serve the Director in initial checking of how well prepared the actors are, helping guide their last-minute adjustments of their performances toward what the Dialogue Director knows the Director will want, and making any suggestions which are felt can be helpful.

The Dialogue Director will probably come over to you and ask---very casually of course---if you'd like to come to a corner of the sound stage and "run the scene" with the other characters involved in it. It may be the first time you've met the actress who's going to be your wife, or the killer who's going to kill you in Scene 23, or the child who's going to run into your arms crying in a few minutes calling you "Mama" or "Daddy".

When you're "running the scene" you may think you're just doing an innocent little warmup rehearsal. Not so. After the Dialogue Director is finished rehearsing you, watch where he wanders to...apparently without any special purpose. He'll probably go stand next to the Director, apparently "just watching the filming". Actually, he's sotto-voce-ing to the Director things like "Mrs. O'Brien in Scene 48 doesn't know her lines...she's nervous as hell"..."John the Hit Man has a cold today...sounds awful"...."The Sexpot in the pink is lousy"..."but the Bartender's sensational!"

What all this is for is to save the Director valuable time when those scenes come up for filming and sometimes even prepare the Director to make hasty reblocking plans with regard to how to shoot the scenes the actors are involved in.

Mrs. O'Brien's lines will be cut to smithereens, with apologies that they've seemed overwritten. John the Hit Man may be encouraged to make his voice even huskier---in case it should become worse during the shooting day and not match the morning's takes. He might even be asked to add a habitual sniffle, for the same reason. The sexpot in pink who was "lousy" in the runthrough will be told something like "Oh, my, you're too sexy...we'd better just have you stand there wide-eyed and inviting. Your lines would distract from the great way you look. We'll give your lines to Helen."

The Dialogue Director has helped speed the day's filming by preparing the Director ahead of time for what can be done to save the time and retakes that would have been wasted if he weren't forewarned about things that would have to be coped with.

And don't be worried if you happen to be the Bartender whom the Dialogue Director reported ahead of time was "sensational". The Director probably won't even look at you, and you may think he's ignoring you or doesn't think you're worth saying anything to. Directors in these moments are usually extremely complimentary, hospitable and kind-voiced and charming as they deal with the potential problem people. They're trying to relax those people with kindness while doing what they must. If they ignore you in those last-minute conference and adjustment moments it usually means only one thing...that you're perfect without any changes, and the Dialogue Director has given you a good report.

Even before that moment when the Dialogue Director collars you to "run the scene", there may be a few moments to simply go _stand near the Director_ and maybe say a quick "Good morning" or something else just as brief. Carefully choose a good moment...if there is such a moment, since directors are always under extreme pressures. The reason for even going to stand next to him is to give him a brief opportunity to look at you, to approve or disapprove of your makeup or wardrobe, and avoid any delay later if something isn't to his liking. Remember, it's usually the first time the Director has even *seen* you since the casting session which resulted in your getting the job. He has probably almost forgotten what you look like. And the wardrobe you have on for that scene coming up soon has been the Wardrobe person's guess of what he'll want. He'll (almost unconsciously) be grateful for this brief "checkup" opportunity. If he doesn't call Wardrobe, Hairdresser or Makeup for some change, he thinks you're fine as is.   Go away quckly. Don't hang around. He's busy.

Finally---about the time your nerves are shattered from the long wait around the set, you'll be called to rehearse one of your scenes, first for blocking and getting your "marks", then on camera. It may be the first time you'll meet several people close up that you've only watched from a distance throughout the many hours of waiting for your turn.

OTHERS ON THE SET

The *First Assistant Director* (called simply "The First") is the guy who bellows out "Quiet!...Give us a bell!...Kill the blowers!...Roll' em!", etc, before takes and last rehearsals. He's the Sergeant Major on the set. Those yells are his easiest job on the picture. He's basically the "Straw Boss" on the set, and his work began long before shooting started.

He accompanied the Director on location scoutings, noting details that he felt would waste money or speed location moves between sequences. He sat in conferences advising on rounding up of crews. He helped pare budgets with the Budget Depsartment. He argued with Set Decoration and Carpentry people. He worked up the Breakdown. He either arranged for use permits to shoot on private property locations himself or supervised and checked on whoever arranged all those details. By the time he's on the set for the actual filming he's 'way over halfway home.

At the end of each shooting day he won't be going home when everybody else is dismissed for the night. He'll probably be starting another long night of trouble-shooting with regard to the next day's filming. If weather is questionable; if some equipment can't be gotten for what was planned earlier; if a star is suddenly sick and schedules have to be revised---these and other unexpecteds and unpredictables will keep him burning the night lamp until about two or three o'clock in the morning and he still has to be up and ramrodding all the physical elements of the filming by daybreak!

His main (often only) contact with actors...since he's in charge of literally everything else...is when an actor bumps a light stand setup or coughs during a take or reports in late on the set. He's the one responsible for the picture staying on schedule, for saying determined no's to fussy directors who would exceed the budget with their sudden inspirations, etc. His mind is on how many pages and how many story minutes are shot in the least amount of time and how to get the crew and company to the next location before lunch break...or on how to change the day's schedule to avoid going into overtime or even "golden time" later that night. Simply *don't bother* this extraordinarily busy man!

The *Script Supervisor* is the person on the high stool with the script on a clipboard or stand, with a ruler and stopwatch hanging from around his or her neck, who's usually seen marking off each take on pages of the script one after another. The Script Supervisor's copy of the script is the one used later by the Editor as reference about what takes there are of every scene, how much coverage (different versions of the same brief scenes) there are, etc.

The Script Supervisor also constantly monitors "matching" details as to wardrobe, hair, etc. He or she may yell "Cut!" at any time when something is missed in dialogue and the Director himself hasn't caught it immediately. Be nice to Script Supervisors, if you have any contact with them at all. They're usually doing their hard job in preparation for their own directing career goals down the road. From the strictly technical viewpoint, they're among the best qualified to make that transition when the time comes. They know film!

The _Cinematographer_ (whose other titles are _Director of Photography_ or simply _Cameraman)_ rides the camera dolly setting up best angles and frames with the Director during rehearsals for shots. After making sure that lighting is perfect, that the right filters are being used, that actors are going to remain in focus and not move too fast for the camera to pan or dolly with them, etc., he climbs off the camera and---union "featherbedding" being what it is, at least in Hollywood more than on locations out of town---turns the camera over to his second, the _Operator_ or _Assistant Cameraman_, who will probably actually shoot the scene most of the time, unless the Cameraman opts to do a few special shots himself.

During rehearsals the actor should have a bit of communication with the Cameraman. He expects that experienced actors will ask him things like _"When am I in?"_ ---which an actor needs to know when walking into a shot, _"When am I out?"_---when exiting a continuing scene and having no other way to know when he's out of the camera's frame, or _"Where are you cutting me?"_---to find out where to hold props to have them appear in the frame, etc.

Other than these brief but important questions from actors, the Cameraman's too preoccupied with the visual aspects of shots to have time for small talk. Often if a Director is inexperienced and tends to miss film "no-no's" he cautions the Director about the actor who is continually talking with his hands (making his head jump around distractingly in closeups because the talking hands aren't even in the shot) or tells the Director that he'll have to pull back wider because the actor is unpredictable and can't stay in the desired frame.

Others around you, with whom you'll have little or no contact, include _Slates_, who holds the clapboard with scene number, location, director's name, participants in the shot and the take number chalked on it, and claps it loudly, barely missing your nose---because it has to be in focus as well as your face is, for the Sync Room to read it easily and "sync up" its visual closure with the loud clapping sound it makes on the shot's sound track, in order to put work picture and track together for viewing of "dailies" (sometimes called "rushes") the next morning. Slates usually rides the side seat on the camera dolly and continually adjusts focus to preset marks during camera or action moves.

The _Grips_ are the men who move things and carry things and hold things. They're headed by the _Key Grip_.

The _Lighting Crew_ folks, who adjust the "seniors", the "juniors", the "sun guns", etc., and the big silver foil reflector stands which bounce that harsh sunlight into your eyes during exterior shots, usually include the _Gaffer_ (the head honcho), the _Best Boy_ (his No. 1 assistant) and several others you'll seldom glimpse as they adjust lights on the high catwalks and grids above the set.

The _Sound Crew_ includes the _Recorder_ (whom you probably won't ever see, because he stays hidden away in the soundproof truck at the edge of the sound stage), the _Mixer_ (who adjusts the dials on his console next to the set for best recording of dialogue and sound, with as much as possible shutting out of unwelcome "noise" otherwise) and the _Boom Man_ (who stands on the high platform next to scenes in progress most of the time and extends the microphone boom out over the actors' heads, flipping the mike back and forth toward whichever person has the next line).

Your only real contact with any of these folks will come if you don't speak loudly enough to be recorded comfortably or make the amateur's mistakes of rustling paper or hitting a table or desk with your first or something.

Others you might never actually meet personally are the _Stand-ins_, including your own. But there's something you need to know, if you don't: When you hear the call _"First Team!"_ that means you, the actors. You're called back for shooting with that yell. Before that, the director has rehearsed you and blocked you into positions, establishing your _"Marks"_. Then you'll probably hear _"Second Team!"_. That means you should leave the set as the Stand-ins (the "Second Team") come to the set and literally "stand in" your positions while lighting is being adjusted painstakingly on your marked positions.

Stand-ins are usually members of the Screen Extras Guild. Sometimes they're people with similar clothing, hair, size, etc., to your own. Stars often have their own special stand-ins, called for personally on picture after picture, who do look quite a lot like them, so that the same hair coloring can be lit most effectively for their own filming later, and everything being photographed of their own later performance can be lit and prepared perfectly while they relax and avoid becoming sweaty under the lighting being prepared.

WORKING WITH THE CAMERA

Some people go through disastrously traumatic experiences time after time on film sets, and raise a lot of tempers around them, because they don't know how to work with the camera and feel the Director will take care of everything. Unfortunately, the Director expects the actor to know quite a few things and usually becomes frustrated and very upset if he doesn't.

160

Remember, The Camera Lies A Lot!

Picasso must have been talking about film when he said that often-quoted line, "Art is the lie that makes us realize a truth." There's a lot of lying that goes on...very skillfully...in filming.

First, there are the _lenses_ that lie about how close one actor actually is to another. This gives theatre actors accustomed to huge proscenium stages a very strange and quite uncomfortable feeling...as directors block them to stand just inches from other players---which in the film will look as though they're perhaps feet apart. There are _camera angles_ that lie about where the horizon is, because it moves up or down depending on how high the camera is. Those _avalanche rocks_ cascading down upon characters or the _tiger_ apparently leaping down on them from a tree are both on film and simply being rear-projected on a giant screen behind the actors while the actors cower on a sound stage floor with a few rocks around them, in no danger whatsoever as the camera films both the rear-projected film and the actors in front of it in a composite shot. That _car_ speeding along a city street or down a country road is also probably on a sound stage of the "process stage" kind (huge, two-stage setup) with you at the wheel, looking like you're driving---again with a rear-projected film rolling on the huge screen behind you with either city buildings or country road trees passing in the film, and with some grips shaking what is probably just a mockup car (part of one) with you sitting in it and "driving" it, coordinating their shakings with supposed road bumps, while someone else stands beside the camera motioning to you (the driver) the steering wheel turn coordinations to match the corners or curves projected in the picture behind you which you can't see.

That _accident_ in which the car apparently hits the actor for real and knocks him down has been shot in reverse action, with the "dead body" (when "_Action_" is called to start the shot) seen lying in a heap in front of the stopped car, then leaping disorganizedly to life after a second and throwing itself against the standing-dead-still car bumper, then walking away backward as the car slams into reverse and screeches away backward also...all of which, when reverse-printed and with the sound of the body crunch added in a Dubbing Session, will create a damned convincing disaster.

The _gigantic Roman Forum_ behind Caesar's throne is a skillfully painted canvas hung behind a small number of robed extras, with the rest of the crowds being painted on the canvas and animated with computer generation later, or else the whole big crowd background action is actually filmed freshly on a small set.

Also, that _many thousands feet jump out of a plane_ by the star---who appears to jump out of the plane looking scared to death---has really just meant that the star dropped about four feet or so from a tight shot of the plane's door onto a nice soft pad. Later that jump will have been cut directly up against a cutaway of a stunt skydiver falling through vast space. Then, in Editing, they've cut back to the star in another shot...in close, bone-crunching detail...as he landed (having been dropped from a crane harness release to the ground...a total of perhaps ten feet or even less!   Often even the ground-plop will have been the stunt man, then with a quick cut it's the star himself in a close shot as he writhes in pain and then laboredly pulls himself together and wobbles to his unsteady feet after his terrible "fall".

These are only a few examples of the thousands of "lies" film actors must learn to work with.

Another form of the "composite lies" involved in the very simplest of film sequences might involve the star walking along the street, stopping in front of a store window, turning back to check his pursuer, then walking on.

The star is using only about one-tenth of his very alert thinking to deal with the Hit Man pursuing him in the story.   The rest of his thoughts have to be, or at least should be _technical_. They have to be.

First, he's had to (1) make what's called a *"clean entrance"* from behind the camera, (2) stay in the exactly right section of the sidewalk crowd for the best camera framing, (3) "indicate" slightly when he started to turn toward the store window and stop---so the camera could still hold him in center frame, (4) hit the carefully laid "chalk marks" there---so the camera could catch the reflections in the store window over his shoulder and the "sun gun" light could cast just the right amount of light in just the right place, (5) remember exactly how he stood as he looked into the window's reflections---because he's had to be in exactly the same position when they've shot his closeup in that position later, (6) turn to look back at just the right angle to indicate the direction from which the Hit Man was approaching him---which wasn't the actual direction at all, but the camera's lens said it was, then "indicate" that he's going to turn away and walk on---because the camera was cued to "dolly" on its laid tracks when he was starting to walk away...and then (8) finally walk away in precisely the right direction along the sidewalk!

A longtime director friend, Lawrence Dobkin, once put it in a nutshell: "In theatre, for the actor, it's ten percent technical and ninety percent involvement, but in film it's ninety percent technical and ten percent involvement...and within that ten percent you have to be brilliant."

The sidewalk sequence may appear on the screen for only about ten seconds if at all after final editing of the picture, but it will have taken hours to set up, light and rehearse on the blocked off street location...with off duty real policemen and street barricades keeping regular pedestrians and traffic out and allowing only some rehearsed Extras to pass through...with constant yells of *"Cut!"* because cars or sirens a block away made too much noise to be matched or dubbed for next cutaways, or because a cloud came over and the lighting didn't match other shots of the sequence.

There can be perhaps ten or twenty takes of various types before the right amount of "Atmosphere" (the extras) are paraded by in the right manner without covering the star as he walks along the sidewalk, or the right amount of passing motor traffic is achieved to appear convincing without

162

distracting, and the star's actions are carried off without minor problems. Sometimes there's even a long delay until the sun comes back out, or until a Production Assistant can get to the construction site two blocks away and pay them enough to get them to stop their loud construction noises for a few minutes at a time.

At the end of a shooting day the film actor is tired more from waiting so long for camera setups and lighting and filming conditions than from actual working in front of the camera!

You're Expected To At Least Know The Basics

First off...*Left frame* is to your right when you face the camera. *Right frame* is to your left in the same position.

Before your scene is shot there's at least one *Dry Run* or rehearsal of it---often no more than just that one or perhaps two at the most---for setting your positions and giving you your marks on the floor or sidewalk, to set camera angles and movements, and to make sure everything that happens in the shot is not only possible for the camera to catch and hold in frame in the desired manner but also is perfect as to all details.

When everything's right, the guy with the chalk will *give you your marks*---outline where your feet must wind up when you stop someplace or stand someplace. You'll be expected to be able to walk into those marks skillfully without looking down at them. Actors who can always hit their marks time after time work more often than the less accomplished in this always required, very technical feat.

There are various approaches for "hitting marks". *Backstepping*, recommended by some, isn't all that dependable. Some oldtimers swear by it, though. Backstepping means first standing on your marks, then stepping your normal steps backward while counting your steps, so you can (hopefully) return the same route when the move is called for. The problem with this manner of working is that if there's any curve involved in your move, as there often is, or if the approach is too long a distance for accuracy at judging distance and final stopping point, backstepping can fail dismally as the answer.

What might be called *peripheral vision* or *relative position* means estimating how far you're to wind up from one or two objects...perhaps a chair on one side and a table on another; a tree trunk on one side and a rock pile on the other. You need to estimate how far you are to wind up from these objects both to the side and to the front. But this way still isn't always exact enough either.

There's really *only one very exact method* for hitting your marks. It involves what surveyors and photographers use: *Sighting*....or call it *Lining up* or *Crosshairs* or whatever you like.

It means that, when you're given your marks as to where you're to wind up after a move, and the direction you're to be looking is established in the blocking, you can *line up*---both vertically and horizontally, one near-

163

er and one more distant object, or a point on each, making sure neither object or point is going to be moved. Stationary objects only!...buildings, trees, desks, lamps, windows, streetlights, pictures on walls...whatever. Notice exactly where the two imaginary points intersect. Then, if in moving back to that spot later you wind up even inches to the right or left or in front of or behind your marks the intersecting point won't be quite the same and you can easily correct your position as you "settle in" on your marks without anyone being aware of the adjustment. Such available sighting objects---for your use in lining up these two imaginary points of intersection---are there on any sound stage or city street or country road, as long as you remember to not use anything which may or can move before or during the shot.

First, when called to the set by the Director, you'll rehearse the action of the upcoming shot. After your movements are carefully blocked and camera positions and framings are carefully set, while lighting and the camera and sound crew are getting things placed and set, there'll be one or more brief run-throughs to "warm up" the action. Then you'll hear *"Second team!"* called out. Get off the set, so your Stand-in can come and stand in your various positions, one after another, while the lighting is being adjusted and your makeup is probably being freshened by the Makeup person. When *"First team!"* is called, you, the actor, being a member of the "First Team", should get back into your previously blocked *first position* to prepare for filming.

This is the moment at which an amusing but also catastrophic thing happened once...to the same New York stage actress who was already a nervous wreck after having trouble getting the sound stage door opened, mentioned in the "Inside The Lot" section.

After the rehearsals---just before actual filming of the scene, it's usual to hear *"Powder Down!"* called out, because just as a shot is ready and "Slates" stands ready to clack his board loudly right in front of an actor's nose the Cameraman often detects some perspiration shine on the actor's face. Makeup will scurry to the actor and "powder down" the offending perspiration spots.

On that occasion involving my New York friend, at precisely that moment, with "Slates" hanging his clapboard in front of her face, the Cameraman did call out "Powder down!" She---accustomed to doing such things for herself on Broadway---reached out and grabbed the "powder puff" eraser hanging on the slates right in front of her and literally powdered down---with the *chalk* from the slates eraser hanging there so handy.

Her makeup had to be completely redone by Makeup and an already terrifying first day was that much worse for her as she heard everybody snickering and guffawing...everybody, that is, except the poor Director (who was trying desperately to cover the heart attack he was probably having on the spot because of the lost quarter of an hour) and John Wayne (who had already sighed audibly several times that day about his co-star's first film day mistakes). By the way, the same actress won a long overdue Academy Award in one recent year, but she never forgot that first day's experiences on a film set.

There'll probably be _Master Shots_ first...shots which involve large or moving action usually; often some complicated camera dollying or panning, etc. If you have a stopping place in a "master", bear in mind exactly how you stood, how you held your head, how you used your hands or perhaps held any prop in each such position, because there are normally more and different camera angles (called "coverage") taken of you in each of those positions later. Those "coverage" shots include _Closeups_---your head only, _Medium Shots_---usually the top half of your body or a bit less, _Reverses_---probably shooting from behind your head at someone else's "closeup", _Over-The-Shoulder Shots_---the same as "reverses" but usually framing the shot with the side of your head and neck or shoulder, or some else's when aimed at you, etc. There are others in addition. These "coverage" (several versions) shots later afford the Editor in the cutting room several selections of the same moments, progressively, moment after moment through the sequence, so the most effective sequence of brief cuttings can be used.

The observing and remembering of your body-involving positions and movements is called _"matching"_. Your positions must match all those previous and later shots at all times in every detail, so you can be cut in easily in the Editing Room. With the footage of actors who don't skillfully match having to be thrown away in the Editing Room, imagine how much more of your own footage will wind up in the picture if you've skillfully matched at all times!

One of the _Script Supervisor_'s jobs is to watch carefully, make notes and tell you if you're not matching, but it's better for you to be able to observe and remember by yourself. It makes you appear more professional and more aware of how important this requirement is. Only newcomers don't know they have to document all moves and positions in their minds for this matching aspect. Some newcomers---nervous in their first jobs---forget (or simply don't know) that as a Master Shot is being filmed, many more angles and versions of the same moment will be filmed shortly afterward. Such forgetting or not knowing can make several people on the set very irritated and waste a lot of film.

For film acting it's ideal to make _extremely conscious, definite and precise movements_ at all times...not only for the "matching" reason, but also so the camera can comfortably keep you in frame in a particular way. The camera doesn't like surprises. Movement for film is generally slow enough that the camera can do this without too many retakes. One top Director has said "It's like moving under water." Those who've walked on the bottom of a swimming pool or the ocean floor will know what he meant.

Top film actors also know that it helps keep film frames interesting visually---while it also duplicates real life body involvement more truly as well---if a hand is used in some manner around or on the head some of the time. Lean on a hand, perhaps, to think...remembering exactly how you do it, of course. Play with a collar or something...again remembering exactly what you do. Hold your disturbed forehead...and remember how you do it. A face and nothing else in a closeup can become a little dull after a few moments. Use your taste and judgment, of course, but it's worth keeping in mind and trying.

Hold the _head and face fairly up_ most of the time. The face and eyes need to be visible to the lens. Naturally, there are exceptional moments in sequences when this isn't observed, but it's fairly standard as a requirement...and experienced film actors know it.

On film sets where there are newcomers or even more experiencd actors who don't know, you see the Director stand near the camera during their closeups or some two-shots and hold his or her hand at _lens level, about three feet from the camera, to its right or left_....and tell the actor or actress to "Think, and look at your thoughts, over here most of the time." There are several reasons...some being simply technical; some being more aesthetic...for this being the spot where he may ask you to look and think most of the time:

(1) The lens is the viewer's horizon level as the scene is viewed later in a film or television piece. The viewer, with the actor's horizon being the same as his own, can forget that it's film being observed and feel like an unobserved bystander to the action;

(2) When looking or talking at that angle the actor's two eyes and the thoughts and processes behind them are clearly visible to the lens;

(3) That point where the Director is indicating is where the other character's face supposely is in many cases, since most camera recording of interaction is done at an angle which places the viewer almost (but seldom exactly) in the direction talked toward. Almost never will you be asked to talk directly to the camera, except as a spokesperson in a commercial or as a threatener in a horror picture.

(4) The "horizon" level is really more truthful for the actor as well, since people being talked about, things being reenvisioned, etc., literally lie out there on the true horizon over which they disappeared. Similarly, tomorrow's hopes and dreams lie somewhere out there on the same true horizon also.

Actors who come to recognize this source of a more complete and truthful experience work this way by choice forever and don't even need the Director's instruction to do it. Remembering someone or something being talked about, you certainly wouldn't naturally see them up in the air or down at an angle near the floor. They're "out there somewhere" on the horizon, just out of present view---which is probably exactly where they really are. It's simply the most truthful place for actors to do the visualizing of what they're thinking or talking about. So cultivate the habit...before the Director has to stop to "teach" you one of the things you're expected to know.

Whenever somebody yells _"Cut!"_ a shot is either finished or is being aborted before it's finished. If the latter is true, something has happened. If it's technical, it's simply corrected and there's an immediate retake...unless there has to be a wait for the plane noise overhead to go away or the buzz saw on that nearby hill to be turned off. Some years ago quite a number of the films and television episodes shot on the Universal lot picked the lot's hillside slope next to the always bumper-to-bumper Ventura Freeway for certain exterior scenes. Some shots got by without retakes, when the Freeway traffic sounds from below were at their lowest noise level. Other shots required waiting for better sound conditions. Others required all the actors involved going to the _Looping Stage_ at the end of the day to re-record their dialogue without any Freeway noises in the background.

Just in case you're sent to the Looping Stage at some point for re-recording your dialogue, its procedure needs a little explaining.

You'll be shut into a small glass-enclosed booth with a shelf on which you'll find the dialogue you're to re-record. Short phrases of it, rather than complete sentences, will be lined up down the page. When everything's ready you'll start hearing that first short phrase on the sheet over and over, with silent spaces between. Listen for a few moments, then start attempting to duplicate exactly what you hear...between the playbacks of the loop. When you've satisfied the man at the controls you'll hear a beep and you'll immediately start hearing the second phrase and be expected to repeat the process until all of those short phrases on the sheet of paper have been successfully duplicated.

Often when _"Cut!"_ is called out on the set it's the fault of one of the cast members and, aside from the forgetting of a line or being off "marks" given the actor, it could be one of those seemingly unimportant things that the actor simply has never learned and which give directors, cameramen, editors and lighting and sound people headaches whenever an unenlightened actor is on the set. While the actor might think such items petty and unimportant, they're deadly important to the people he'd like to work for more than once. If one of these things crops up and causes some "teaching" necessity before a shot can be redone, it might be one of the following items that an actor just hasn't known:

Some Definite No-No's!

Are you a _word-jiggler_ or _syllable-shaker_ when you talk? If you are, you're probably not even aware of it. The "word-jiggler" throws his or her head around just to utter words or even syllables. It's a teenage habit some never grow out of, usually resulting from the insecurity (at least in the teen years) about how effectively the young person is communicating. On occasion a bubbly teenager will be allowed to bring the habit into her performance, since it starts as a phenomenon of that particular age group. It works well for a bubbly, bouncy Car Hop role at a drive-in, or in a "girl talk" scene in a high school corridor, or a teenage boys' gym desciptions of their previous nights' conquests.

In adult film roles it might be allowed for a glib, talkative character having little or no depth and probably little honesty, even, but for few other types of characters. Yet we see so many people who exhibit the habit---and the personality signals that go with it in the eyes of shrewd personality judges---and some of those people are actors. Most who throw their heads around just to talk have no awareness whatsoever that they're _working so hard_ to get their words across to other people.

Most actors and actresses stop this summarily after viewing their first work on film...if the Director hasn't stopped it somehow during the filming. It's one of the most distracting habits an actor can bring to a film set, and the camera hates it. It forces the attention of the viewer away from the characer's mood and feeling and inner thought processes; forces attention instead to be focused on shaking hair, bouncing eyes and head and shoulder twitches! Actors with this problem eventually come to understand why the Cameraman or Director will ask that they hold their heads still and why, if they can't, their dialogue has been cut to almost nothing in Editing.

Watch leading actors and actresses in film and television more closely. Do they word-jiggle or syllable-shake to simply talk? No way! Observe how much more clearly you can see their inner thoughts, attitudes, fragmented inner processes...because they're not shaking their heads and jerking around when they're talking. Get some dialogue of your own on tape and observe whether you're working in the same manner or perhaps throwing your head around unnecessarily in delivering dialogue. If you are, and your coach (if you have one) hasn't caught it...change coaches.

If you currently require "word-jiggling" or "syllable-shaking" to simply talk, work to get rid of the habit before walking onto your first film set. Better yet, get rid of the habit before you go in to read for a role. It doesn't work for film and it's seldom allowed to get onto a film set.

Quick, unpredictable or jerky movement of any kind is sometimes impossible for the Cameraman to hold ideally in frame. Experienced actors know how to "indicate" ever so slightly that they're starting to move, and they know that the camera makes most movements appear a little more rapid than they actually are anyway. They also know that if the camera must start to dolly or pan with their movement they simply start left on the left foot or right on the right foot to avoid the "wavering" in the other direction at the start of their move.

Covering another actor who's behind us in a shot usually means that we're a little off our marks. Tight shots require very conscious holding of our position in a frame while staying as "loose and un-stiff"-appearing as possible at the same time. This is just something you have to get used to, perhaps in film acting workshops or in time after time playing foreground in actual film shots.

Weavers and _Drifters_ are the most guilty of wasting film. The "weaver" is the actor who keeps unconsciously shifting his weight from one foot to the other for whatever reason. The "drifter" is the "I'm very involved" actor who drifts across the shot in order to achieve the ultimate in his or her version of deep feeling experience. Usually this is the actor trained in "action"-playing classes who therefore feels he must lean forward toward other characters. Both the weaver and the drifter cause many interruptions of shots by the Cameraman.

The _Bouncer_, too, causes problems. He is one of two things...either an actor talking with hands too much (therefore causing his head to jiggle up and down in the shot) or an actor who's so nervous that he simply bounces up and down like a self-conscious Freshman, pressuring himself to remember his lines successfully...meanwhile making the wallpaper or trees in the background bounce with him if the camera is to hold his face in center frame as may have been planned.

There are *Haystack* actors too. When their heads and face are constantly down and you can't see anything but their blonde or brunette "haystacks" of hair, someody's going to yell "Cut!" pretty quickly.

Some actors are incurable *Overlappers* of others' dialogue or action. In your closeups or other shots involving only you, you should wait a beat before responding with your lines, no matter how false it may seem the first few times. This isn't true in group shots or shots involving two people, but it's highly desirable in your own closeups.

Sound recording of the dialogue track is on tape. Scissors have to get in between the last sound before your words and the start of your voice, so that your closeup can be cut into the picture...otherwise you're "overlapping". If you're a hopeless overlapper who can't be persuaded out of the habit on the set you'll spend a lot of time at the ends of shooting days in the Looping Stage's soundproof booth re-recording your own dialogue. But the bigger problem with overlappers is that the other players whose dialogue you've overlapped will have to be sent to the Looping Stage also. It becomes costly for the production. The actor is not only messing up his own dialogue track but also the other characters' in scenes with him as well. It's costing the studio or production company additional time and payroll money.

And there's *visual overlapping*. Body movements which are to accompany dialogue shouldn't begin too suddenly after the other person's speeches in closeups or individual shots of any kind. Otherwise, the Editor will have to cut into the end of your body's adjustments in the Editing Room, losing some of your action in moving, so that the previous speaker's speech can be totally cut into the film. The Editor cutting the picture detects such problems quickly and the number of your closeups eventually cut into the picture may be approximately zero as a result. The leaping into physical movement the split second the Director yells "Action!" will be overlapping, because his voice is still ending on the tape and, again, there's no space for the scissors to cut between the two.

Audibility and *speaking volume level* can present problems and calls of "Cut!" also. Speaking at the "living presence" level is usually fine, since the boom mike is directly over the scene or in the best spot for recording the particular take. This is sometimes a little uncomfortable for actors from Broadway and other large stage experience, for instance, because they're so accustomed to projecting their voice. Directors are quick to caution these folks to simply speak on "living presence" level.

But if you're not speaking loudly enough to be easily recorded (without also recording a lot of noise because the Mixer has to leave the mike turned up too high), the Sound Crew will yell "Cut!" and, again, you'll have wasted film and time for many highly paid people on the set. The last ditch effort they might make is to pin a _lapel mike_ on you after every other persuasion has failed. This certainly doesn't add to your attractiveness for more jobs with the same people at later times. The other extreme, of course, is the aforementioned "projecting" too loudly as for a large theatre stage. Most leading actors have had to learn to modulate their speech and volume to adapt to the film camera.

Hands-talking must be underscored again as one of the biggest problems actors may have and may not know they have, and may suffer from in the Cutting Rooms when their film footage is being edited. "Matching" becomes involved, even if constant "frame-jiggling" doesn't. The "hands-talker" (who can't talk without using his hands to help say words and accompany every speech in some manner) can't possibly match in a later shot what he did in an earlier version of the same sequence.

Hands should be basically part of _the character's experience_ rather than having anything to do with its mere communication. The hands should work with---in fact be part of---the character's mood and feeling, and should work in a more real life manner with the feeling instrument. If you're a hands-talker and it's not being stopped it's something you should take up with your acting coach.

An example out of the past: There used to be what were called "Zasu Pitts cutaways." Miss Pitts, in those old films, constantly fluttered her hands along with her quavering speeches and still fluttered them in her silent moments. It was one of the things audiences found "charming" and certainly unique. But it was impossible for her hands to be in the same fluttering positions in all the versions of shots in continuing sequences. Her closeups couldn't possibly be cut directly into any other kinds of shots of the same scenes. So the solution became one of shooting "cutaway" shots of maybe ducks on a pond (for no reason) or of an old hound dog scratching fleas outside a screen door (again, for no reason). This allowed for cutting away from one of Zasu's closeups to the scratching dog or the ducks, then back to Zasu, and it didn't matter what position her hands had been in in the previous moment.

In our more rapid-paced industry now, few people are afforded the luxury of such Zasu Pitts cutaways!

Some Positives To Bear In Mind

Learn to "cheat"! When playing a tight foreground (closest to camera) position in a "two shot" of the increasingly popular kind which involves two actors---one in closeup and the other farther from the camera with both facing forward toward the camera----which saves money and time by obviating the reversing of lighting and camera positions continually---you need the "soap opera actor's" ability to be talking to another character who's standing behind you on the other side of the frame of the shot. Some actors have difficulty making this convincing because they've been trained in classes where they've always worked straight into other characters' eyes all the time.

Foreground acting requires expert, convincing "cheating"...when talking to people behind you; when listening to them; when sharing and relating with them equally as much as if you were also looking at them. Actors who can't do this in a convincing and comfortable manner usually wind up in the background---and as a result smaller in the frame---but even there they need to be able to talk to where they know the foregound player's eyes are without having to lean out on their side of the shot to try to lean around the head and look into those other characters' eyes.

It's best to learn to do this "cheating" convincingly and become totally comfortable with doing it. As mentioned above, the soap opera actor has to do it in almost every single shot where there are two actors. Learn it. Get used to it.

For the actors who are trained to focus on their characters' own experiences (rather than on the other character) it's "duck soup" and totally fulfilling, but for those who are taught to "get everything from the other character" or "do something to the other character" every minute---which is lousy training for a film actor to begin with--- it can be an uncomfortable manner of working. Face it. Get used to it. Come to enjoy it. It's an often encountered manner of working before the camera.

Also, get used to _stopping and standing still_ just out of the shot when you have to exit a continuing shot. Don't continue walking. You might trip on one of the many lighting cords and sound cables which lie around the set, or knock something over, causing the shot to be stopped. Experienced actors simply step out of the camera's frame, making sure ahead of time they've asked the Cameraman "When am I out?" during a setup rehearsal. They exit the shot, then stop dead in their tracks till the shot in progress is completed. The reason? Their footsteps which would be disappearing in the distance will be dubbed in on the Dubbing Stage later. They'll be the right kind of footstep sounds, whereas yours, stepping from a carpeted set onto a wooden sound stage floor, wouldn't match sound-wise. And your disappearing footsteps, after you're out of the frame, might cause some problem with the dialogue of those remaining in the continuing scene and cause several people to have to go to the Looping Stage later to re-record their dialogue. It's simply the way this is done. You're expected to know.

When you're in a group scene of any kind but have observed that for a time you're not on camera, _stay in character anyway_. Don't goof around, even in a camera rehearsal or run-through of any kind. And don't just "go dead" just because you know the camera's not on you during a part of the shot. If you believe that what you're doing won't be in the shot you might even be mistaken and cause a stoppage and be bawled out.

If you remain in character and keep doing what your character should be doing it's even possible that the Director or Cameraman might notice and, even though they haven't planned to "cut away" to your piece of activity, they might suddenly decide that they should do an extra shot of you and what you're doing...affording you some more footage in the scene. Act and react, in other words, even when the camera's off of you, until the scene ends. It has often paid off for the actors who do it. Anything else on your part can be distracting and annoying to the Director.

Bring more than your lines to the set! Generally, these days, you won't even have gotten past the reading for the role if the lines are all you know to bring. You will probably have gotten the role in the first place because you brought to the reading more of the character and its personal experience than others did in their readings.

Once you've gotten the role, the process mustn't stop. You've been hired because the Director realized that he wouldn't have to spoon-feed to you those meaningful "character's experience" moments or inventive ideas. He'll expect that, in homework preparation, you'll have come up with still more little touches for those generally "between the lines" moments as well as for those moments involving dialogue.

One Director we know tells actors to *"Bring something from home."* That's exactly what he means. And another, in Russian-English, says *"Make from yourself something before you come."* Of course each of these directors, and most others, will bring ideas too, and maybe won't approve of yours, but if he does he'll love you all the more for making him look like a more inventive director!

By the way, cooperate with the man or woman who comes up to you with a still camera of any kind and asks you to be in a shot somewhere beside the set. He or she is the official *Still Photographer*....otherwise he or she couldn't have a still camera of any kind slung over their shoulder on a film set.

Anything the Still Photographer takes goes into the official *Still Book* of the film, which is a standard production process record of the filming. Not only will you be able to get a copy of such shots in which you appear through this person's work---which might be valuable to you if you're in a still shot beside one of the stars, right?---but also bear in mind that choosing you to be in stills hasn't been a mere whim of the Still Photographer. Different departments tell the Still Photographer what shots they want. If somebody in charge has decided there should be a number of still shots made of *you* off-screen that means that somebody thinks you're worth it, that you're doing a good job and that somebody may be considering using your face in some manner in publicizing the picture!

Something which may be impossible for you to bear in mind in early jobs---with your mind full of new and unfamiliar details---is to become acutely conscious of how often takes end with "Cut!", "Cut, print!" and other stop calls for scenes you're involved in. "Cut!" (and nothing else) usually means "Go again immediately"; something went wrong. "Cut, print!" could mean that the one take worked beautifully, or...and this is what to look for...if "Cut, print!" is followed by one or more takes of the same shot then there will be one or more *"Out takes"* later. Only one of the printed takes will be used in the Editing Room. The others will be "Out Takes".

They won't be used in the picture after the best of the two or three is chosen when dailies are being viewed. "Out takes" and _"Trims"_ (something else) can be used later if you can obtain them for your own promotion purposes. (See "After The Job...Using It For Promotion".)

Between shots it can be a good idea for you to jot down on your copy of the script, in the appropriate spots in dialogue and action, any _changes_ that occured to your hair, wardrobe, props or body during the scene just finished, to assist in the matching process in immediately following scenes. The production's _Continuity_ person or the Script Supervisor will probably have caught the change and noted it too, but you can help. And they'll appreciate it if they see that you remembered. If the wind blew your hair awry during the scene, notice it, so that in the next shot it will be the way it wound up in the other shot. If a cigarette was half smoked, notice it for matching in the next shot. If you buttoned or unbuttoned something, notice it and mark it in the script.

Lighting and preparations for the next upcoming "angle" of the scene, or the next subsequent scene, can take hours, and there might be time for you to forget and have egg on your face if you have to be reminded. These notes are especially vital when, out on a location somewhere, you go up to a building door to enter (at which point the action will be "Cut!") and perhaps a week or a month later must enter through what looks like that same location-filmed doorway, with everything about you in the same exact shape...on a sound stage back in Hollywood!

A small point...sort of a "grace note", but not just that: If you don't have to go off and woodshed your lines for upcoming scenes, stand or sit and _watch some of the other scenes being filmed_. Often the people involved are favorites and often-used friends of the Director. They're often part of his "stock company", and seeing you interested enough to watch their work might...just might...seem an indication that you like his choices among actors and that you're interested in and enthusiastic enough about _his_ work to watch it. He may not even look in your direction in any obvious way. After all, he's busy and rushed. But he's probably at least conscious of who is _interested_ in what he's doing and who's _bored_ by it. It's a very minor point, but it could be a productive one for you. It could even illuminate for you the Director's points of view and biases, as well as his personal style, for your own work in your later scenes with him.

Another little-known point: Often a Director will ask you to make some adjustment in your position, the manner in which you move from one point to another, or the manner of handling a prop. Don't try to read his mind and jump to make the adjustment you _think_ he's going to ask for. _Listen carefully until he's finished_ telling you what to do. You may guess wrongly and he'll be annoyed to have to start all over again telling you exactly what he wants. Simply wait till he's finished, then do what he asks. He'll appreciate it and time won't be lost because of your well-intentioned but over-eager leaping to the wrong guess.

When you're on a film set you'll frequently see some of the other cast members---usually the older men and women you've seen in many, many

173

character roles in films and on television---playing cards in a corner or telling jokes and horsing around between scenes in which they're involved. That's perhaps fine for them. Usually they're experiencd enough to be very secure with their lines and what they plan to do in upcoming scenes and are perhaps just keeping themselves relaxed among some good friends with whom they've worked many times. But for the newcomer to do any such fooling around on the set could be disastrous and distract from the concentration required to do the many things which haven't yet had time to become "second nature" and automatic in their work. You're not playing when you're on a film set. Best to stick to business if you're one of the newer people there.

AT THE END OF THE DAY

If you're still on the set at the end of the shooting day you'll hear *"It's a wrap!"* called out. It means that everything's finished for the day. But it doesn't mean *you're* officially released to go home yet. If you've been released earlier in the day the "Second" will have been the one to release you officially. At either time...before the shooting is finished for the day, even if you are, or at the end of the day's filming...you'll probably be given your *next day's "call"* ....again by the Second. If there's some problem, though, and he doesn't yet have the calls (which happens often), you'll get yours by telephone later that night at home when the next day's schedule is finished in the Production Office. Be home to get the call, to avoid somebody else getting a detail or two wrong. If they can't reach you personally they'll call your agent, but agents are human too, and they too might get some detail incompletely or wrong.

The Second will have you sign the *Time Sheet* with the correct releasing time shown on it before he lets you go.

Some amusing and some tragic things can happen with new actors on first jobs at the day's "wrap".

If the Second comes to you and says "You're *slopping!'*, it doesn't mean you're doing a sloppy job, as a nervous newcomer might fear at hearing those words. It means they haven't finished with you as expected and that you're to work the next day again, or at some later time, and are still on salary unexpectedly. Actors love to "slop" after they've learned what the word means.

Don't wear any of your filming wardrobe home at the end of the day. Hang every bit of it in your dressing room closet where you found it (unless you brought your own from home). The Cleaning and Laundry people must have it available so they can have it freshly readied and back in the closet for you before the next day's filming. This applies whether it's studio wardrobe or your own from home. Somebody may have a heart attack the next morning if you've taken something home and forgotten to bring it to the set the next morning.

If you're held into *overtime* on the set, don't even mention it to the

174

Second when you sign out on the Time Sheet. He or she knows it all too well. The time of your release will be on the Time Sheet before you sign it. If you're due any overtime pay you'll find it faithfully included in your next paycheck. Exceptions are so few...usually only in very low budget pictures when---probably once only and never tried again---somebody producing his own film on his own money and running low on funds tries to overlook this item. Any _meal penalties_ due you---those penalties assessed against the production for shooting past the time when you're required by SAG contract to be released for or served lunch or dinner---will also be handled faithfully on your check. It doesn't popularize an actor with a film crew to see him clock-watching to make sure the "meal penalty time" is observed. If any such charges or payments for them aren't added to your paycheck, nine times out of ten it's somebody's very exceptional oversight and can be handled easily with the production company..._by your agent_, not ever by you.

At the end of the day it's not a bad idea to be cordial to the people of all kinds that you've worked with. If it's the end of the job, or the end of your work in the picture, it's good to thank everybody personally. Even the director, who may have yelled at you during shooting and left you thinking he didn't like you or was impatient with you. Thank him especially. He was only yelling at you so he could more easily be heard over the noises on a busy set.

The Director has been operating under stress throughout the filming and at the end of it all he's grateful for even a cast member's appreciation. He's been on the griddle even more than you feel you have. The actors who---out of embarrassment about something---simply slink off into the night feeling they've done poorly, therefore neglecting this small grace note, are more quickly forgotten by the Director. Even if he did upset you at some point during the filming, he may not have realized it, or if he realized it he may very well be sorry. Forgive him easily and leave him with a smile and a thank you...because it's probable that with that small gesture you'll be called to work for him again.

Before even leaving the lot, or at the latest when you arrive home, be sure to call your agent and let them know you've finished. Let them know that you enjoyed it. After all, they were probably instrumental in your getting the job. If they weren't, you probably won't know it that often...and it will make them feel good that everything went well. Also, they'll know that you're then free to go on more interviews immediately. Otherwise, agents have no way of finding out for a day or two that you've actually finished, since even "one day" jobs often and unexpectedly turn into longer employments due to production delays, added scenes, location unavailability at scheduled times, etc.

For those who don't know, your paycheck is required by SAG to be mailed immediately by the production company and will reach your agent's office usually within about three days if you've signed those _Check Authorization Forms_ which direct Payroll Departments to send your checks to the agency rather than direct to you. Or you'll receive your check direct from Payroll within the same period of time.

If your check has gone to the agency the agency will quickly deduct its commission and issue its own check to you from its *Clients' Account*, set up for that purpose. SAG requires that this be done promptly. Some agents even call their clients to come in and pick up their checks, to get them to them more quickly. If you don't hear from your agent or receive your check from them within seven days, call them. It's highly unusual that there'll be *any* delay in your receiving a check, SAG regulations and the resulting standard procedures being what they are.

Before you go to bed that night after you've finished filming, why not enter the new credit in the appropriate place on your own copies of your résumé? You might want that credit to be on the copy of your résumé that you'll be handing out at somebody's office the very next day.

So....the job's finished! Some actors forget it and quickly get their minds onto finding the next one. That's important too, of course, but there's still more one can do to exploit what's just been added to your list of credits!

AFTER THE JOB....USING IT FOR PROMOTION

There are so many things that actors don't realize they can do, or just forget to do, after film jobs, in order to promote more jobs and their careers.   Some do think to send thank-you notes, but with many that's about it. And there's so much more possible!

Remember the man or woman who came around with the still camera and asked you to pose setside with Marlon Brando that day on the set? The *Still Department* of the studio will have it's *Still Book* ready and available for checking through within a period after filming of the entire picture is finished. Call, make an appointment and go there to look through the Still Book, to choose some shots of which you'll want prints. There'll probably be a minimal charge for any such copies, but it's great stuff for your carry book, or for your publicist if you have one. That shot of you and Brando, by the way, doesn't indicate how small and unimportant your role may have been in the picture. There you are, beside him!

Also, you might *try* (I use the word "try" advisedly) to get some *Out Takes and Trims* of your performance's footage. It's less and less possible nowadays, and usually depends on whether it's a major lot or major production company with edicts out that *no footage of any kind* is to be allowed off the lot, or another, smaller company that may not have issued such an edict. Some are disposed to be kind about this item...so it won't hurt to try. Here's the best---almost the only---manner of trying for this:

Soon after filming is completed for a television show, or about a month after a motion picture is completely finished filming, call the Producer's office, or the Editorial Department of the studio, and ask for the name of the Editor who's cutting the picture. Call the Editor. Identify yourself by *the character you played* . That's how the Editor will immediately recognize you if you're not yet a well known player, since Editors usually don't have the cast lists. Ask whether he or she expects there'll be some Out Takes or Trims of your performance. There should be some of both, actually.

An _Out Take_ is one of those extra takes of a scene which was printed up but which for some reason isn't being used at all in the final editing of the picture. If they can't or won't release an Out Take to you, the performer, there's a whole spool of film that will simply go into the trash can.

Trims are what are left of your performance---with perhaps much closeup footage included---from any shots involving two or more characters and involving you as one of those characters---when in editing the other character's face and dialogue has been cut into the final picture in alternate splicings with your own footage. Your closeup was filmed continuously, remember---in one continuous shot, therefore there will be many portions of that closeup shot which will become "trims" later. Such trim pieces and many out takes will be thrown away later unless you can get them.

Some of these can even make fantastic _professional headshots_ for you, by the way, since you've been photographed in expert film makeup for the camera, in some kind of costume or wardrobe, in front of an authentic-appearing background...all under ideal lighting and other conditions!

If the Editor feels it's alright to let you have some of the out takes and trims he'll say so, or ask you to call back at some later time to find out. If he knows there'll be some, and that you can just as well have them, ask when would be the best time to call back to come and pick up any he can let you have. As previously mentioned, many Editors can't let you have any at all...but some can, so ask. Maybe as early as when the editor is finished cutting the picture even into a "work print", probably by the time it's into "rough cut" and even more probably by the time there's an "intermediate" or "final cut", he or she will know whether there'll be anything you can have.

And by the time the Editor has cut all those separate, continually revised and refined versions of the picture he's probably an old friend of yours...that is, if you didn't do some things in the filming process that have given him problems in editing! Although he hasn't met you, he knows what you look like and knows whether you're a good enough actor or actress to warrant some special treatment if it's possible for him to provide it. He'd probably enjoy meeting you face to face. Some film editors are fans, and they seldom have opportunities to meet the actors they labor over so many long hours at their Movieolas. You might get a very warm reception, especially if you invite him or her to lunch to say thank you as you pick up the material.

Next---if you can get some out takes or trims or both, at home cull through the entire footage under a bright light and choose the section or sections you like. Use gloves, just as the editors always do in handling the film strips, so you won't leave fingerprints. Cut out about five or six frames of the sections that you especially want to use and put them in an envelope---again, to protect them from smudges or scratches. Take them to one of the Photo Reproduction shops. Ask the duplication people to check the five or six frames for the best one and have them make up a _"dupe-neg"_ (duplicate negative) and print an 8x10 enlargement of any you want. And have maybe 100 copies run off.

Naturally, _write in your new credit_ on your résumé. Do it in pen, to more vividly point out the fact that you've worked too recently for printing of a new résumé. Show the title, the billing you got (if it was any good) and the role you played. Some agents like you to list the Director's name too, as it indicates quality in so many cases.

Then ask your agent if he'd like you to come around and make the entries on the résumés which are being held at the agency for its use. The agency might delay putting the new credit in, and it's important to get the word out quickly that you've worked. Making sure it's entered on all your résumés right away can help, and whoever's responsible for making such entries on all the clients' résumés at the agency may be backlogged or may forget to enter yours right away.

Send those _Thank You Notes_ that many actors do think to send even if they overlook or are ignorant of so many other things they could do. Send a note to the Casting Director---saying how much you enjoyed doing the role; to the Director, in care of the studio or production company if you can't get their mailing address elsewhere---saying something nice, of course; and maybe to the Producer also....although the best time for that particular note is later, after you've seen the picture and know that you've even been kept in.

Sometimes producers of motion pictures or television series episodes will send cards notifying actors of scheduled air dates or movie premieres or sneak previews of things the actor has played in for them. But often these notifications, if sent at all, are received by the actor too late to be used effectively in the actor's promotion.

So, for a television program, the best way to be informed ahead of time is to find out what network it's going to run on and then call the network from time to time until they can tell you the air date. The _Network Scheduling Department_ will usually be cooperative in response to such inquiries. If you forget to do this, at least keep checking the _TV Guide_ so you'll know maybe a week ahead of time.

In either case, do some promotion. If you have an important role and if you can afford the cost, _take out an ad_ (of whatever size you can pay for and whatever size seems warranted by your role and billing) in both _Daily Variety_ and _The Hollywood Reporter_, even paying the premium rate for the back outside cover if you can afford it and if the role warrants it.

Paying that much money, you'll certainly want to dominate the ad with your picture---if possible even in the character (from one of those out takes' or trims' individual frames), or simply one of your own most appropriate professional shots. A good rule of thumb is to consider the kind of character you played and then, if you have a photo that suggests the same casting type, use it.

A special note: If you've been successful in obtaining some out takes or trims from the Editor you must remember that he or she may not have had official permission to give them to you. You could, however, at that point, call the Producer or Associate Producer and ask, at that time officially, whether you can have some footage from which to choose a shot (in character) for use in the ad. If such permission is granted, then of course you can get all the out takes and trims you want from the Editor and everything's okay. But *don't* tell the Producer that the Editor has previously given them to you!

As to the ad, be sure your agent's name is at the bottom, also your personal manager's if you have one, and your publicist's if you have one. In italics above the agency name put *Representation*; in italics above the manager's name put *Management*; above the publicist's name put *Press Relations* or *Public Relations*. Be sure the ad includes the airtime and air date and the network as well as the show and the character you play, noting the billing, whether it's *Guest Starring*, *Starring* or *Costarring*....whatever. Perhaps somewhere in the ad refer to "the (some nice, choice adjective here) performance of (your name) as Shadrach", or something equally attention-inviting.

Discuss the ad with your agent ahead of time, of course. He or she will most likely give you permission to head the ad with something like "The (name) Agency invites your attention to...", etc. It's better to give the impression that somebody beside yourself, perhaps your agent, is inviting the industry's attention rather than you having to do it for yourself, and the agent is the logical one...or your manager if you have one. One or the other is fine. On the other hand, if the producer and director have raved to you about your performance you might even ask them if *they* will permit you to start the ad with one of *their* names, or the company's name, or the show's name, as the one inviting the industry's attention.

Be sure, of course, that *your name* stands out more prominently than anything else, dominating the ad. You're paying the money to promote *yourself*, not the other folks mentioned in smaller print at the bottom of the ad. This kind of ad is a major expense. Justify it with the fullest possible impact of your own name.

Either of the two publications mentioned will often provide the layout from your typed copy sheet and photo, or you may want to have the ad designed independently by someone else and take it to the publication "camera ready".

There's much more description of how to prepare and place such ads in the next Chapter, *Self Promotion, Self Publicizing, Self Advertising For The Actor.*

Also *send cards and notes* (short, to the point ones) to Casting Directors, Producers, Directors, etc. Give them all the details on the card or in a brief letter and ask them to watch your performance. If they do watch, fine. If they don't, at least you've used a dignified opportunity to remind them of you and show them that you've had a very good role.

179

When you know the air date and time _notify your agent immediately_. He or she can start promoting viewing by people. It gives them something to talk about when they're in offices, too. And an agent whose clients are playing roles worth this kind of promotion is a popular, respected agent.

Maybe get a friend to videotape the television show directly off the tube for you, or do it yourself if you have a good VCR. You may want to later edit parts of that role into your building audition tape. There are companies that offer to tape off the air, but they're fairly expensive, and it can be done on home VCR's almost as effectively and for much less...probably just the cost of the cassette.

If by the time the show is in "answer print" stage or about ready to be aired you've had any meaningful contact with any of the Production Office people...the Producer, the Director, the Associate Producer, the Editor or anyone else involved in post-production on the picture, you could ask permission to go to one of the _screenings of the final cut_ which are customarily held with Dubbing and other folks there (that Department's work having just been completed recently). In that viewing you'll be able to find out whether you're still even in the picture when it's finished and find out how effective your performance is in the version which is going to be aired.

Immediately _after_ the show airs...or just after you've been allowed to sit in at one of those final production company screenings, _then_ is the ideal time for the short letter to the Producer. Thank him or her for the way your performance was handled in editing the picture and of course comment on the outstanding quality of the picture itself.

Everybody enjoys being thanked, and maybe they will at that very moment have another role in an upcoming script sitting on their desk when your note is received for which they might otherwise overlook you.

Producers receive many complimentary letters and comments about their pictures, of course, but it's surprising, a few have said in Seminars, how seldom it is that any _cast members_ let them know that the way they've been edited in a picture is appreciated. It's a far more personal comment...especially since the Producer is the one who has shepherded and dictated the manner in which the film has been edited and how it turns out.

If it's a motion picture you want to promote, on the other hand, then there's not too much you can do to promote viewing of it until the time arrives for its release and openings in theatres. At that time, although many producers and others will have seen it in industry showings ahead of time, send out cards or short notes to some (or all) asking them to be sure to catch your performance in the picture and if they like it consider you for upcoming things.

There aren't many more ways in which you can promote a single film job into creating more film jobs. As for _general promotion_....it's the upcoming Chapter.

Chapter Eighteen

Self Promotion, Self Publicizing, Self Advertising For The Actor

There are usually looks of acute disbelief and disillusionment on the faces of new actors when they're told by someone that most career advancement for an actor is seldom based on a fine talent as much as on promotion----promotion of one kind or another, but still promotion with a capital P!

It's a regrettable fact that an actor's talent is sometimes slow to be discovered while many people who somehow manage to be skillfully promoted----even if they have comparatively less talent if much at all---burst forth with television series starring roles and feature motion pictures in no time at all.

The easiest way is of course to take on a publicist (press agent) as soon as possible. But it's also expensive and usually beyond the reach of the newcomer's pocketbook of saved-up pennies. The rent has to be paid and even hamburger diets become more expensive every year...so a press agent has to be put out of the mind for a while.

Still, promotion has to begin somewhere, and that somewhere is right at the starting gate, not later.

Even the decision to leave your small hometown for Hollywood was an act of self-promotion, wasn't it? Taking that small, cheap apartment right in the heart of trashy Hollywood, rather than somewhere else in Greater Los Angeles...wasn't that promotion too? After all, who back home would respect you if you settled on Toluca Lake, of which they've never heard---even though it's where Bob Hope and many other luminaries live and is right nextdoor to Burbank Studios, Columbia, Universal, NBC Television, etc.? And that flashy red BMW convertible that barely runs....why not a plain black Chevy in far better shape? Face it. Those were early self-promotion decisions. You're aiming for stardom, or at least an important film acting career, and you wanted everybody to know it!

Right from the start, once in Hollywood you need to call attention to yourself in the vast sea of faces. So this Chapter and the following one are aimed at showing you some things an actor can do _on his own_ at first; the things you can get others to do better for you later; and some ways to keep control of your goals when the bigger promotion is being handled or being potentially mishandled by others when you reach the point where you can afford to hire them and really need them.

First off, let it be stated in no uncertain terms that your first self-promotion steps will help or hurt your next ones. In their eagerness to start letting people know they're in town many newcomers plunge in blindly, getting their photos and résumés out to everybody in town and hoping for a miracle reaction from just _anybody!_, for _anything!_. not caring who or what happens as long as somebody and something does. It's the first big mistake.

Stop and do a little self-evaluation. Get advice from a qualified acting coach. Consult with people who you know will know what they're talking about in the industry. You need to decide...before you start promoting, _what_ you want to promote yourself _toward_, and what logical first steps you can take toward that goal.

The decisions you need to make very objectively at this early moment---and with some help and advice---include (1) whether your talents are ready, without any further study, to be exposed and judged by industry people who'll afford you just one chance upon which your future with them will be based; (2) what if any special quality you have, in addition to talent, that can help people remember you; (3) whether (when ready to start) you should start in "handout bit" roles and hope to work your way up gradually, or (4) whether you seem to be one of those special people who---because of your particular qualities and uniquenesses as they apply to film and television---should be able to start in good co-starring cameo roles if you're willing and able to hold off a little until you're better prepared.

Don't decide these things by yourself, certainly. Get some advice from friends in the industry who know something. Don't just ask that "moonlighting" casting director who's using his or her name to draw swarms of opportunistic "pay to audition" actors to their Cold Reading Showcases or Cold Reading Classes. Many of those doing this are last year's secretaries and casting receptionists with no acting background themselves who may not even know why the directors to whom they bring actors by appointment hire the particular people they do hire. If you can, ask directors---who do happen to be in good positions to judge your qualities and your talents, or more experienced casting people---who after many years of casting can more ideally judge who is "*special*" for some reason and should hold out for good, effective roles, and also can judge who *isn't* special and should grab anything they can get and then work their way up from those bottom starts. Ask agents or any established actors you may get to know during this starting-out period.

It should be said that most actors may well have to go that "bit role beginning" route, but there is this other group of actors who shouldn't even try for smaller bit roles because their personalities, their charisma, their total intensity and depth or even their special looks suggest that they won't ever get those bit roles anyway. They have "leading player" and "boxoffice star potential" written all over them in some way from the start. They're not many in number, of course...but they're out there, and you might be one of this very special group.

You may not look like "a cop", "a bookkeeper", "a doctor", "a housewife" or "a nurse". If you don't, you should know ahead of time that nobody's going to hire you---with your special look and quality---for those tiny roles. Even in a brief appearance on film you'd distract from the stars of the piece. It's a tough row to hoe, but if you're told by enough people who know that you're one of these "special" people, contain your frustrations till somebody is there to light that first bonfire in your career and you'll be able to start on a much higher level than most...probably at least co-starring in your very first film or television role. No, it's not impossible. It happens, and it happens often.

Maybe it doesn't sound like promotion, but the first big step is to get with the best acting coach you can afford who'll recognize and can help bring out those individual and unique qualities you have while developing your talents----a coach who works in a sufficiently personalized manner with the people he or she teaches to even notice those special things about you and help you keep them along with your development; a coach who opts to prepare you for strictly top roles rather than for more general, functionary ones.

If you're in this special group, don't even consider starting to "buckshot" your photos and résumés around. Recognize that you're an exception. Don't start doing your own promotion at all yet. To obtain those important first outings for you, _somebody else_ is going to have to do it for you when you're ready to try for and get a decent starting-off level of roles. It could be, and might very well be, your acting coach. It often is. Or a friend of the coach to whom you're introduced by him in a manner that allows you to display your very unique talents and special qualifications for top roles.

Sometimes it's simply somebody...anybody...who knows what you have that's very special and who knows somebody who can help bring you to people's attention in the right places.

Now, on the other hand, if you're fairly sure that while you have a fine talent and maybe even some degree of attractiveness you don't stand out as being that "different", then one of the best ways to start is to try out for and hopefully land a number of roles in the small theatres that are located in the more or less central areas---not too far from studio and production company offices, to increase the chance of casting people and agents coming to see the productions.

Another way is to pick up _Drama-Logue_ religiously each Thursday morning and quickly get your photos and résumés out to seek interviews for any roles that fall within your age and category...whether they're film, television or theatre roles. Often if you manage to be interviewed for a role, even if you don't get *that* role you'll be remembered and at some later time you might be surprised that you're called back (without even applying) to try for a role that's exactly right for you in the producer's mind...and you'll probably get that role, which may even be better than the one you originally tried for. Low budget, financially limited production companies do this all the time. They remember that you were a good actor and often remember your personality and your look if you've impressed them at all...and they're quick to think of you for a good role later simply because they know you're still "starting out" and can be gotten cheap so they can spend more money on those people they want for their boxoffice draw starring roles. Many, many actors who are starring today started exactly that way, in those low budget films as their first jobs and in small roles which gradually led upward to where they are today.

The point is, for you who must work your way up from the very bottom through bit roles that lead to more bit roles and eventually obtain promotions for you in subsequent outings into better roles and the beginnings of billings, practically _any_ opportunity must be sought and grabbed when it's presented. Credits are credits for you. Even an embarrassing little film that may never obtain release or distribution...any non-union industrial film...any small theatre role, no matter the theatre as long as it's in the central area...any acting at all shown on your résumé---especially if it's here on the West Coast...is better than none, certainly, and indicates that you're here, you're serious, you're trying hard, and you have enough talent that some people have hired you.

There are very few in Hollywood who haven't had to go through those early struggling years, and they respect those who are currently going through them and working to advance and grow.

Keep in mind this comforting thought: All those producers, casting directors and agents whose doors you're knocking on feel exactly as you do, regardless of the level you think they're on because of their titles.

In the film and television industries there are few stars, even, who think they're as high up as they should be, and for production people like those others named above it's even worse. They play those important roles in their offices---appearing so secure and impressive---during the daytime. But they too go home at night and look at themselves in the mirror just as you do, feeling they're still pretty much on the bottom rung of the ladder with a lot of climbing ahead of them. The producer with some boxoffice failures recently probably has an ulcer and is on the edge of a heart attack. He often doesn't even have this month's office rent or any bank credit left. The director has to be hired in order to work, and most of the time is "between pictures" while he watches so many others for whom he has little respect being signed to direct the pictures he'd like to direct. And the casting person is never successful in his or her own eyes. Casting, as a profession nowadays, means constantly pitching for employments, most of the time losing out because of asking too much money or else taking an embarrassing picture to cast simply because, out of desperation, the salary asked was among the lowest bids and succeeded in eliciting the offer.

Try to remember these things about those "important people" who could frighten you otherwise with the importance you (but not they) attach to their positions. You'll walk taller.

SUPPORT YOUR LOCAL POSTMASTER!

You'll find yourself doing this whether you want to or not. When it's tax countup time at the end of the year the actors who are newcomers to Hollywood---unless they're brought by a studio or scouted on Broadway and brought to town for a top level start by a top agent---find that one of their biggest career expense items for the year has been _postage_. Mailings to agents to get representation, mailings to casting people, mailings to production companies, etc. Too bad these are so necessary, but they are.

As mentioned earlier, for the _agents_ you need to mail your photo and résumé with a very short cover note simply asking in one paragraph for an interview regarding representation. Use the current issue of _The Agencies---What The Actor Needs To Know_ to decide which agencies you should submit to because they sound right and probably most receptive to you. Use this publication also to put together your address list for the mailouts. It's the only source we know of that's continually updated, and agencies do move around quite a bit.

For mailings to _casting directors_, mail your photo and résumé with, again, a very short cover note if you like but no cover note is necessary. If you do send a note simply ask for a general interview at the casting person's convenience. And don't expect any response or any immediate result.

However, miracles do happen once in a blue moon and your look or something else about your photo or your résumé might arouse some interest and produce a call.

For the always most dependably up to date mailing addresses and phones of casting people get the then current issue of _The CD Directory_, published by Breakdown Services, Ltd. The Breakdown Services also offer self-adhesive mailing labels that are at least fairly current. You shouldn't trust any other publication listing casting people's locations to be as dependably up to date.

Mail your photos and résumés to the independent film production companies and television production companies. As this is written one of the best sources for these addresses is the *Hollywood Creative Directory*, usually available at actors' bookstores but if sold out there can be ordered from the publication office at 451 Kelton Avenue, Los Angeles, CA 90024 (213-208-1961). This publication is updated every three months---which is more often than most---and includes the names of the heads of the organizations with what they handle specifically. The other most reliable source for these addresses is the *Studio Blu-Book* published by and available at the offices of *The Hollywood Reporter*. However, this large, all-encompassing publication is published only once a year and some of the addresses will certainly be out of date.

Any mailings to these independent production companies should be sent to the attention of "Casting Director" on the outside of the envlopes.

While some of these are only "sometimes" producers, most at least file and keep the pictures and résumés they receive in the mails...primarily because, again, you're still at the stage where you're probably available for minimum slary. A number of them even prefer *un*-agented actors because they don't like to have to negotiate for higher salaries and worry about billing requests as they would if dealing through agents.

If you feel like "making the rounds" to some of those smaller production company offices and can gain access to them---those not inside studio lots being much more accessible, of course, by all means take your photo and résumé around to them personally. And if you can somehow get into a studio lot it's even better for "rounds-making" to drop off pictures and résumés---at least for leaving them with secretaries, since in all those many-officed production office buildings there are scads of producers' offices right nextdoor to each other in every hallway, usually with their companies' names on the doors for your records of where you left your materials.

It would be unusual for you to actually meet any of the producers themselves, since on-the-lot producers are usually in high-level meetings with studio executives, and most of the independent (usually off the lot) producers are only parttime in their rented offices because they earn most of their livings working for others in jobs other than producing. But some of them don't even have secretaries or receptionists in their own offices and might happen to be there when you drop by and might even meet you at the door and accept and look over your material while you're there.

For any such "drop-in" visits, morning times are usually best, when they're probably at their offices to read *Daily Variety* and *The Hollywood Reporter* and check over their bills. Afternoons are more often scheduled conference times for these folks.

For self-circulating of photos and résumés to *studio and larger production companies* about the only time of the year that's fairly unproductive is April to June. That's "hiatus" time for television series, for instance...the time when there's little if any television except special programs; when agents tend to be out of town on brief vacations (it's their best time of year for grabbing a few days for travel); and when production slows in all of television.

However, the _low budget filmmakers_ are usually _more_ active during that same period...the smaller companies capitalizing on series leading players' free periods in which they can do films of their choices for outside companies. Casting people are generally more unemployed during this period too, so it's less productive to try to get any results with them until about late June or into July, when television is booming again and when good weather is more predictable again, insuring more feature motion picture scheduling then to avoid winter weather surprises that delay shooting.

By the way, the earlier caution to always keep cover notes short applies to any and all mailed requests for _anything_ in Hollywood. If one sentence can say what you want to say, make it that short. It will be appreciated. Longwinded life histories or discussions of your theories about acting or the industry go immediately into the "round file" sitting beside every desk in Hollywood for just such well meant but misguided nonsense.

In one of the author's out of town Career Guidance Seminars---I believe it was in San Diego, with talent agent Steven R. Stevens on my panel of industry guests, when the subject of "always short notes" came up Steve pulled out a six-page, single-spaced letter which he had received from a young actress asking for an interview regarding representation. He proceeded to read marked parts of the letter as an example of what _not_ to do when writing people in Hollywood. She had devoted much space to her opinions about what was wrong with most actors, which acting methodolories she felt to be excellent, the responsibilities of actors to roles they play, etc. Don't use even _two_ paragraphs when _one_ will do.

On the subject of notes to agents but equally applicable to any notes to those low budget producers, as frightening as the prospect may seem to someone who's new and just starting out, it's perfectly alright to call those offices where you've left off your materials about a week later to ask whether your picture and résumé were received. You might get a very abrupt response from a secretary, perhaps from most...but don't let that deter you. Get used to _at least asking_. There's probably no other profession which is so full of constant rejection, but actors have to get used to this and live with it. The feelings of diminished self worth that accrue from these many rejections could be devastating if you let them be. Simply keep trying. There are some offices where if you _don't_ follow up with a phone call to check nobody will ever look for your material and check it. It will remain in the big pile of others' material, doing you no good whatsoever.

Several casting directors on my seminar panels have said that _follow-up calls_ are almost musts for them. That way they hear your voice and can tell more from that personal contact than they can from your photo and resume, no matter how encouraging your materials may appear.

It's too bad, but for the actor starting out the foregoing represents a lot of postage, a lot of telephoning, a lot of photography and printing outlay, and a lot of time. If it's too much for you to handle...probably out of a part-time job's salary or paychecks from some nine-to-five drudgery at a job you hate, then give up and get into some other career for a while.

Many would-be actors have to work and progress in other fields for many years, preparing toward that "someday" when they have the "venture capital" that starting out in acting usually requires. Any field that involves private enterprise...as acting certainly does in the early period...also involves the outlay of "venture capital". Many actors discover that they have to delay the starting-up money outlay until they've made enough money at some other trade. While building their bank account preparations they pursue acting more or less as a hobby, keeping their hands in by doing small theatre in some suburb, or doing small roles for little or no money in Hollywood. Many of these folks get their acting careers going considerably later than was originally planned, but when they finally turn off everything else to devote all their time to an acting career they are prepared financially and are able to stick it out long enough for things to happen.

You simply must do what you can, of the many kinds of self-promotion that are available, as quickly as you can do them.

GET OUT INTO THE MAINSTREAM!

Perhaps the first thing to think about is _showcasing your talents_. Showcasing comes in many shapes, sizes and ranges of potential effectiveness, as mentioned earlier.

There are acting workshops that are money-grabbing schemes, offering weekly meetings with casting people and opportunities to read for those folks whether you're ready or not. It's chancey for newcomers to pay their money and take the chance that they'll be found sorely wanting at a too early point in their development. If this happens, the actor or even his or her agent later will have little hope of obtaining a role interview with that casting director because the actor was seen and "auditioned for pay" at a too early, unprepared moment.

Commercial Acting Workshops, on the other hand, are excellent showcasing opportunities. At most of these the teachers are qualified professionals. Commercial acting is a finite art of and by itself, and the people who head these workshops (at least most of them) are in some way actively engaged in the field of commercials every day.

In most of these there are commercial producers, directors, casting directors and agents either speaking or at least there to observe you and your work...usually themselves scouting for talent and often looking for special casting needs that are on their desks at that very moment. Many, many jobs result quickly from attending these good training workshops. The best known and reportedly the most respected among them are listed in the Acting World Books quarterly _The Hollywood Acting Coaches And Teachers Directory_ with special praising comments about their excellence.

THEATRE....AS STRICTLY SELF PROMOTION

Many actors seek theatre roles exclusively for showcasing, and this is more true in Hollywood than anywhere else. A decent role in even a small theatre in the Hollywood vicinity can obtain an agent or a casting interview, and that's what much of the small theatre work in the Greater Los Angeles Area is aimed at.

What makes theatre in these small Los Angeles theatres even more attractive is that here even a newcomer who's still non-union can be cast to play a decent role in a theatre production that acually boasts a recognized star or name player in the lead. This was made possible by Actors' Equity as of 1972 and still obtains today. And, in spite of their claims to the contrary, even the stars appearing in these small Hollywood Area theatre productions are "showcasing" something about themselves. Some have slipped and are trying to regain their former positions or fresh starts. Some want to be seen in new lights by the industry. Some are showcasing a writer friend's work because they believe in it and want to help it get off the ground through their good name's participation in its premiere showing.

Whatever the reasons for the top players' participation in these productions, the result for the newer actor can be the opportunity to appear with a name player or two for the first time---hopefully in a decent role, and enjoy the good industry attendance that results when there's such a name player in the lead and the reviews turn out to be excellent or even fairly good. The industry will come. It's curious. And it might just discover _you_ in the bargain when it attends the performance.

For locating the most theatres' addresses and information, use the _Christmas Week Issue of Drama-Logue_ and its big list of all levels of theatres. Most of its listings remain up to date throughout the year. It's the best and most reliable place to find such listings of theatre information.

Mail out photos and résumés and request consideration for upcoming castings. Since we're still talking self promotion, choose the theatres located in the central areas where casting, agency and other production people might conveniently come to see your work. Give first consideration to the Hollywood, Burbank, Studio City, West Hollywood, Beverly Hills, North Hollywood areas. Some industry people wouldn't even consider coming if you're in something in Pasadena, Santa Monica or Venice.

If you're using theatre to promote yourself for film and television, then your first consideration---rather than that "The show must go on"---is _you_. You've probably approached the getting of a theatre showcasing role rather coldbloodedly from the start anyhow, so don't waiver. If the play isn't going to be excellent, find an excuse and leave the cast. If it's obviously going to be fine, send out those cards with your photo at one end and details of the production on the other. Offer complimentary tickets which you'd be happy to leave at the boxoffice in people's names if they'll call you and let you know when they can come. Offer two tickets, rather than just one. Most who do accept to come will want to bring someone...and it might in many cases be bonus industry guests whom you haven't invited personally, affording you a second industry exposure instead of just one.

Back to the question of "follow-up" calls after you've sent out your card announcements: The majority of the industry people who've offered their advice about this on the author's Seminar panels say that the people who do call their offices perhaps a week after mailing their material---to ask whether they arrived---more often get what they want...an acceptance to attend. The actors who don't call can have their invitations get lost in the huge piles of incoming photos, résumés and similar invitations that eventually have to be thrown away.

Some industry folks do consider these follow-up calls pestering and turn-offs, feeling that the actor should realize that in the absence of any call from the office there's probably also an absence of interest or ability to attend. But the former advice at least offers some hope, so it's being passed on here.

Call the office. You might get lucky. And at least if there's no interest and you're told that...you haven't really lost anything. If you don't call you'll be just one of the fifty or so inviting them to come to something the same night or weekend and their decision and selection will be made without your chance to influence their choice.

If the production doesn't give complimentary tickets to cast members, as many do, it's still worth the cost to you, probably, if some of those you invite do come to claim the tickets you've left at the boxoffice for them. Simply try to make sure in some manner that you don't have to pay for any tickets that aren't picked up by a certain ticket-pickup deadline prior to the performance. If you don't make some arrangement on this you could be out a fortune on tickets held at your request and never picked up.

Even some of the largest Off and Off Broadway productions in New York afford their people limited numbers of complimentary tickets; don't charge the actors for tickets not picked up by given deadline times; at those times promptly return those tickets to available seating racks. If your guests arrive too late, after their tickets have been put back in the rack and sold, they should have to pay for their own tickets anyhow, and probably will if you've taken the precaution to notify them ahead of time about a "pickup deadline" which "the theatre requires."

ORGANIZATIONAL WORK AND JOINING

No, we're not wandering from our subject. We're still on self promotion. There's one kind of self promotion open to all actors, regardless of the current level of their careers. It's *Organization Work and Joining!*

Some excellent contacts and ongoing friendships that can speed career progress can come, believe it or not, from volunteering to work with and for industry organizations, industry clubs, industy charity fundraising groups, etc.---including, of course Screen Actors Guild, AFTRA and Actors Equity committees and activities.

In fact most organizations in Los Angeles, Hollywood and Beverly

Hills, as well as in the other cities surrounding have many film stars and name players, production company heads, studio executives, directors and agency heads in their committees. Most of those organizations are heavy with clout and names but usually short on "gofers" who are willing to "go fer" whatever's needed. You can usually find one or two or many of them ready and happy to have your help in some "gofer" capacity.

The point, from the standpoint of your self promotion, is that in an organization that has a number of industry people in its committees or special activity groups you may be able to rub elbows and become acquainted with people who are in a position to help you if they happen to take a personal interest in you.

One of the first avenues of this kind that should be considered, if you're a member of SAG, AFTRA or Equity, is to offer yourself as a volunteer to help the union in any capacity where you can be of value. If you have some special ability or professional knowledge in a peripheral field that committees and projects often need---typing, wordprocessing, printing, envelope addressing, etc.---all the better.

You can rapidly gain a far broader overview of the industry and industry practices, and probably have occasion to meet producers, directors, agents and others for the first time in a peer relationship, either on union business or socially, through this contributing of your valued help. If you have the time, the energy and an amount of intelligence to devote to such helping activities on a volunteer basis it can be one of the best investments in your career that can be imagined.

Even as a "gofer", you'd probably be in some of the photographs taken at special events, standing beside someone important, and as a result looking more important yourself than you yet are. You might be called to attend emergency meetings at stars' homes if they're chairpersons of committees having trouble getting things together.

You might even be paid to go on jaunts for fund-raising. You might appear before City Councilpersons and have your picture taken in a group standing beside the Mayor in one of the shots made in that City of Los Angeles mural room behind the Council Chambers. You'd be meeting people by the dozens that you wouldn't otherwise stand a chance of meeting for many years.

And even in running errands as a "gofer" you'd find out where many top people live, what their phone numbers at their homes are, where they like to eat, what projects they're working on at the time which might offer a role for you, etc. Your participation in their activities can be just as calculated as the next gofer's probably is, but you'll also be earning your keep...and earning many people's attention and gratitude at the same time.

Since it may be hard for some to envision how productive this volunteering can be as a manner of early (and even much later) self-promoting, I'm going to give you some examples out of my own biography to illustrate how the many things you involve with in this manner can mushroom into huge and unexpected results later.

I should say out front, though, that in my own personal case I rather got drawn into most of these things one after another more than calculatedly getting into them with thoughts of what they could do for me. In hindsight I have certainly recognized the great richnesses they've later produced in my life and my career, so I feel the benefits that can accrue from this kind of "pitching in and helping things"...volunteering yourself...should be stressed for readers of this book as a means of self-promotion that can be of cumulaive benefit over many years.

In New York in 1946, my first professional "volunteering" was for the Equity Library Theatre's Executive Board. Equity Library Theatre was and still is today a special "showcasing production" organization subsidized by Actors Equity Association. The Executive Board Members receive no pay. Their administering of the organization is strictly volunteer work for them. I think it was simply my knowledge of Robert's Rules of Order, known about by a friend who was a current Board Member, that got me nominated and elected, or perhaps it was the words "Good Gofer Material" which were probably written all over this energetic newcomer's eager face. In any event, my friend said the organization needed volunteer help and I offered any kind of help I could give.

Soon there was the post of Assistant Executive Director to be appointed for the exciting new Equity Community Theatre project which would be taking specially produced ELT productions to outlying theatres after their closings in Manhattan. Who better than the new "gofer" in the ranks to do all the hard work that the Executive Director, busy character Leon Askin, didn't have time to do?

Working my tail off on promotion for that project put me into unexpectedly close and continuous contact with the New York Times' dean of New York critics, the late Brooks Atkinson, and the New York Post's theatre editor Vernon Rice. Both of these gentlemen becoming friends, together they soon observed my hard work and results and delegated me, as their representative, to go out and meet with many of the separatist, unconnected Off Broadway producers---then still opertaing in isolated aloneness without any central organization, to urge and foster the forming of an Off Broadway League with those two critics' support in their columns.

The Off Broadway League became a reality shortly thereafter and still exists today as the League of Off Broadway Theatres.

Working my tail off on that worthwhile project, I learned so much that was to benefit me tremendously many years later toward helping form both the Equity Library Theatre West and the ANTA Repertory Theatre West in Hollywood in 1958 and be appointed Co-Chairman for those organizations' inaugural seasons. But what I learned was to be even more important when in 1972 it provided the base knowledge and perspective for me to personally bring together fifty Hollywood and Los Angeles theatres to form the League of Los Angeles Theatres and president that organization---most say very effectively---for its first three terms.

It didn't hurt that among the first theatres to join the League were two that were headed by producers who had been part of the original cadre of the Off Broadway League in New York, whom I'd come to know personally by then.

There were other benefits from that very first (Equity Library Theatre) volunteering, too. Peggy Wood, its president at the time, became a friend, invited me to join her and others in the Episcopal Actors Guild--- where I met and worked closely with more leading players that I wouldn't have met so soon otherwise. And almost eight years later, I'm sure it was Peggy who had me brought in as Papa's Office Manager, Mr. Jenkins, for the last season of her "Mama" television series.

And there's still more. From working closely with top critics Vernon Rice and Brooks Atkinson on the two projects mentioned came the surprises that Mr. Rice, in 1947, after confiding that he wouldn't have found time to come see *"A Doll's House"* off Broadway if I hadn't been in it, honored me with his Off Broadway Award for my performance as Torvald in it and, two years after that, while we were still involved with forming up the Off Broadway League, when he made a special trip to Keene, New Hampshire to meet with me on details of the then rapidly progressing League and saw my summer theatre production of *"An Inspector Calls"*, voted me his Summer Theatre Direction Award that year.

And Mr. Atkinson too, by then a supportive friend, after a meeting about the League, stayed to sit in on my acting class and, later commenting briefly about my teaching in one of his columns, afforded me one of the critical comments of which I shall always be most proud.

And I firmly believe that I should attribute some of my early "Golden Age of Television" roles as an actor to contacts made and visibility promoted during the helping of those organizations I've mentioned thus far. At least many more people had become quickly acquainted with me than would have if I'd been simply "making the rounds" daily begging for roles. I'm sure it all helped.

By then I was "an experienced gofer" and one was needed at that time by the new United Cerebral Palsy Foundation headed by Leonard Goldenson---a Hollywood producer himself, and someone suggested "Gofer" Parke to do the promotion and phoning to form up the National Sports and Entertainment Committee for the UCPF.

In setting that up and arranging its kickoff at 21 Club, I became acquainted with world champion fighter Sugar Ray Robinson and noted playwright Ben Hecht. Some results? In 1950 Sugar Ray and his then wife Edna Mae helped finance and support my first summer theatre venture as a producer-director, at Pompton Lakes, near his training camp, and in 1960 (ten years later in Hollywood) Ben Hecht had me work with him on the adapting of his play *"Winkelberg"* into its musical version *"Bodenheim"*.

As another result stemming from that very earliest gofering for Equity Library Theatre, Equity Community Theatre, Off Broadway League and United Cerebral Palsy Foundation, national touring children's theatre producer Edwin Strawbridge asked my "gofer" help with reorganizing and ne-

193

gotiating his Equity contract with the then Executive Secretary of Equity, Willard Swire. That association soon saw me directing most of his touring productions, which in turn got me assignments directing several for his friend, Broadway and touring theatre producer Hillard Elkins.

Still more volunteer gofering followed, with somewhat similar results: My friend Peggy Wood, always a bigger star in London than in New York, volunteered me as official New York boat meeter and liaison for Colonel Alexander, at the time head of International Artists and Artistes, a leading London talent agency for stars. Meeting Sir Laurence Olivier's ship when he arrived to play the "Cleopatras" at the Ziegfeld Theatre in the 50's produced an acquaintance with Sir Laurence which was to later make possible his fervent endorsement of one of my plays, *"The Cage"* during its commercial run in Hollywood in 1964-65, which helped obtain several productions of it in world theatre capitals later.

In 1956 it was handling English television star Terry-Thomas's arrival and early managerial details in New York---again for Colonel Alexander's London agency, that put me in first contact with Ziv Television Programs, which eventually---I hardly remember how now---led to my role as "Luke" in Ziv's *"The Harbourmaster"* television series, filmed at Rockport, Mass., and during that filming it was my help---as a New York actor who knew the people being proposed by the New York casting office for guest shots---that led, when the series finished shooting, to my being brought to Hollywood by the studio in 1957 and being afforded a hands-on education in all departments of film and television production...at a very nice salary.

The much earlier experience with the forming of New York's Off Broadway League certainly prompted me to observe the need for, and to call the theatres together in 1972 to form, the League of Los Angeles Theatres, and as its first three terms' president to do all the hard "gofer" work that, as its president, brought appearances before City Council, Chamber of Commerce gatherings, etc. Meeting and becoming acquainted with two top City Councilmen during this period resulted in both of those gentlemen helping me obtain the financing for the European Festivals appearances and the subsequent European theatre capitals tours of my environmental theatrepiece *"Minus One"* which had been selected by the Festival as that year's American entry.

Now? Well, I've long since stopped "gofering" to devote myself to my own activities. But the foregoing are put down here as indications of advantages which can accidentally and unexpectedly accrue from volunteering your help, especially in your early years, wherever you observe an organization that needs it. Organizations of all kinds need all the help they can get. And you can use the exposure for self-pomotion if and when you want to. Just don't become so hooked into the "organizer", "helper" and, yes, "gofer" syndrome that it takes too much away from your time and the energies needed for promoting your own career in all the other manners available!

MANY WAYS IN WHICH YOU CAN PUBLICIZE YOURSELF

Self-*publicizing* is the "toughie" for actors to handle, since it's difficult for actors to realize that even in their early years there are some (admittedly not too many) ways in which they can make what they do newsworthy enough to appear in print where it can matter.

The print media is jealous of its limited column space, and radio and television media are geared to timeslot sales to advertisers, but both have room for anything which can interest the public. Both print and broadcast media would prefer to have everybody pay for every ounce of attention-courting, but they're also hungry for anything that seems important enough to rivet the attention of a reader or listener or viewer to their particular announcements for a few brief moments.

It's some distance down the road that an actor can afford $1500 or $2000 a month or more for a top publicist, and unfortunately that's what it takes to keep your face and name and what you're doing in the public eye and ear. But there are some things you can do long before that.

First, decide what you want to achieve through publicity. Do that at every step on the upward journey, of course. But first, for the actor, is probably just *more roles* through your name or face or both being in print or talked about on the air. And in this section of the book we're talking exclusively self-publicizing (the free kind), not self-advertising (the paid kind), probably with that goal in mind.

The dictionary confuses the two labels, with "publicizing" being defined as "making widely known; advertising", while "advertising" is defined as "turning attention to; making publicly known; informing". For the actor, simply bear in mind that until you have a press agent publicizing means getting *free* public attention through print and broadcast media and advertising means **paying** *for it.*

So...first, how can you publicize yourself toward getting more roles? If you're a sports celebrity, don't stop what you've been doing every season. You can get lots of free press as you turn to acting, just as you continue to get on the field or court each season. Joe Namath, Mark Harmon and many others have profited from their sports bases simply being brought into support for their acting careers. If you're a politician's offspring, help your parent's campaign and of course let the press know that you're now an actor. If you're neither of these but are doing *anything* in your private but seasonally public life...while going to acting classes at night and auditions during your days off...no matter how dull and uninteresting that daytime stuff may appear to you after involving with it for so long, maybe you can find what the press calls a *hook*...something to make it and you newsworthy or of enough interest to attract the media's attention to it and to the few words that say you're also an actor.

If you're making your living as a teacher, put out a press release that you're starting your own voluntary class for underprivileged or disabled children...and of course notify the press, also the network and local news departments...of some kind of event or inaugural ceremony with a celebrity speaking at it. If you're operating a small store of some kind while starting your career at those nighttime workshop classes, call a press and local television and radio news conference to talk about your idea for improving Hollywood's image. If possible, get somebody with a bit of a name to hold the conference with you, and hold it at the Los Angeles Press Club on Vermont. Columnists are often there for lunch anyhow, and it's a good glace to insure that some press will be there and perhaps write it up afterward. Plan your press conference <u>before</u> lunchtime, in the late forenoon...that way those there for it will maybe talk among themselves over their lunches and you might get more provocative coverage through their sharing their views with each other freshly after your conference.

Get ideas. Write "Letters To The Editor" of all the papers on anything you can feel strongly and express yourself lucidly and forcefully about. Find out what's happening in the industry; who's saying what, who's doing what to whom...and especially write "Letters To The Editor" of _Daily Variety_ and _The Hollywood Reporter_. Take sides on public, especially industry, issues of all kinds, and write your views. Initial contacts with some of those important people involved in what you're writing about happen often in that manner.

If you're really a "publicity hound", find out when and where premieres of films are scheduled. Rent limousines and tuxedos. Go with attractive escorts---at least semi-known escorts if you know some. If you have the money, find out where many celebrities eat and drink and spend much time there. Become close friends with some of them and go on their arms to important parties and charity events, etc. Many have done all these things---some with remarkably quick and impressive results. A lot of us <u>cringe</u> at these so obvious publicity-grabbing <u>stunts</u> and consider them in bad taste, but in Hollywood nobody seems to look down on people who do it because publicity is the name of the game in Hollywood, and we've seen these embarrassingly ambitious ploys work.

On a much more legitimate level...when you're appearing in a play anywhere---even in Indianapolis or Albuquerque, notify the press in Hollywood with a philosophical discussion of why doing the play there was important to you. If it's in Hollywood, spend hours on the phone and send pictures with captions (discussed further on) to the press. Invite everyone...with nicely prepared cards with your picture on them (as mentioned earlier). Of course we're crossing the thin line here between "advertising" and "publicizing"...but so does the dictionary.

Write letters to any critics who plaster your production unfavorably, arguing its worth in areas they may have missed noting. Call for a debate with one of them on a local station, in the company of the director or producer, if you have an important role...and if you have sufficient guts to even suggest something like this.

Write intriguing letters to the local radio and television interview show hosts that will make them curious enough and make them respect your outspokenness enough to feel you'd be interesting to have on their shows. Remember, you have to have something of interest in order to be "newsworthy" or be "public interest"-worthy. Again, no publicity will come anyhow if you're not.

If you decide to go the "gofer" route (discussed earlier), volunteer for those items especially which will put you on the scene where the photographers and remote television crews appear because of the projects' public interest worth. Make sure, anywhere like that, that the photographer or the newscaster assigned to cover the event gets your name. You probably won't have the guts to do this...but somebody else in the event organization will, you can bet, and their name will appear instead of yours.

If you have your own theatre, incorporate on a nonprofit, tax-deductible basis so you can get all those _free_ public service announcements on local and maybe even some network stations for your productions. Notify national theatre foundations and organizations of your experimental or special slant theatre work toward getting their attention at grants time (if you can learn to make up grant applications when they invite you to do so), and so they'll list you as noteworthy in those national theatre organization publications. Inquire for details on all national and international theatre festivals and conferences...and apply to go to as many as you can, or apply to have a representative come see your theatre's work, just in case.

An example of the previous item was my own experience with my first venture into "experimental" and "environmental" theatrepieces in 1970. After many fairly or completely "rave" reviews from the Los Angeles critics for my William Inge, Tennessee Williams and Thornton Wilder revivals, and some successes with a few of my own original plays of the same genre, I had enough respect among critics that the first production of the new kind that I'd ever done was extremely well covered by the press.

Apparently the critics were sent into shock by my departure from the traditional theatre forms, and the reviews (I think as a result of pure surprise) weren't all that enthusiastic. Critics' comments being omens of public audience response, we knew that our Actors Equity contract production ---the very expensive kind!---would be short lived. But some quotes, disseminated, helped spread the word and we were able to limp along with at least half houses for a time, barely meeting the Equity actors' contract salaries and other production costs. Knowing that carefully culled quotes from the semi-favorable reviews would help, my publicity folks and I got those out.   Determinedly publicizing what we could, both locally and nationally, we kept getting the words out and those words apparently traveled all the way to Paris somehow, because at our unhappy _closing performance_ there showed up, totally without any advance warning, the Executive Director of the French World Theatre Festival and Andre Berkoff, Theatre Editor of Paris's prestigious weekly _"l'Express"_ . After the performance my theatre, Theatre Today, was officially invited to be the American entry at the following Spring's French World Theatre Festival! So...if there's anything unique about your theatre, get the word out in all manners possible.

Even when just in a theatre cast, have it in you contract, or in a letter agreement---no matter the size of the theatre or whether it's union or nonunion---that you'll receive prominent billing in "typesize equal to (or larger

197

than, if the latter is appropriate because of your role) all other cast members' billing" Any time what you're doing is important, do everything you can to make that fact known.

Having your own theatre or production company does help tremendously. Of course the work produced matters also, but heading the organization puts you in a position to be mentioned in all press coverage and interviews about the productions. In that position your name appears on every piece of mailout information...a side effect connected with the theatre's advertising, but still in a sense "publicity" because it's the production being advertised, supposedly...not you. In that position you'll also become acquainted with the theatre reviewers...by phone and in person...to the point that they'll be more inclined to bring your name into items they write about the overall theatre scene in the city, state or perhaps entire region of the country, and perhaps consult with you for quotable comments on overall theatre scene topics to use in their articles.

Any time you're cast in a film or television role, send a card (not a letter) to _Daily Variety's_ "Film Casting" or "Television Casting", saying so. Also to _The Hollywood Reporter's_ same column. Just a few words...perhaps "John Doe cast in the 'Ballyhoo' episode of 'The Fallout Guy'". For a feature picture or a television Movie of The Week, list the name of the director, the producer and writer as well, with the start date of filming and the location planned. (The latter kind of release gets more attention, because you're also providing details for the Editor to use in other manners, and sometimes it's information the Editor hasn't previously obtained.)

Tell your agent to be sure to tell certain friendly and supportive casting people of your good fortune anytime you have some. Also, have him or her tell those folks when you're in the hospital, or having a baby, or getting a divorce, or are in New York interviewing for a play, or doing a commercial, or are in the Bahamas. If you know some casting people, directors or producers well enough, write them short personal notes to tell them your news yourself. They rather like to hear from good friends too, and if they're really supportive they enjoy knowing these kinds of details along the way. And such short notes might also possibly remind them of something coming up that you'd fit nicely.

A much dreaded kind of publicity, but one that ironically benefits actors' careers enormously if they're brave enough to publicize in their own behalf, is that airing of any kind of controversy encountered in connection with leaving a television, film or theatre project under way or in the process of preparation or presentation for the public.

If you leave a production of any kind after you're announced as being in the cast---of course for just cause in your own eyes, either write or call or send a press release to everybody, voicing your views and reasons for leaving. You can bet that the producers are voicing their own reasons for your being replaced in their cast.

The hullabaloo this sets off gets you lots of publicity for a time. You don't even have to be very important yet for it to be effective. You'll want to hide in a corner, probably, from what you've set off, but the phone will keep ringing...and some of those calls will be new offers. Try it once. See whether you can stand the heat; perhaps abandon the idea forever after if you can't stand the aftermaths, or keep publicizing these unfortunate experiences if you find you can take the guff. These publicizings of such controversies by the actors themselves---to counteract what the employers will have said---have revived careers, created stars overnight, increased salaries and billing value because they've put people in the public eye...and of course also caused some nervous breakdowns in the bargain. How brave do you think you can be in such circumstances? You must consider that.

Even before you're a star or anything else in the public eye, volunteer to appear in those celebrity athletic events, on those yearly telethons' telephones accepting phone-in pledges, on those yearly ushering jobs at the Academy Award, Tony, Emmy, Golden Globe and other ceremonies, as well as all the other kinds of big, newsworthy events you can think of.

Go to all the SAG and AFTRA meetings and raise your hand and speak fervently on any items that matter to you. If you're forceful enough the photographers covering the meetings will want shots of you for their reporters' articles. Watch how many do this at SAG and AFTRA meetings, making themselves fairly ridiculous in the eyes of some of us with their pettiness and obvious limelight-grabbing for a moment...but also later look for their photos waving their fists in news photos of those events. They'll be there. It's still publicity.

If you're invited to a special emergency meeting of some organization and if you smell possible newsworthiness of the emergency, personally notify the press and the other media of the event and the problem, in case the organizers haven't wanted any coverage. The press will be grateful. Then go, and be noticed by those media people whom you suggested should be there.

By now you have a picture of what "publicity" entails until you have a press agent. It's a vast ocean of faces out there. Everybody wants to be noticed. Some make it. Some set aside their own personal taste and judgment to do these things; others who don't do them sometimes wish they'd been able to do them comfortably. Some are too embarrassed by the obviousness and horrified at the callousness which publicity-seeking sometimes---actually often---entails. Others, who force themselves to obtain publicity early on through some of these borderline ploys---because they know the incalculable value in public awareness---can later sit back in an interview lounge chair on a network morning show and chide themselves good-naturedly in the interview for doing some of those "awful" things that got them going toward where they're sitting for that television interview.

When the time comes when you really need one, and when it's possible financially to take one on, take on a press agent. Even a top manager (who usually has a press agent at his or her heels around town on a 24-hour basis), as well as a top press agent you may later want to hire, will appreciate all the publicity that you've already gotten through your own devising in the early years, and their chances of quickly boosting your public visibility still higher will be increased by the fact that the columnists already know you.

For either a press agent or a top manager, building a totally new face that's fresh over the horizon is a more difficult one...and your first year's fee with them may be higher as a result of all the ground-laying which you perhaps could have done before but didn't.

In publicizing for print or broadcast media---even before you have a press agent who'd do the job much better, you must know how to make up your own press releases in a manner that offers hope of gaining some column space or broadcast mention. If you haven't studied Journalism One you need to have the basics of how any news story (which a press release must be) needs to be submitted.

PREPARING YOUR OWN PRESS RELEASES

When you send out a press release on anything you should hope that the Editor who decides to run your story will only need to blue-pencil _part_ of it and for the most part be able to run it almost as it is. For that to happen it has to be well enough worded to be run in essentially the form in which it's received.

The two Hollywood trade papers, _Daily Variety_ and _The Hollywood Reporter_, and other directly competing publications in any industry published for the same readerships of course don't generally publish information submitted in releases verbatim because they want their editorial matter to avoid duplication with their counterpart's items on the same events or other material. But the same rules as to how to submit in "release" form apply to these two publications as well.

First...straight out of Journalism One classes: Use the "_Who, What, When, Where, Why and How_" sequence as your first paragraph. Examine most news items in the columns of your daily newspapers. It's there, that form. It's how any news article or anything else should begin. It's that simple. (1) Who... (2) Did or is going to do what... (3) When... (4) Where... (5) Why...and (6) How. In some standard-form news and other items even the _Why_ and the _How_ are reserved for the second paragraph; sometimes they appear briefly at the end of the first paragraph. It depends on the material.

After the opening paragraph, round out any details in the subsequent paragraphs...but the lead-in first paragraph should be presented as a brief capsule of the total story. A short, concise capsule containing the whole story in one or two sentences is best. No elaboration on details yet. Many releases simply go into the wastebasket beside the Editor's desk otherwise.

Editors quickly scan many, many releases every morning or night at their desks. They want to know---by the time they finish that first paragraph---whether the stories are worth their reading any further and whether they're worthy of being edited for their columns in time to meet their upcoming deadlines. So don't start with any flowery details or philosophizing. Jack Webb, on the old _"Dragnet"_ television series, had the answer for those first paragraphs: "The facts, Ma'am. Just give me the facts."

If the story or event or whatever is worth something, send a photo with it, with a caption pasted on at the bottom containing just a few words to identify the person or building or whatever is in the photo. But first, to the rest of the details of a good, professional-appearing, standard-form press release:

At the top left, indicate after the word "From:" either your name or someone's name or the organization's name from whence the release is being received by the Editor. Next, under that, type "Contact:" or "For Further Information:" indicating whom they can call if more details are desired before the article can be printed. After the name of the person indicated as "Contact" a telephone number for reaching that person.

Next, consider whether a date should appear on the release. Many advise leaving it off, because of the possibility that if it's received or looked at off the pile some days later it will be considered "old news" that another publication has probably already used, and will be thrown away. If you want a date on it at all, it should go across at the right top of the release.

Then drop down about two inches and at the right margin print in capital letters and underline, "FOR IMMEDIATE RELEASE, PLEASE".

If a heading (title) for the release is desirable (obviously for the purpose of "hook"-ing attention), put such a brief heading (what the release is about, perhaps reducing the original paragraph's "Who" and "What" items to a three, four or five word title), centered, in capital letters, without any underlining.

Then drop down again at least two spaces, but preferably three---so the title will stand out, and begin your first paragraph. Indent five spaces at the start of each paragraph. The body copy of the release should always be double-spaced on your typewriter or wordprocessor, to leave room for editors' blue-penciling of parts they want to cut before running the story or for making other notes. They need the space between the typed lines for editorial markings.

Use perfect grammar and punctuation, so the Editor won't lose patience at having to correct so many things and wind up discarding the whole thing. Paragraph the double-spaced material expertly. If you need help with spelling or paragraphing, get it. It's that crucial.

At the bottom of each page, if there's to be more than one page, put "---1---" or "---2---", etc ., without quotes of course. And two spaces below the last sentence of the whole release, on whatever page the end of the copy appears, type, in the center of the page, the age-old newspaper story-ender "---30---", again without the quotes.

With these pointers anyone can write a standard press release that will at least make it apparent that he or she knows something about the public information media. The same kind of release applies for network and local television and radio media, by the way. Most publicists and news-mongers of various kinds submit standard "press" releases to the networks and local stations, rather than preparing submissions in any other form.

Everybody's used to this.

Back to the "_captions_" mentioned earlier which should be part of any photo submission to the press and television media. They're simply strips of paper pasted onto the bottom of the photos with a brief line or paragraph about the photo, as mentioned earlier, to identify any person or anything else in the photo itself.

Be sure to rubber-cement the strip of paper, after its caption is typed onto it, onto the _back_ of the bottom of the photo, not the front. The entire photo might be deemed desirable for plating or for televising on camera with the story. Don't cover any of it. Attaching the caption on the back will avoid that.

If a newspaper or magazine does print a picture of you at some point, the _plate_ (if the paper is letterpress rather than multilith) will go into the _Morgue_ at the publication. Sometimes if you ask for it you can obtain that plate and use it at some later time for your own purposes. If the publication, on the other hand, won't release the plate to you it's a sign that they feel you may be newsworthy and insist on keeping it.

In the event that an article about you, or one in which you're mentioned for some reason, does happen to get into print, get a copy for photocopying or offset printing in quantity to use in your own promotion. Photocopying is fine. Offset isn't necessary for most professional promotion use. One hundred copies should run you between $2.75 and $5.00, depending on the city in which you have the copies made.

Also, you shouldn't take for granted that all the people you'd like to have seen the article will have seen it. Mail out those copies to all the people you want to make sure see it, and mark it or color-accent it for easy and quick focusing on what you want them to note. If you do this, it's sort of nice and makes it more personal to pen in some short comment beside the marked portion of the article.

Before leaving this Self Publicizing material, mention should be made that you shouldn't just be interested in the Entertainment columns and Entertainment programs on television and radio. If you're getting married, it's also for the Society pages. If you're doing a telethon, it's Local or National News, or for the Happenings column. If you're appearing in those Handicapped Olympics it's also for the Sports pages. If you're modeling a friend's designs on a runway it's for Fashion and Women's pages. Those are all separate editors, by the way. Know where to send your releases to have the best chances of seeing them in print. Simply send them to the publication or network or wherever, marked to the attention of whatever editor is appropriate.

And don't overlook those other "listing" columns in the trade papers..."_Who's Where_" for any traveling you may do---perhaps to your film's location or to New York or to something, anything, with a word or two that makes your going look important; to the "_Rambling Reporter_" and "_Just For Variety_" for any "gossip of the Rialto" columns of Hank Grant and Army Archerd, respectively; to the "_Hitched_" editor for wedding announcement;

to the *"Television and Radio Briefs"* column for small items; to the *"Actor/Agent Pacts"* and *"Agents Alley"* columns for when you change agents or sign with one. Anyplace at all where your name can justifiably be mentioned is good. It's called cumulative visibility.

Lastly, as you become known by editors influential in your particular sphere of the entertainment world, don't overlook them at Christmas or, if you can find out somehow, on their birthdays and at other holiday times. It doesn't hurt, and should be made to look like a simple "thank you" for column mentions and a growing friendship, since it probably will be just that anyhow. They're actually lonely people behind their desks in those night-time hours and these small "grace notes" mean something...to them, and to your future through their constantly keeping their eye on you. They'll still be there years later, and they will be helping you or will be secretly enjoying hurting you, when you're more newsworthy.

You're simply doing what a hired and paid press agent would have to do later. Later those press agents on your staff will be sending those gifts to a lot more press people when they start representing you. If they have many clients they'll usually pick up the tab, or ask all their clients to share the costs. If you're their only client when those gifts are due to be sent, get out your checkbook.

Those columnists also appreciate getting calls from friends---or from anyone, in fact---alerting them to something which is newsworthy. If you happen onto some tidbit that you think such a columnist might appreciate, be sure to call them quickly. If they already know, fine...but they'll still appreciate your thoughtfulness in calling, and if they haven't already heard about whatever it is they'll appreciate it doubly. They scour the entertainment industry daily and nightly to come up with their column breaks on new stories. It's a tough job. Those who stay in their positions for years are great columnists, you can be sure. It's good to have them on your side as early as possible...and to keep them there.

So much for the *free* side of "making widely known" what you want to be known about you. The other side of the coin of "information disseminating" is called *Advertising*. It can cost big bucks!

HANDLING YOUR OWN ADVERTISING IS EASY

Everything about advertising is really quite simple, if you have the money to pay for it. Those printings of cards to notify casting directors and others cost money. Your photos and résumés cost money. Postage to mail them out costs money. Ads in trade papers cost money. Brochures and mailers about projects cost money. But advertising, if carefully planned, skillfully handled and placed with some awareness and consideration of the market or readership you're seeking, makes all the difference in the world...for actors just the same as for other "products".

Of course an actor is a one person business in the early years, and if you don't have a bit of experience working in an advertisding agency it can seem a formidable thing to start tackling. But tackle it you must...and it's really not all that complicated.

Anyone can design an effective ad. There needs to be, again, some "hook" to capture attention. "Hooks" come in all kinds of wordings, from conservative to ridiculous, embarrassing and insane. Sometimes the latter kinds capture more attention than the former. It's a question of your own taste and judgment of the kind of attention you want, and what you perceive to be the common denominator of taste and judgment of the people who matter out there where you're going to put your message.

You don't need to rent big billboards along Sunset Strip like an actress did once and have your likeness and physical attributes beaming down on the Strip traffic. We've never seen her name or face since, so it probably didn't help much at the time. You don't have to strew streets around studio lots with flyers like an actor did in the 60's. I don't think that helped much either. I don't know whether some of those ads covering the outside back covers of _Daily Variety_ and _The Hollywood Reporter_, with names and faces that nobody has heard of before, help any if they're just of the "Who's Jack Macho?" or "Meet Cuddles Available" types. If you're in Hollywood long enough, sooner or later you'll see one or two of this variety. Of course if they showed a semi-naked body or a hairy chest and huge biceps and a home phone number they may have brought responses, and of course they're a form of advertising...but let's return to sanity.

The first advertising an actor can do constructively is the mailing out of those photos and résumés. I've heard that a few of the "actors' promotional service" organizations do a conscientious job of circulating actors' materials to casting people for a charge. Casting people have said they do receive bundles from these folks and sometimes do take the time to look through them quickly, so at least it appears they may be a legitimate advertising help, depending on their charges and their manner of doing what they promise to do. Using their mass mailing service would certainly save lots of postage on your own.

But we'd strongly advise steering clear of any and all publications that print big magazines in full color, containing many hundreds of photographs of would-be actors, would-be models, etc., and claim they're "used by casting people and producers to find new talents."

One such publishing company, headquartered in expensive offices on Sunset Strip in Hollywood (offices paid for by all those gullible people all over the country who've paid to insert their photos in the company's publication), even sends a group of shills out to nearly every large and medium-large city in the country each year to hold one day "Hollywood Comes To (City)" Seminars that are really nothing but "sales pitches" to get people to send their pictures and their checks to the company. In Hollywood---where the organization tells all those outlying towns' hopefuls that their magazine is "used by everybody in casting and talent searches", the organization is recognized for what it is..._a big money-making scam_ that dupes many, many thousands of naive dreamers and indulgent parents from all parts of the country who are sure their little child was born to be a star and that his or her face merely published in such a magazine will start the telephone ringing. That's not how talent is *ever* found. Don't fall for it.

The one advertising that no actor should fail to do, even if nothing more...is the *Academy Players Directory*, which has its offices on the 6th floor of the Academy of Motion Picture Arts and Sciences building at 8949 Wilshire Boulevard in Beverly Hills (90211). The telephone is (310) 278-8990.

The Directory is published every four months as a cooperative service to players and production companies for casting research and talent locating. It's distributed free to casting departments, directors and executives of all the studios as well as to most others concerned with the employing of motion picture and television talent. You're *not advertising* if you're not in the *Academy Players Directory* as soon as possible. When a casting person suggests an actor to a director or producer, the question isn't "Is she in the Directory?"; rather, it's simply "What page is she on?" That's how much this Directory is used by the people who count!

To be in the Directory you must either be a member of the Screen Actors Guild---with or without an agent or manager, or have an agent or manager submit your picture and information as being represented by them. Those are the only two restrictions as to who can place their photo and information in the Directory. The cost is small for the value received. At this time it's $20 for a single photo in a single category in a single issue. There are categories for men titled "Younger Leading Men", "Leading Men", "Characters and Comedians", and for women titled "Ingenues", "Leading Women", "Characters and Comediennes". There are also categories for Children, Native Americans, etc.

Some casting people advise that even if age-wise you're a "Younger Leading Man" you should consider also inserting your photo in the "Leading Man" category. Two insertions cost $40, of course. If you're an "Ingenue" age-wise you should still consider going into the "Leading Women" category as well. If you're a "Character" (man or woman) you should also be inserted in the "Leading" pages, since the time is long past when "leading" men and women had to be attractive.

The reason for inserting your materials in two different categories is that when confronted with a role for casting, if a casting person wants to think of some additional faces to suggest after jotting down first thoughts that come to their minds, the age of the character or a "leading" or "character" look may be what suggests which section of the Directory they'll go through. They may not even look in any other section, and might miss you if you're in a "just over the border into a different category" section of the books.

By the way, "Leading" in the Directory doesn't mean that you have to be a star. You may never have played a leading role. In fact you may never have had a single role. It refers more to a general type...and as mentioned above the old-fashioned "leading man" and "leading woman" cliches don't exist anymore and most actors realize the benefits of being advertised in the "leading" pages. Even if you're fairly ugly, and of course would think to insert your material in the "Character" catgegory, put yourself in the "Leading" category also.

The mechanics of inserting your photo or photos in the Directory are: If your agent or manager customarily handles this for all their clients, simply provide them with an original print (not a photocopy) to submit along with your check or cash to cover your insertion(s). If you're to handle it yourself you can take the original print to the Directory office and pay the charge, filling out the form with your name printed and some kind of contact information...if you have an agent or manager, the agency or management company's name. The Directory will add the address and phone of the agency. They have records of all agencies and managers. If you have no agent, as long as you're a member of SAG you can simply put down your home or message service number for contact. If you have both agent and manager it's customary to put both into your ad's space along with your name and photo.

Each time you do something worthwhile in role terms, consider running ads in both trade papers. If it's a starring role you're proud of, consider placing a full-page ad on the back covers of both _Daily Variety_ and _The Hollywood Reporter_. Those two publications are read avidly by producers and directors who want to keep up to date on all the news---as 99% of them must, and they'll see your ad if it takes up a whole page. Casting people, too, read these two publications daily.

The reason for suggesting the _back outside cover_ of such publications is that it's more sure to be seen, whether first by someone because the publication lies upside down on their desk, or last as the publication reading is finished. And it's still there, saved for other items the publication contains, sitting on the desk or coffee table, usually at least for the rest of the day, and often upside down with your photo ad staring up.

Smaller ads on the inside pages of these same publications are certainly of some value, but how much can't be calculated. Some casting people say they don't notice the smaller ads at all, since they're usually taken by actors to announce performances in very small roles. Others say they do notice them because they're often calling attention to nice cameo performances at least and sometimes even outstanding costarring or even starring performances by actors who don't have the money to spend on full-page ads. So it's good to at least consider some kind of "announcement" ad----in both trade papers----when there's something worth calling attention to. None of the busy people glancing at the ad may bother to watch the show, but even for a split second they'll have seen your face and your name.

In any large or semi-large ad of whatever size it's good to use as the "hook" at the top of the ad a phrase like "The...Agency invites your attention to the (Starring, Guest Starring or whatever) performance of (your name) as (the character's name) in (show title)..." and follow with information as to when and where it's showing, whether in movie theatres or on television.

(Other details for such ads appear in the section describing what you can do after film jobs to promote your appearances in them.)

For placing your own ads in trade papers, better take a standard sheet of prepared copy along with the photo you want to use to one of the Advertising Desk people at the two publications. Ask for their help. They give it all the time to those who ask. They'll often prepare a layout of the ad more skillfully than you could, with type font and typesize suggestions, and available art they know they have at the paper...in many cases not even making a charge for this help. They'll later offer you a proof for your checking before printing the ad.

If you'd rather have somebody design a fantastic ad for you, you'll be expected to take it all the way to "camera ready"---usually a PMT (photo mechanical transfer) for offset publication or to "engraver's plate" for letterpress publication before submitting it to the paper or magazine.

You'll be submitting your ad for one of these: "R.O.P." (run of paper, placed wherever the publication wants to place it), or "Request Position" (meaning that you're asking for a special positioning, which in addition to placement in a particular section usually also should include the phrase "Right hand page, right hand column, next to reading matter") for the most readership attention), or "Guarantee Position" (the publication committing to run your ad in a definite place). For the latter there'll be an additional charge.

For full-page ads, costly as they always are, you should definitely obtain "Guaranteed Position", whether it be on a particular inside page where you think the people who should see it will be looking for their own category of news also, or on the back outside cover for its obvious advantages. Find out all the prices and extra charges ahead of time and see what your budget can handle.

Especially be careful of the costs that may be added to the "space" charge. Sometimes "publication typeset" (from your provided typed copy) costs extra; sometimes it doesn't. Sometimes "layout" is another charge if they do it for you; most often it isn't. Certainly the adding of a color or two, rather than black and white, shoots the costs sky-high and requires a special coated stock, and availability depends on any already planned special stock pages for that issue because of others' ads involving second or third colors.

When you've ascertained the costs it wouldn't hurt to ask your agent whether he or she would consider sharing the costs with you. Many agents will do this. Many won't, some can't...but it's worth trying.

Also, if you have a friend working at an advertising agency, no doubt they can have all the preparation done for you much more cheaply than if you have others do each step for you separately. The agency will know how to handle all the steps ideally....from first layout, with any graphics and type-font suggestions, through to the "insertion order" and any other paper-work, including getting the ad the best position and date for appearing as is possible.

One reason for the agency's charges to you being less than otherwise---as long as you have a friend on the agency staff handling things for you---is that 15% of the display ad's space cost (not the artwork and design, of course) is the standard agency commission on all advertising in all ad media, meaning that the trade papers will simply charge any recognized advertising agency 15% less for the display ad space than would be charged of you if you paid for the space yourself. Your agency friend might even be able to pass along the whole 15% saving to you, but that depends on the higher-ups at the agency, since that 15% commission is what advertising agencies live on.

A suggestion which comes from some agents is that you pay to have your photo inserted in their "*agency book*", with the assertion that casting directors refer to such books. Rubbish! Casting people almost never even look at such books, even if they're provided by such agencies. This gimmick is usually a way for a few unscrupulous agencies to make a few bucks on their clients, even though they're fully aware that such "agency books" are completely useless.

Sometimes personal brochures help, but they're certainly not a necessity. They can be attractively prepared by personal managers especially (who sometimes suggest having them made up) or by actors themselves, with a photo on the front cover of maybe a single-fold brochure with whatever can be put inside to further the actor's promotion. Often the typesetting costs of such brochures and their reproduction and special mailing envelopes render them too expensive...and they're a questionmark as to their effectiveness anyhow, unless there's something very special that casting people and others will find important enough to really read.

When you're mailing out advertising to industry people, some say to mail it on a Thursday, or even a Wednesday, so it will be in the bundle of take-home-for-the-weekend mail that the casting or production person hasn't had time to read on Friday at the office and may even take more time to look over at home than they could afford to take at the office.

As an actor not yet known, it doesn't hurt to think like a door-to-door salesman with your own advertising and promotional materials. If you can afford the time it won't hurt to personally "make the rounds"---just like a New York actor must all the time---dropping off your advertising material. Certainly it takes a lot of time, but you do have a reason---your own---for dropping in at places, and you never know what you might find out, or whom you might accidentally meet when their secretaries are out for coffee, if you do this rounds-making. Otherwise, the mail is fine, and cheaper, and usually just as effective...except for those unexpected and accidental encounters with a few people in person.

Be careful to avoid those monthly or quarterly magazines of the slick, full-color variety that are sold at newsstands. Some offer cooperative agents "kickbacks" on ads they persuade their clients to run in such magazines. Your agent, if he or she is inclined to cheat, would be told by the publication to charge you $250 or so for the running of your photo, $50 or $100 of which would be the agent's! It's been done. And nobody's going to see your

208

photo in those publications anyway. Those publications prey on the ego and on the dreams of the very naive, mostly would-be actors who pay for their ads and later even buy the publications to see their pictures in them.

As mentioned earlier, there's one such magazine with posh offices on Sunset Boulevard that is a very impressive-looking, full-color publication that's full of would-be actors', would-be models', would-be dancers' and scads of fresh young kids' faces. It sends representatives about once or twice a year to most fair-sized cities across the country to advertise and hold one-day "Hollywood Comes To Willow Creek Junction (or whatever city name)" Seminars.

The "seminars" are expensive sales pitches proclaiming that their magazine is used as the main source for casting people's searches for "new talent" and urging each of the hundreds of naive folks who attend these sales pitches each time they're held to pay to insert their photos in the magazine. The gullible folks caught by this scam pay anywhere from $300 (the minimum) to something like $5,000 for a full-page, full-color photo ad! These gullible folks, because they aren't in Hollywood and don't know that the magazine is never referred to by _any_ casting person, _any_ producer or _any_ director, happily and hopefully send their photo and their check to the Sunset Strip address.

And there's even more scamming involved with this particular magazine! There's also the enticement to come to Hollywood and study and be "star-tailored" with the magazine's "star-making" workshops...of course for substantially more money.

Then there are those "Casting News" publications on newsstands in Hollywood that are stapled shut! They're stapled shut for very good reasons. They too encourage advertising by actors. But this kind of publication, once you've unstapled it to eagerly find its "casting news", contains almost none of what its title proclaims. And if you look at the faces of those who are foolish enough to advertise in something like this publication you'll observe written all over those faces the kind of mentality that would fall for this deceptive come-on. What's especially ridiculous about even the thought of advertising in something like this is that nobody would even think of buying a "casting news" publication except actors. Those advertising with their photos in this one are advertising to fellow actors! But some actually do.

An afterthought with regard to those large, full-page ads in _Daily Variety_ and _The Hollywood Reporter_: When you have one big role that you want to advertise, if you have _other_ recent roles or some coming up, mention those too in the same ad! A heavily-in-demand actor or actress is indicated, and it's even better advertising to indicate this. Along with the big, single announcement that dominates the ad, include at the bottom some headings like "Just Completed..." with those titles, "Coming Up..." with those titles, "Also..." or whatever. The space is costing a lot of money. Use it for all it's worth.

At the publication offices, in such advertising of whatever kind, don't fail to ask for some "tear sheets"---which you might not have to pay for, or some "special run" copies of your ad---which you obviously would have to pay for. Tear sheets are just as good, and if you can't get some tear sheets you can always buy a copy and have many photocopies made at a print shop. You can make sure that some of the people who might not otherwise see the ad do see it by mailing it to them after the ad appears, with a clip-on note saying something like "I hope you saw this!"

If you do some or all of these things effectively it's quite possible that at some point your career will speed up and you'll have a manager or press agent, or both, and one of those folks will of course be suggesting, planning and handling the details of your advertising. Have ultimate faith in their suggestions.

But until then, be smart. When you're placing costly advertising for yourself, consider readership demographics and profiles first. Compare circulation figures and cost-per-thousand of readership impressions the publication can promise, etc., as well as the simple costs. Any advertising is going to cost money, be assured of that. But advertising poorly handled or essentially wasted in wrong publications costs much, much more!

Chapter Nineteen

A Top Career
Needs A Press Agent

Normally it will be much later when the actor needs to hire a Public Relations person or firm---after his career has begun to roll upward. There are exceptions, as we'll note, but they mostly apply to well known sports figures, ex-presidents' sons and daughters and others who've achieved some public visibility or even notoriety before turning to acting.

For the actor who's inching upward simply through fine performances that gradually bring him or her preeminence it's silly and financially draining to employ a press agent or public relations firm before there's some _newsworthiness_. The PR people can't do much for you until at least some people know who you are or there's some good reason why they should find out about you.

Since some reading this may be at the point where they can and should take on a publicist, and since even with a hired publicist you're still (by checkbook and contract) handling your own press relations to an extent, even though with important, expensive help, some things should be said about that important step into increasing your career support team.

Unless you're able to find a press agent who'll be willing to handle you on some more "personal favor" basis, expect to pay about $1500 minimum per month for the hard work these folks do. The handling of someone before there's some kind of newsworthiness already available which only needs more exploiting in all media can be sweaty, time-taking, scheming, rat-racing and columnist-bribing hard work. The good press agents are worth whatever you have to pay them.

Press agents, to earn their money, must be constantly seeking inspirations as to what they can say about or do for you. Each of them has a personal list of columnists, TV interview hosts, party-throwers, clubs and organizations and special event sponsors whose favors they can ask once they get an idea, but it's the getting of the next idea and the next one after that which keeps them awake at night and keeps them on the phone and at the typewriter all day.

When you decide the time is right to hire a press agent, some of the first things you'll be asked to do is to provide him or her with:

(1) a resume of your whole life---either a narrative bio starting with your birth in that small town and continuing up to the current moment, or a step-by-step, year by year life resume in some form;

(2) a list of known personalities who might help you in some way, whether in the industry or public sector;

(3) plenty of photos and professional resumes---since they can sometimes get these into papers and magazines along with stories that are either true or fictitious;

(4) clips of any publicity you've previously received anywhere in the world;

(5) lists and data about any special skills, hobbies and interests, clubs and organizations you belong to, what pets you have and their names, your marital and family information, where you spend most of your time and what you do there---perhaps with whom, what your life goals are, what food you like, the names of your fan club presidents across the country (if you have fan clubs by that time), and your lawyer's name and address and phone---in case something comes up at some point which requires the cooperation of that member of your staff quickly.

There'll be talk about the initial campaign tactics and goals. The press person can probably get special boxed items in trade papers immediately when you appear in something. You couldn't get those by yourself. The press agent can get you radio talk shows and television interviews that you couldn't get for yourself. The press person might even suggest a large ad in trade papers---the expense of which you'd bear--- announcing that the well known press person involved "announces the worldwide representation" of you. Actually, this kind of ad can sometimes bring surprising results, often including some interesting film or television role offers. It's that phrase "worldwide representation", suggesting that something is suddenly happening that makes you much more important than everybody may have thought.

Shortly after taking on a press agent it's usual to be asked to be a runway model for one of the press agent's couturier clients, or to be one of the bake-off contestants in Julia Childs' next bake-off if the PR person represents Mrs. Childs. You might be persuaded to attend the Academy Awards event on the arm of a top starring bachelor or beautiful starlet whom the press agent also represents. You may find yourself suddenly being invited to many industry parties and events in the company of different stars who, being clients of the PR person, would otherwise be going alone to them.

When one of the press agent's stars is doing something or is at something there's always the possibility of another celebrity-linkup photo with that star at the event...which is what your press person has hoped when asking you to go. All PR people have a few stars and other celebrities as clients who've agreed to help the PR person's other clients in these manners when possible...mostly because it helps keep the press agent coming up with ideas for them, too, if more than one client can be involved. And if you're already some kind of celebrity you must expect to be asked to agree to do the same for the press person's lesser known clients.

There are PR-created love affairs that really don't exist; marriages about to break up---the papers say---that are still solid and happy; awards received from New York or Tuskegee organizations which, like the organizations themselves, are actually nonexistent. There are trips made in somebody's company that didn't happen. There are clever comments attributed to clients of the PR person which come solely from the busy mind of the PR person, just to create what's called a "column break". There are notes in the "Who's Where" columns about trips you didn't really make, to make you appear more in demand, and a few million other PR-conceived and PR-buckshotted lies and half-truths.

The foregoing are examples of the continuously fanatic and continuously inventive catalog-thumbing desk work of the typical PR person. Along the way, working with them, you have to judge whether those things your particular press agent comes up with are helping you achieve your goals or hurting you with respect to what you personally want the public to think of you. Remember, even though it's through a press agent---and with due respect to those folks, it's still _you_, handling your promotion by participating in all of it, as long as you pay the press agent and do what's being suggested by him or her.

Pressagenting is both image-building and image-erasing. There was a top star who died in recent years whose press agent and agent once agreed that the agent's secretary should become his wife to quash the growing rumors in columns that he was homosexual. There have been top stars committed to sanitariums whose press people have managed to keep word about it quiet through pleas and bribes and through influence and friendships with the top columnists.

213

In the days of Hedda Hopper and Louella Parsons there were careers made and careers ruined overnight, often by single sentences in those two ladies' columns that their press agents couldn't keep out of print. Press representatives of even the top stars had to bow and scrape to those two imperious muckrakers and stay on their good sides, just in case they might need some favors when some of their star clients had problems that those two battling columnists would love to use, even if just to "scoop" their competitor.

There was one leading sex symbol some years ago who had little interest in acting but fell into a career which thrived but later began to falter because of her limited talents and well known personality problems. Her eventual studying with a leading acting coach in New York was pressed upon her by a press person. This might have succeeded in affording her a new image if critics of her subsequent work hadn't begun to note that she had strayed from the one real talent she had. When her millions of fans, too, began turning away the press was persuaded by her press agent to bring her back to her old image in their columns. Careers can be turned around, aimed in new directions, etc., by top press agents...nobody else. And _nobody_ but a top, respected press agent can persuade columnists to _not_ publish juicy tidbits about stars' when they're in trouble.

Press agents have to handle these things very carefully. When stars are caught by John Law doing things stars shouldn't do their press agents are the ones who quickly call the columnists---who of course have ways of hearing about such things immediately---to keep whatever happened out of the columns or at least play them down. Once you're really newsworthy for some reason you'll need either more building up or more protection, and often both at the same time. The press agent is the person who can do both better than anyone else in the world could.

Cooperating with this team member, you should help your press agent by telling them everything. Repeat, everything! Tell them where you went last night, and with whom and what for. Better yet, tell them ahead of time that you're going there and with whom you're going, and they may be able to send their own photographer or alert a publication's photo people as well as the columnist who'll be most interested.

If you join a union committee of any kind, or an animal cruelty prevention committee, or some other committee or organization, tell them. There are ways in which they can use these items, either in publicity or promotion or advertising, even though you can't conceive of their possible newsworthiness or how to use it.

If you're in an accident, call them immediately, even before calling your insurance broker or your lawyer. They may want to get a photo so it can appear in the paper or on a newscast quickly. If you're caught in a raid of some kind, call them even before you call your lawyer. The trade papers will need to be called quickly by the PR person in such a case to try to stop the story in time.

If you're throwing a party for even a bunch of no-name pals, tell your

PR person. In the trade paper and daily paper articles the next day about your "big Hollywood party" you'll probably see a number of names of celebrities who weren't there at all but whose names make your party look like a major industry event. This is done often by pressagents, because all those celebrities are clients of the PR person and they've given him or her permission to use their names anytime in this manner because it provides more visibility for them too....even though they were actually at home watching television or playing with their dog that night!

Even if you're out of work and desperate, tell your PR person that straightforwardly too. They know how to jump in and make you look busy and very much in demand, helping you over the hump and helping make it possible for you to keep their checks coming regularly. You'll probably discover in the trade and daily papers that you've been in Mexico discussing starring in a noted director's next film, or in Berlin to confer with Ingmar Bergman, or returning from Paris after meetings with Roman Polanski or somebody else. Of course your agent or manager will be clued in on the publicity fib by your PR person, so the story won't be denied by them if it's brought up in an office and might otherwise surprise them.

Usually such a publicity fib includes a phrase like "...will return tomorrow from..." or "...is expected back Thursday, after....", just in case the publicity could result in an instant call from some production here in Hollywood that would otherwise think you'll be out of town and unavailable for a time or just in case the production might decide to call the person in Europe or Mexico that you're supposed to be with, to get to you.

Any time you see photos of stars in fan magazines doing whatever they're doing at the time, with whomever they're "caught" with, it's not the magazine that's been snooping at random. It's the stars' press agents who've had those shots taken by their own photographers and rushed the photos to the magazines. Visibility, constant and intriguing, is what keeps stars in the limelight. And it's their press agents who have that job.

When a star appears on Johnny Carson's or Jay Leno's talk show at night it's not a call from Johnny Carson's or Jay Leno's staff that occasioned that appearance. It's been a call from a press agent suggesting that the star has some interesting details---not about their career at all but rather about their private life---that millions of people would find interesting. Press agents' calls are always answered quickly by those talk shows' staff people. Other calls may get no response at all.

And it's well nigh *impossible* to become an internationally-known star without a PR person continually peppering the foreign press of all kinds---fan magazines, major periodicals, entertainment columns of worldwide daily newspapers, the Associated Press, etc.---with tidbits and photos of their clients.

Bottom line: It's the press agent's job, more than anyone else's on your growing staff, to put you on top and, once you're there, keep you there by hook or by crook. *You* should help by occasionally supplying the "hook"

---something to inspire releases and phone calls to columnists, and the press agent will supply the "crook"---the distortion that accomplishes more than the truth would.

If you're starring in a television series, any good press agent you employ knows that they must check with the studio or production company as well as with the network PR people on much of what they release about you. This is often written into the small print in television stars' contracts as they come down from the network in first draft form, but the more publicity-hungry stars know to strike it out in negotiation---before the final contract is prepared and signed---to leave themselves freer to get whatever kind of press they can. If they're important enough and if the network and production company want them badly enough they get by with it. After all, there's also a "morals" clause in all such contracts, in case the star or the star's PR person makes a boner involving behavior of the series star.

The same of course applies to any studio or production company which has you under any kind of term contract or multiple picture contract, because that studio or company also has a vested financial interest of huge size in you for the duration of that contract. Certain kinds of publicity can make you less valuable to them and some can have a devastating effect on their projects.

Perhaps you haven't known before that often those "second TV season series contract renegotiation" demands by series stars for more salary---and the fact that they're refusing to report at the time of the series' projected resumptions---are blown up intentionally and far out of their actual proportions through the cooperation of the networks', the studios' and the production companies' press people in friendly collusion with the stars' own press people, after they've all met in joint conference, just to increase their series' ratings with media coverage all the while such a squabble is boiling and again after the stars "finally agree" to re-sign and report for work.

Look at all the media coverage that's so often gotten in that manner...for both the stars and for their series. Who cares that the squabble over this or that---if it isn't in fact just money---is ridiculous and suspect? The stars, their series, the production company and the network with which they're supposedly "battling" are in the public eye and ear for days or weeks on end, and the series can use the publicity just as much as the star can. Newspapers will print such stuff joyously and the networks love it. You might even break _The National Enquirer_ for the first time in your career with such a nice, juicy---even if nonexistent---squabble!

And there's nothing more certain to keep your name, your face and your every going and coming in the tabloids, the consumer magazines of all kinds and often even the daily newspapers than a name star's divorce squabbling or property settlement. The more ferocious the bickering, the more outrageous the property settlement hassle, the more dirt that's raked up by one party or the other, the longer the period the story will continually hit the headlines. These continuing squabbles are of course sometimes real, but sometimes, both parties agreeing, they're less simply divorce and

216

settlement battles than they are publicity-grabbing by two secretly cooperating stars.

Even the "palimony" cases---usually the dirtiest of all---are sometimes voluntarily continued in the press by both sides, with still dirtier stories thrown to the press wolves daily. Some years ago a world famous female tennis star's palimony suit, involving her former female partner, provided continuing publicity for her for months on end, and with the story being aired publicly it was intelligent press relations for her to obtain equal coverage for her own side of the story, thereby gaining a certain amount of sympathy with the fans that that kind of story may otherwise have alienated. More recently, in the early 90's, a second world famous female tennis star and her female palimony case opponent allowed themselves to be interviewed together on network television to air their battle. Sometimes when very private and potentially fan-alienating publicity is inevitable the press advisors of stars and other public figures feel it's better to bring all the details out voluntarily and let the chips fall where they may.

As an example, one top female star was fired from a picture some years ago because she refused to do some quite total nude scenes and threatened suit against the studio for firing her without sufficient justification. The studio retaliated swiftly with a story that the star's recent rib removal operation that had left telltale scars was the reason she couldn't do the mostly nude scenes, and stated that she had failed to tell them in advance of the problem. The star or her press representative realized that the wisest course was to publicly admit that she had indeed had such an operation, at the same time pointing to many other female stars who had had the same surgical procedure to maintain their figures.

These are examples of unwanted, possibly public-alienating publicity being turned away from the ultimate career damage such public airing could generate.

And there are secondary sources for publicity available and ready to be exploited at all times:

Along the way, you might have a second career that you maintain even during your top starring years that's good for still more television appearances to promote things you perhaps design---even though in name only, and manufacture---again, even if in name only. Watch the Home Shopping Club on television and you'll see Farrah Fawcett, Phyllis Diller and Vanna White making regular personal appearances to sell their jewelry. Rue McClanahan, Vanna and Jacqueline Smith plug their dress and casualwear designs. Connie Stevens and Frankie Avalon sell their own lines of cosmetics. Ruta Lee hawks her own vitamin spray line. Those appearances on the Home Shopping Club's pitching programs, in which the stars take on-the-air, in person calls from viewers calling in about the products, are pure gold in publicity terms. Viewers are thrilled to be able to call in and talk personally with stars. Some stars get into these secondary publicity activities when they're on top; some come up with them later when their careers are fading.

217

Then, too, you might be prompted by a PR person into some high visibility appearances at political conventions and other gatherings and, rubbing elbows with the right people, be talked into at least running for Mayor somewhere---like Clint Eastwood (Monterey) and Sonny Bono (Palm Springs) and get a lot of additional publicity when you're elected, over and above the publicity you're getting for acting career things.

Later, should your career droop or sag a little and a "comeback" is the only answer, that's a time when press agents are sorely taxed---if you can still afford one at the time, or if you've paid a lot of money to one in earlier years and they still love you and will help you "on spec".

That's when you're prompted by a PR person to turn to discussing health foods on TV interviews and putting out your own line of cosmetics and ghost-written books like silent film star Gloria Swanson did in the 70's before her death. That's when you might, like Miss Swanson, do commercials and talk shows to show everybody how good you look after your fifth face lift. You might donate your memorabilia to some museum or university and be photographed doing it. You might be booked at women's clubs around the country to discuss your career and your love life. And of course it's a common career-reviving ploy to write (or have ghost-written for a star) an "expose" book about themself which implies many star-studded liaisons on every page whether they're there or not.

In many of these cases and in other variations on the same themes which do reach print or media exposure at those later times when stars have faded some, it's hoped that some, any kind of attention will provide the hoped-for comeback. The ideas may come from the PR person or from you, but you still need a press person and his or her network of connections---if you can obtain the help of one at the time---to do the most effective job of getting your story out and some promotion working.

In other words, at any point in your career when you need and justify, or don't want and need to hide, what must go into or be kept out of public print and media dissemination, the press agent is the one to turn to.

Simply keep in mind---early on as you handle all those things by yourself as well as later as you pay those checks to other people to do the work for you---that it's still basically _you_...still self-publicizing, self-promoting and self-advertising in a sense---who must in the end call the shots if you're to keep any control over your career.

Chapter Twenty

Contracts...Big Items
In Small Print

As in any other profession, contracts are negotiated and signed by employer and employee to insure the providing of services, the conditions of their being rendered and the remunerations for them during specified terms or upon completion of employments. It's the same in acting, whether it's a "SAG Minimum" contract for those on the bottom rung of the career ladder or a multi-million dollar contract with a hundred special and very specific clauses for a top star.

There is a minimum salary for an actor employed for just one day for an acting role in either television or motion pictures. There are escalating salaries for three-day employments in television that depend on whether the shows are half-hour or hour shows, hour-and-a-half or two-hour shows, etc. There is no such three-day contract for motion pictures. But there is also a weekly contract for both television and motion pictures.

If the actor is hired for a "minimum" salary there's usually 10% of the total salary tacked on above the minimum rate so that the agent can take its 10% commission without cutting into the actor's basic salary. These current minimum salaries can be learned from SAG's current information packets for new members or by simply calling the "Contract" office at SAG and asking. They're not quoted here because they keep changing from time to time.

Even in the "minimum" or "scale" level (both words mean the same), as in all others, there are standard extra benefits insured the actor by the SAG contract:

If you must be fitted for wardrobe at a studio wardrobe department or perhaps at Western Costume or if any other special trip is required of you for that purpose, there is a *Fitting Fee* which will be paid on your paycheck later. If only telephone discussion of your available wardrobe is necessary with the Wardrobe Department people there's no fitting fee paid. If you supply your own wardrobe there's a *cleaning fee* paid on your paycheck. At the time of this writing it's $10 for streetwear and $15 for formal wear.

There's a *Meal Penalty* payable to you any time a lunch break or dinner break during a work day isn't afforded you at the appropriate time. At the time of this writing it's $25 for the first half-hour, $35 for the second half-hour or fraction thereof, and $50 for the third half-hour or fraction thereof.

Overtime Pay is calculated at time-and-a-half for over 8 hours (for the 9th and 10th hour), except that there are two days in a weekly contract player's work week allowed to go up to ten hours without any overtime being due. Over ten hours on a working day is *double time*, based on the hourly percentile of your day's pay rate.

The biggest bonus for actors applies to "minimum" and "scale" employments just as it does to leading players' salaries....*Residuals!* On any filming done since 1958 actors get these wonderful surprises in the mail periodically for many years after they've worked.

The residuals structure keeps changing in most new contract negotiations so for the latest percentiles it's best to check with SAG literature. The different residual structures for television include network prime time, out of season prime time, non prime time network and syndication. When someone has done a network series which is "picked up" later by many, many stations across the country---like the old *"I Love Lucy"* shows and other mostly sitcom series, the actors who appeared in any episode or episodes---even if a "minimum" or "scale" player---continue to receive residuals practically forever. They receive from the syndicators (usually the original producers but not always) residuals that start at the equivalent of their original salaries for the second run in network prime time of any show. Beyond that one item the residual structure is complicated, depending on rerun timeslots, many syndication considerations, etc.

All checks for residuals due from production companies for the actors in the casts are due at SAG no later than 30 days after the runs involved, but it takes SAG a certain amount of time to process them and mail them out to the actors. Actors shouldn't count on receiving residuals they know are coming---because their friends have told them they've seen their shows again---until at least sixty days after those rerun dates.

A television *series* player may, if he or she wants to, consider a *buyout* of residuals which would otherwise be received in all those future years if their series is rerun in any of the aforementioned situations. To arrange this, either at their or the producer's suggestion, such a buyout must be negotiated in the original contract for the series. It must be indicated as being *in addition to* the original series salary. The minimum amounts allowed by SAG for such buyouts keep changing, so for the latest figures it's best to inquire with SAG if the occasion comes up and you want to find out about this possibility.

Those *buyouts* need to be very carefully considered, though. Look at all the old television series that, years later, are picked up for syndication runs on both networks and individual local stations all over the country. If the series stars *hasn't* gone for the tempting "buyout" while the series was running they've continued, some almost forever, to receive residuals from all that later use of their performances. For those who didn't have much faith in the potential longevity of their series and went for the "buyouts", forget it. They won't see a penny of residuals later.

If a movie made for television is later released for *theatrical* exhibition (in motion picture theatres), the actor who did the television show is to receive 100% of his original salary for "domestic" (the US and Canada included) and 100% of his original salary for "foreign" (other countries). However, at the time of "theatrical" release in *either* of them the actor is to receive 150% of his original salary on the assumption that the other market release will soon follow.

Other benefits applying to *all* SAG employment contracts include the following:

Looping, if required at the end of a shooting day or otherwise, is paid as overtime if at the end of the day, or as a half-day's salary if less than four hours on a non-work day, or a full day's salary if more than four hours on a non-work day.

Rest Period Violations are often incurred by producers with companies out on location, for their convenience and because of weather or other conditions. The actor is assured a minimum of twelve hours of rest period between shooting days or such a penalty will apply, except that on the first day of employment on location the minimum is only ten hours.

Mileage is payable to actors who are asked to drive themselves to nearby locations within a thirty mile radius from Beverly Boulevard and LaCienega Boulevard in Los Angeles. The actor, as this is written, gets thirty cents per mile under the SAG contract, usually in hand upon arrival at the location.

Location Travel Time is payable under all conditions. Even when the actor reports at a studio lot to be transported to a nearby location, work time and salary begin at the time of reporting at the studio and continue until the actor is released, back at the studio dropoff location, at the end of the day.

Travel to Out of Town Locations is usually by first-class air, where it's available, paid by the production. The actor is paid for the travel day enroute to the location at his full day pay rate. If air travel is more than four hours a rest period of ten hours is due him before reporting for work if the producer wants to avoid having to pay the rest period violation penalty. As mentioned earlier, producers are often happy to pay the penalty in order to save location shooting time and the far costlier salaries of the crew members, etc.

Returning from out of town locations, if the actor is transported on a working day and it remains inside the day's allowed working hours, there's no extra pay due. If it's not within working hours a half-day's pay is due. If on a no-work day, also a half-day's pay.

Per Diem Allowance on locations means meal money, figured as this is written at $8 for breakfast, $12 for lunch and $22 for dinner. The total is $42 per day, but if the producer opts to supply one meal or more the appropriate contract amount for that meal is deducted from the day's per diem allowance. These are the minimum amounts, by the way, and stars and top players often negotiate for far higher allowances on these out of town locations.

The SAG contract also insures *consecutive employment*. Day players are paid for each day worked, at their daily rate, and for any days when they're not required to work as long as their employment isn't finished. Three-day players are paid for three days whether they actually work all three days or not. Similarly, the weekly players work as needed within their weekly employment periods and are paid their weekly contract guarantee even if they only work two or three days of the week.

There's one exception to the "consecutive employment" provision that some actors may not understand. It's called *Drop-Pickup*. It's an option afforded producers if they have a role which needs the actor heavily *later* in the filming of something but also needs him *only briefly* toward the beginning of the shooting schedule. They may hire him on a *daily* rate the first time he's required. His daily rate can be terminated at any time and he can be recalled later, if arranged in the initial employment contract. There must be an intervening time span of 14 days for a motion picture or 10 days for a first-exhibition television picture prior to recall; otherwise the actor must be paid for the intervening time.

Availability is a rather touchy matter. Once you sign a contract for employment in a picture for either television or feature filming you're signed to work until the picture is completed. To cover the production company, unless you've negotiated a *stop date* and it's written into your contract---because you know that you have another job coming up on a certain date, you have no out. You must stay with the contracted filming until it "wraps" and you're officially released. Stop dates are seldom granted by production companies, since the productions never know what delays may occur and unexpectedly extend the time required to finish your work in their project. They can be talked into affording stop dates only in the case of major stars....and then only if they can't get those stars without them.

Not too many years ago Ed Asner was working in a film, confident at the time of signing for it and starting that it would easily be completed in time for him to commence on schedule with the upcoming season's shooting of the _"Lou Grant"_ series. When he wasn't finished---because the motion picture went considerably over schedule, Ed's agent Jack Fields and Ed himself were in fairly hot water with the series producers until it was straightened out amicably with a delayed start of the series. Of course Ed _was_ the series. Be very careful in matters of finishing and starting dates that may conflict, especially if you're not in as secure a position as Mr. Asner was. You can lose a fully contracted next job if you're not available for its start date.

There is a clause in all actors' contracts called _Force Majeure_. Any major catastrophic interruption of filming which prevents continuity and causes temporary suspension of the work can be handled in one of several ways: All players can be terminated with the paying of one day's pay beyond their last filming day if they're day players, or with a half-week's pay if they're on weekly contracts, if the production has decided it must shut down completely. If there's hope of resuming production soon, the cast may be maintained on half salary for up to three weeks, but if there's no resumption by then the actors are free to leave the production, and resumption is subject to the actors' availabilities at the time of the new start. An exception is possible, in that the production company may want to offer a _Holding Fee_ of a size that warrants the actor's remaining available for an extended period, but this has to be approved by SAG.

As an example of the latter item---the _Holding Fee_, some years ago Paramount was planning the first motion picture version of _"Star Trek"_, using the original series stars. This author was representing two of them at the time, and watched these details unravel over a period. Contracts were signed and a tentative start date for filming was announced.

Then Paramount and Gene Roddenberry decided that, instead of a motion picture, the series itself should go back into production. Time was needed to prepare scripts and production details. They wanted to hold the series stars available, so a very large holding fee was offered to all the actors. Expecting a start of series production within a time, they remained available in return for the holding fee payments.

Then Paramount changed its mind again; decided to make the motion picture after all. Another production start delay. Another large holding fee was paid to the actors. Eventually the motion picture was produced. The stars had already had two huge pay checks even before reporting for the first day of actual filming!

There are also _Favored Nations_ clauses in some contracts. When the actor agrees to accept a salary which is less than his usual quoted salary his agent will often ask for the "favored nations" clause to be inserted in his contract, stipulating that if any other player is ever paid more on the film or series guest starring list the player having agreed to work for _top of the_

223

show in television---meaning the salary the show never exceeds, instead of his usual salary---is guaranteed to receive the difference between what he has received and what is later paid to someone else.

A not too widely known "secret" regarding "favored nations" cases: The contract with the player is executed by the production company, and _it_ is the company committing itself to the favored nations conditions. So, later when it wants to pay much, much more to a top-magnitude star for a guest appearance, in order to avoid violating its earlier favored nations contracts---because it has maintained a "top of the show" salary, all it has to do is consult with the _network_ involved and if possible arrange that the _network_, not the production company, pays the _over_ "top of the show" amount, removing any threat of action by the lesser paid actor. Occasionally it's not even _money_ laid out by the network as a persuasion to the superstar; it might be a Silver Cloud Rolls Royce or a Mediterranean villa or something else that the superstar has hinted he or she would like. There simply are "favored nations" and _more_ favored nations.

Re-use of Photography means that if any footage of a player's performance is desired to be used for any subsequent purpose other than that for which he was employed originally he is to be paid at daily rate minimum or better for such usage. This is not negotiable at the time of original hiring. It has to be negotiated separately at the later time, prior to any such proposed usage.

Personal Appearances by actors who've been in motion picture roles which warrant them, when pictures are opening out of town or in town, may be bargained for by the producer at the time of executing the original contract. At the actor's discretion, they may also be negotiated at a later time, since they also promote the actor. These trips or appearances are negotiated at a level commensurate to the player's worth, but in all cases no less than the player's minimum daily rate must be paid for periods involved with personal appearances for the productions. Travel, per diem, first class hotel accommodations and all other standard working conditions must be satisfactory as well.

LOW BUDGET FILMMAKERS HAVE TO BE WATCHED!

Most low-budget pictures leave contract-signing till last minutes, usually because they're still trying to get a star who's holding out. The star, if they can get him or her, will then be squeezing out some other player who's been held waiting for the answer on that role. Also, the star who finally accepts will be robbing some other player who's been expecting top billing in another role of the top billing he's been expecting but which isn't contracted on paper yet. Reshuffling and phone calls are still going on up to last minutes before filming begins. Some production company people will even urge the actor to report for filming start without a signed contract, for similar or other reasons. This is not allowable for the actor by SAG, for diametrically opposite positions...to protect the actor.

Often on low budget pictures the agent's negotiations are only as effective as the last phone call, and each phone call changes the conditions, can change the salary offer or the billing previously offered. Per diem allowances are often lowered suddenly because the budget is ballooning and there isn't the money for what was originally agreed to. A four week guarantee of employment for a nice juicy starring role or costarring role might be suddenly reduced to a few days because they've found a way to use the actor and get him finished earlier...after he may have turned down another job or two that he could have accepted if he'd known sooner.

The motels and hotels at those distant low budget filming locations are sometimes too expensive for the budget, so the actors might be persuaded at the last minute to even sleep in tents....and again, if it's a SAG signatory picture at all---low budget or not, the answer should be no.

The actor hired at a daily rate for three days, expecting to receive $1,000 per day or more, might not notice when signing his contract--- again, rush-rush at the last minute---that his "conversion rate" (meaning that his contract can be changed to a weekly if necessary) is typed in as being *minimum* for a weekly.

Simply watch out....at every turn. Low budget filming is desperate, fanatic determination---and promises to investors---to bring a film in at the lowest budget figure possible, and every step along the way is watched to see if there's a possible money-saving loophole or "accidental oversight" that hasn't been thought of yet.

FOREIGN COMPANIES HAVE TO BE WATCHED EVEN MORE CLOSELY!

If the production company is based within the continental United States it's a "domestic" company simply filming some or all of its footage on foreign soil. But if it's a production company whose headquarters is based in Munich or Tokyo or Israel or somewhere else it's *not subject to the SAG contract or conditions!* *Where it's based* determines whether SAG has jurisdiction. Remember that. If SAG has no jurisdiction to protect you...you're simply and purely *on your own*.

In either case, if filming in a foreign country is involved not only your agent but also a qualified *Entertainment Attorney* should examine the contract you're offered very closely. Don't sign until this has been done!

Most reputable foreign-based production companies are now accustomed to being required to deposit the total guaranteed salary for the entire film engagement of the actor in escrow in an American bank before the actor leaves for those foreign-based locations. The attorney looking over the contract should also require that the manner of disbursing the salary from that escrow account, or from that "Letter of Credit" at that American bank as an alternative, is explicitly spelled out so there won't be any hitch to come up later.

Another thing you should watch out for: The *Monetary Exchange Rate*. It was embarrassing to me once, when I was an agent myself, when I had an actor going to Australia for a Hanna-Barbera series pilot starring role, to discover that the per diem allowance I'd negotiated for food and lodging was less than would be ideal due to the monetary exchange rate. Caught, it was quickly straightened out and bettered with Hanna-Barbera, but you might not always be able to remedy such an oversight. Be sure to check that monetary exchange item ahead of time. It affects the costs of food, hotels if you're to pay out of provided expenses, car rentals if the production makes you rent your own, and how much your dollar-rate actually represents in the foreign exchange rate when you go to stores.

Also, on foreign-based productions the working conditions---unless carefully worked out and checked by your agent and your attorney ahead of time---can be pretty terrible. One of my actors, once, on location for Golan-Globus in Israel, had to be camel-backed across the desert and had to sleep in tents. An actress of mine, on location with a Munich-based company, had almost no rest periods between days of shooting. Another, a loud and fairly unpleasant young star client of mine, was spied drinking American liquor in his location hotel room one night...in a "dry" country...and was reported to the police and, arrested, had to pay his own fine to be released in time to be picked up to be taken to location the next day.

If a foreign-based production goes over schedule, extending beyond the period for which the money has been deposited in the American bank, have your same U. S. attorney require further deposit _immediately_ in order to make sure you can collect your salary for the additional period.

Naturally you must make sure you have your _round trip_ ticket in hand before you leave for the foreign country. Don't trust your return flight ticket to be supplied to you later. It must be in hand before you go. And don't take any _salary advances_ from the foreign company, to buy too many nice things while there. Any such departure from the original salary escrow arrangement will complicate matters and arguing with foreign bookkeepers can be a mess. As the agent of one star who was working---and shopping---in Austria, I know. Moreover, any problem that you'd normally take to either SAG or to court here in the United States isn't that simple to handle abroad. It's difficult to sue a company on its own turf.

Bottom line: Remember that unless all the details of _any_ non-SAG contract...whether with a low-budget producer or a foreign-based production company...are carefully ironed out _well ahead of time_, you can be fired or stranded without much or any cause---even purely for the company's convenience---and be in a big pickle!

CONTRACTED BILLING....INTRICACIES AND PECKING ORDERS

No matter what level you're at in your career, you'll be getting whatever billing your importance to the picture or series warrants only if your agent fights for it or the role obviously demands it. Since billing is negotiated and included in contracts it's being discussed here also.

Early billing will probably be no more than _Featured_ or may even appear in small print at the bottom of the End Credit listings under the word _With_. You're not in a position yet to hassle over billing until you justify it. If there are more than 50 in the cast you're not even required by SAG to be billed at all if the role is a bit role.

After starting to establish some worth and appearing in roles which justify some concern for position in at least those end-credit listings, your agent should start requesting _first, second or third_ Featured positions and start trying to persuade people to move you upward into the _Costarring_ listings as soon as possible.

Costarring billings can appear either at the end, often at the top of all the end credits, or in the Main Titles before the start of the picture. It's at the producer's option unless it's been negotiated and settled that your name shall appear in whatever position in those Main Titles, and that position is a coveted one. Others' agents will be fighting for their clients to appear there.

Since position in the billings is becoming imporant for your career by this time and important for continuing upward mobility, hassles are often necessary in the getting of any billing position ahead of other players, and your agent must be up to the demanding and the getting. You're either more important as an actor or more important as the character if position is to be gotten over others of the same billing level. So, regardless of the role's importance, your agent should always be arguing that _you're_ more important as an actor than that other actor tentatively planned to receive billing ahead of you. However, many, many very important people's names appear in the costarring lists, so don't expect miracles from your agent every time you work.

The next move up is _Starring_, and now billing and position become even more important. Agents will always be requesting at least _Separate Card, Main Titles_ for your starring billing---meaning that when your name appears on screen there will be no other billing name appearing when your name is centered for its moment in a rolling frame and no other billing name appearing when your name appears in some part of a _non_-rolling frame for a few seconds. Sometimes, in this billing level, the best the agent can get for you is _Share Card, Main Titles_---meaning that your and one or more others' names will be shown at the same time. This is often true when there are large casts heavy with important names.

Something the agent will also start asking for in the Starring level is "_Type Size equal to or larger than..._" others receiving starring billing, to guarantee that the actor is not indicated as a second-class citizen in that level by other names being billed in larger type.

Guest Starring and _Special Guest Appearance by_ types of billing come next. Usually they're in the Main Titles up front, on separate cards because these billings are used for "billboarding" of known stars. There are many hassles between production companies and agents as to whether this billing is justifiable in relation to other equally valuable people in the same casts.

About the only alternative which might be acceptable in this level would be billing, either in main titles or in end credits, _after_ all the rest of the names---sometimes even after the "Featured" players list---as _With (the star's name) as (the character's name)_ . This is often the compromise that some stars must wind up with due to large cast lists or fairly stet opening credits on major television series. In recent years two series stars, Joan Collins of _Dynasty_ and Susan Sullivan of _Falcon Crest_ have opted for this kind of billing. When it's what's negotiated, of course the star's name is in quite large type, on a separate card with no other star's name on the same card.

If you're starring in a series it's best to have it stipulated in your contract---in the first season especially---that you are to be afforded starring position in main titles ahead of any guest stars' billing in the same episodes. That way, out front and until it's certain who's going to "carry" the series--- which the production company might prefer to wait and find out before preparing their opening title formats, you're assured of the desired billing prominence. Agents can usually obtain that clause if the producer is fairly certain that you're going to be one of the "fan mail and ratings-boosting" prospects in the cast. If you can't get this clause it may mean they're not that confident as to how much you're going to mean for the series.

SPECIAL ACCOMMODATIONS....WHEN YOU'RE WORTH THEM

You'll know you've "arrived" when you start receiving special accommodations of all kinds written into your contracts and the contracts, with all those nice "extras", are signed by producers without any hassles.

For _domestic_ pictures, whether motion pictures or television, stars who are in demand---but no others, sorry---can also get cars provided for them on location, travel and accommodations for their wives and personal staffs, special wardrobe designed by their favorite couturiers---and may be allowed to keep the special designer wardrobe after the picture is finished, and often by really demanding them can get _Stop Dates_ ---cutoff dates when they're promised they'll be finished, whether the picture is or not. Often they're offered _Points_ in the production's net receipts ---if they're willing to accept this very chancy form of payment in lieu of a couple million dollars of their salary out front, and many other things which SAG doesn't guarantee or provide and which must be negotiated by the player's agent or lawyer.

For _foreign_ filmings---shooting outside the U.S., whether U.S.-based or foreign company productions, usually anyone of substantive worth to the production---whether Starring, Costarring or even very valuable Top Supporting players---will be able to obtain cars for their exclusive use while on location, their choice of hotel in some cases, larger per diems and expense allowances and sometimes (not often) even stop or cutoff dates.

So, when you're filming on location anywhere, and you see the stars able to live in those "ultra-ultra castle" hotels while you and others are holed up in the Excelsior Armpits Motel, simply recognize that they've earned those locations and those frosted-glass convertible limousines and all those other things, and look forward to the day when those things can fall to you as well...*if* you and your agent start demanding them.

MULTIPLE PICTURE CONTRACTS....A DYING BREED

Not many studios still offer *Multiple Picture Contracts* these days, but a few do under certain circumstances. The circumstances that persuade them to offer a player the opportunity to commit himself to doing one or more pictures a year for the studio or production company involved are when an actor is clearly marked for rapid rise to top boxoffice stardom in the immediate future but is still treading water as to money demands.

At that time, and at that time only, the studio may offer the player the multiple picture contract at a somewhat higher rate than he's currently getting---possibly because the agent isn't demanding enough and the studio recognizes this. The studio or company may throw in an *escalation clause* that ups that original salary with each picture completed under the contract. The studio knows in such a case---and its computers confirm---that that player will be receiving lots bigger salaries when he works for other production companies and studios during the timespan of the offered contract. The studio is gambling that he'll actually make that rapid rise and that they'll be saving a lot of money in subsequent years when they want him.

Another set of conditions which suggest multiple picture contracts is when there are major stars being contracted for series leads. At that time, if the production company or studio is also involved in motion pictures as well as television, it isn't uncommon for it to occur to both the studio and the actor's agent that contracting for the star to star in a number of motion pictures for the company during the same series contract term is a good idea. The motion picture appearances can boost the series ratings and help build the star's preeminence, which does the same thing.

However, in the glutted talent marketplace of today there really aren't many of even these multiple picture contracts offered, since every aspect of production itself is in a dubious state these days as to cost and feasibility, and any such contract is on a "pay or play" basis, insuring that the actor will receive the stipulated amount for the given number of pictures during those years whether he or she is actually worked or not. With the current corporate studio deals and bank-financing questionmarks clouding the horizons in Hollywood it's usually too big a gamble to take!

TELEVISION SERIES PLAYER CONTRACTS

There's always the chance that you may be cast in a television series pilot; that your pilot may get a network pickup around April or September of the following year; and that you may be even more lucky and have the show renewed for more than thirteen weeks. It might go on and on forever. Some have run for eight, nine and ten seasons.

Number one...that's a lot of salary, especially with larger amounts each season---either per the original contract's escalation clauses or following dogged renegotiation by your agent while you're told by your agent to not report for work at the new season's start until those higher salary demands are met.

The first step, of course, is to get the role in the pilot, after several callbacks, network executive checkouts and meetings, finalizing of the pinpoint negotiations when it's decided they want to film test you, then the film test that decides whether you'll actually do the pilot. But before your film test there's the _Deal Memo_ that the production sends down to your agent.

A Deal Memo is an "almost contract". It spells out the production company's first offer on every aspect of possibly employing you for the pilot and the series. It's still open to negotiation on some points---and your agent and you aren't even expected to accept the whole contract without some negotiation. Most negotiable points are mentioned in the following paragraphs.

The deal has to be totally worked out and agreed to before they'll put you in front of the camera. The deal memo by that time turned into a _Series Contract_---with all details finalized and ready to be operative if you do get the role after the test, you're already locked in on all the conditions for doing the pilot itself, the option terms for holding you long enough to allow the production company to try for a network pickup of the series, plus all conditions and terms for _the first seven years of production of the series_!

If on the other hand the production company really wants you without a film test, chances are there won't be any "deal memo". The contract will be drawn up and required to be signed before you do the pilot.

In either of these situations you have to remember that you don't have a series, though, unless a network picks up and runs the show after viewing the pilot. Under certain circumstances, even if the network picks up the series, you still may not have a series, since the production company can decide or be told by the network to pay you off and replace you with somebody else. It's all there in those contracts' small print.

Other things in those contracts' small print are the billing you're locked into, the salary you do the pilot for, the salary you receive for each episode of series production, the escalating salary as it rises season after season if the show continues over a period, etc. Normally there'll be a guarantee of how many weeks are required for production of the pilot, the residual basis---whether SAG minimum or lots more if they're desperate to have you in the series, conditions for possible theatrical use (showing in motion picture houses if they decide to go that way after filming the pilot), conditions for any pay-TV release later, profit participation due you if any (usually this is so small it's laughable), the option period after shooting of the pilot within which option to use you must be exercised by the producer.

There'll be stipulations as to whether, how many and under what conditions you can do any commercials for other than one or more of the show's sponsors, the same conditions as they pertain to endorsements and public appearances, and many, many more small print conditions. The details of these contracts are mind-boggling the first time you confront them in your agent's office.

The *Option Period* ---the period during which you and the producer alike are sweating out network pickup and some definite word that the series will go into production, is often governed by Par. 24a (1) of SAG's Basic Television Agreement. It's for twelve months, but the first six months of that period are firm and the last six have the conditions that if the series is picked up but *you aren't* you must be paid for no less than thirteen episodes or thirteen weeks of the series' production period (the lesser of the two), even though you've been dumped from the series. A Par. 24a (2) option stipulates that after six months (again, those first six months are firm) you're free to accept other jobs up to actual exercising of the pickup option by the production company. And a 24a (3) option---the one most often chosen, for obvious reasons---provides that after the first six (firm) months the player must notify the production company of any employment offer for four weeks or more work and that the producer can preempt in order to start production or else permit the actor to take the other job and take the gamble against a sudden need to go into production before the actor is free from the other job.

To obtain any option at all the producer must contract for the player to receive for the pilot a salary equal to or better than twice the minimum freelance salary or pay the difference out front to obtain the option if desired. Certainly there will be some arrangement for an option period, since following the pilot's completion it takes so long for the production to obtain network pickup assuring that the series will roll. Therefore the actor's salary for the pilot will certainly be no less than twice the minimum. The average salary for a pilot of course varies widely, depending on where you, the actor, stand. For new people it can be roughly $5,000-6,000 or more for a normal length shooting schedule. This level of salary is the level for people who have little or no real track record behind them. For others of course it's much higher, and for established stars (as you've read in the National Enquirer) it goes well up into six figures for both the pilot and each of the episodes if the series goes.

While a pilot is an investment gamble for the production company or studio footing the bill, a pilot role is also a gamble for the actor, who can't do another pilot for the coming season because the producer holds that option on his services if the show is picked up.

In those contracts, *Exclusivity* is spelled out...making it a breach of contract for the player to appear in his role by character name under any other circumstances or for any other producer and so forth. As to commercials, the exclusivity is different: Players at salaries of $10,000 or less per week or per episode for a half-hour pilot or $15,000 or less per week or per episode for a one-hour or longer pilot, may not grant any exclusivity with respect to commercials.

231

Also, if the player is not guaranteed at least thirteen episodes in the series portion of the contract he may not grant <u>any</u> exclusivity unless the per episode or per week salary is $130,000 or more for a half-hour show or $195,000 for a one-hour or longer show.

Endorsements are spelled out, meaning product endorsements of the show's sponsor's products, as to number to be required or asked of the actor. This knocks some actors who've done a lot of commercials out of the running early, because they're very liable to have conflicts, having done commercials for similar categories of products which might still be running or might be picked up at some point for reruns. Sponsor commercials are usually required of the series player, so where conflicts exist prior to the pilot's filming there are actors who won't be cast in the pilot. Unfortunately at the time of a pilot's filming and even the "deal memo" which is signed before the actor does the pilot the eventual *sponsor* isn't yet known. This sometimes means that an actor who has done the pilot may still be removed from the cast due to such a conflict when a sponsor is obtained by the network. It has happened.

The amounts of *Per Diem* and *Expense Account Allowance* are spelled out or simply typed in by the production company as being "SAG minimum", which many stars won't accept and therefore the amounts are usually negotiated by the agent and the production company.

A *Morals Clause* is always in the contract, to cover the production company and the network in the event that you do something which is considered offensive to public standards of behavior, in which event you can be removed from the pilot and the series.

Other items that appear in the pilot and series contract include:

Guaranteed Number of Episodes for the first broadast year and subsequent ones; the *Option*---24a (3) usually; the *Period Allowed After Network Option Before The Shooting Start and Before Exercising of Option*; *Escalation Clauses*---the salary raises, season after season, usually for the first seven years.

The *Escalation Clauses* are often the subject of extended negotiation between producer and agent. They certainly should be, since producers will originally offer as little increase for each subsequent season as they think they may be able to get away with. Any agent worth his or her salt knows that if the client is "carrying the show" with his or her popularity with fans and ratings by the end of a first season that client will be worth far more to the show, therefore sometimes the agent will advise the actor that *getting the pilot* is what's most important. If the series' first season run shows the network that the actor is far more valuable there's always the start-of-the-new-season time for "renegotiation" for a far better salary before the star will report for work. Such cases are in the trade papers and dailies every year---the "holdouts" who won't report for second or third seasons' work until their salaries are upped astronomically to the level warranted by the popularity the series has created for them. Most of the time....but not always....<u>not</u> reporting without these big salary increases per episode works.

Participation in Profits is usually next to nothing percent in the original contracts and is usually negotiated anew only if and when the player has established his or her worth. Each year you read in papers that somebody is suing the studio because of "participations" not paid or "merchandising" not paid. *Merchandising*, which also starts at a ridiculously low level in a first season, involves the player's share of net profits received by the production company through selling publications, recordings, music, T-shirts, toys, scooters, posters, caps, school tablets, etc., with the star's picture or likeness on them. Such lawsuits and refusals to continue on series come up periodically. The two well established top series stars of the *"Dukes Of Hazzard"* series, for example, were immediately replaced in their starring roles because of their demands for more participation and merchandising shares as conditions for their returning for the start of the new season's filming.

The *Turnaround* provision in contracts means that as of sixty days following the expiration of employment in the show's current production, or sixty days following the network's cancelling of the show---whichever occurs last---the player is released from any and all options unless the option contracted for in the original contract has not expired by the sixty-day period ending or has been renewed by the production company at some point. There is the alternative that a *Holding Fee*---described earlier with that example of the *"Star Trek"* film-to-series-to-film confusion and the resulting holding fees paid the waiting actors---can be paid to the actor to hold him or her available.

Remembering the *"Star Trek"* experience of its established stars brings to mind another item: *Personal Appearances*. This item should also be included in pilot and series contracts, but it's not a standard item and is sometimes overlooked during negotiations.

With the popularity of the early *"Star Trek"* series came swarms of fan clubs throughout the country, as most readers will remember. Throughout the years *after "Star Trek"* had gone off the air originally, and up to the new productions, the fan clubs of "Trekkies" across the country held big conventions and paid the cast members to make personal appearances at them and discuss the series and their roles in it. There were dozens and dozens of them, from which the actors made personal appearance monies down through all those subsequent years. Then, Paramount got wise and, with the new series and other contracts being made up, required that the cast members make no more appearances at such events on their own and that subsequent requests come to Paramount, with a quite different financial arrangement. I'm sure the reader can guess what that different financial arrangement was.

These are examples of how valuable *Merchandising* and *Participation* can turn out to be for the actor---even *many years after* a series has gone off the air. So...make sure you get what's coming to you. Those toys and fan clubs will be around long after the series is off the air, and you should continue to share in the enormous profits that can accrue from them.

233

MINI-SERIES CONTRACTS

The same conditions apply to Mini-Series as to regular episodic series, since that's exactly what they are, except that they have a small number of episodes of usually two-hour shows each, and then they're over. No hassles about second, third and fourth years.

With regard to a mini-series, however, your agent should be especially mindful that in all probability it will later be released for motion picture theatrical exhibition, at least in many foreign countries, and will go heavy on this particular point in negotiations. It occurs often, these "foreign releases" of what in domestic markets were simple mini-series.

Chapter Twenty-One

Commercials...Selling Products And Selling Yourself

Beginners---new faces not generally known yet, top costarring, starring and even internationally starring players...they all make commercials! It doesn't matter at what point in your career you make that first or that one-hundredth Class A national commercial which can bring you anywhere from about $5,000 bare minimum for a short run up to many thousands more for good long runs that are repeatedly brought back because they produce results with network prime time viewers. Any commercial you can do, do it happily and without any qualms. At one time those actors who also did commercials were looked down upon. Not anymore!

John Wayne made no commercials until he was almost ready to retire. Sir Laurence Olivier waited till sickness caused him concern about his life estate and persuaded him to do those camera commercials. James Garner and his "I am not Mrs. James Garner" TV wife Mariette Hartley didn't worry that *"Rockford Files"* star, and Ms. Hartley's dramatic specials often followed or preceded those commercials for the One Step camera. Sophia Loren didn't bat an eyelash about pushing her perfume. Bob Hope and even Frank Sinatra have done them. John Forsythe, on *"Dynasty"*, was on television far more frequently than most people may have realized with his voice-overs for any number of products, as was and still is the mellifluously hearty voice of Lloyd Bridges for many others.   Sandy Duncan's career started with her old Dodge commercials, and much more recently, by then a top star, she has happily romped through a field or sat on a sofa avidly chomping on those thin wheat wafers....for very big bucks.

If you could read the contracts of those stars and others for those many, many products you'd probably faint!

The actress who cha-cha-cha'd with a cat, Miss Patsy Garrett, became wealthy with her "cat dancing". The lovable character actor who for years squeezed the Charmin regularly and the lady who for years proclaimed that Folgers was "the very best kind" were able to retire on their annual earnings which could have gone on and on forever. And the droll character actor and comic who complained that servicing Maytag washing machines was a dull life didn't have to live a dull life himself in private beause the income more than amply made up for his eloquent boredom on screen and for the fact that too much overexposure for Maytag made him undesirable for the comic TV and film roles that he had previously played.

The foregoing are mostly "exclusive" commercial contracts, and they run into six figures or perhaps even seven for those chosen to be the continuing spokespersons for certain products.

There are different kinds of commercials, though. There are _Class A_ (national) commercials which are set for national network showings by leading national blue chip advertisers for their products. The actors who get a crack at some of these can build mansions atop a Beverly Hills knoll wihin a few years. One of the author's people has done just that from the earnings from a scad of commercials which you see all the time, over and over, season after season because they're favorites of their sponsors.

How much you'll make from a Class A commercial depends of course upon how often it's run and how long it's telecast before being replaced by a new commercial pitch. Some even go off the air for a time and then come back for long runs again. Between their cycles the actor is receiving _Holding Fees_, and when they return to their buckshot scheduling the money starts rolling in again.

In addition to the Class A plums there are _Regionals_, _Wild Spots_, _Dealer Spots_ (types A and B), _Test Market_ commercials, _Non-Air_ commercials and probably a few more kinds.

Regionals are often for beers sold only in certain parts of the country, or supermarket chains and manufactured products which are also regional.

Wild Spots are usually 30 second or 15 second commercials for a manufactured product or a toy or something for which the manufacturer buys the air time for running whenever the station or network likes as long as a continuous spate of them are aired within a specified timespan.

Dealer Spots are produced and provided by the distributor of a national market product to dealers in many markets (cities are markets). The dealers or stores of any kind carrying the products buy the airtimes for

236

running them, directing people to the stores paying for the time. These are _Type A_. The _Type B_ dealer spots are provided by major chains to their own specific branches or franchised outlets, with the branches or outlets buying the airtime and directing viewers as to where they should go to buy.

Most actors are quite happy to accept the fairly low amount usually paid as a one day _Session Fee_. The chance of so much more money later more than justifies the low "session fee" in their minds. There are _On Camera_ session fees and _Voice-Over_ (not photographed) fees.

The basic contract for a commercial is usually for 21 months from the date of commencement of the first cycle of its use. If the producer desires it may also negotiate a separate _Holding Fee_ for another 13 weeks following that, negotiated at the time of the original employment. _Use Period_ is automatically renewed if the player isn't notified by the producer in advance of the termination date of the 21 months or 13 week period. The actor is kept up to date on when termination dates are coming up by the dates being shown on all vouchers attached to paychecks. The player can, however, refuse a renewal period if he likes by notification to the producer in advance.

Wild Spots and _Dealer Spots_ would be confusing to even a fantastic bookkeeper if he or she is not experienced in monitoring the use and revenues of commercials. It all depends on the number and kind of markets in which these commercials are telecast. For Type A's, for their six-month use period which goes with the session fee, there is the additional difference between the session fee and a figure in excess of $1,000 for on-camera appearance, payable 15 days after delivery of the commercial to dealers, if the markets include New York City. That standard figure of difference for on-camera appearance is lower if New York City isn't included. There are lesser figures for off-camera with New York included and for the same if New York isn't included. After these first market-determined amounts are paid the actor must wait for long periods before the rest of the income from these commercials can be expected to start arriving. Those later payments depend on the "units" (market packages) in which the commercials are run.

Type B spots also have their market-determined fees and later "unit" payments.

Wild Spots get unlimited use for 13 weeks. If the producer wants to continue the commercial, a _Holding Fee_ must be paid the actor. Again, the "units" applying to the different market packages determine the pay received after periods of telecasting.

If the actor should make a commercial, or at least participate as a _Principal_ player---whose face can be identified in the commercial, then later not be used in the commercial when it's edited and run, the session fee is all that will be received. This is called _Outgrading_. However, the producer is required to so notify the player within 60 days following employment or 15 days after first use. If such notification is furnished the producer has no further obligation to the player.

Downgrading means that the face is not identifiable in the commercial when it is finally edited. However, if the player still appears---though his face isn't recognizable in the commercial when it's run, "downgrading" means that if the producer furnishes the same notification the player is to simply receive one additional session fee at that time.

Upgrading isn't a common occurence, since the producer usually knows exactly what's going to be featured and what isn't ahead of time and has storyboards approved by the sponsor and advertising agency executives far out front. "Upgrading" means that when the commercial is in final cutting for use there's the discovery that a face not expected to be featured at all jumps out at everybody and appears valuable to be "upgraded". Being kept in the commercial, and in fact being featured and recognizable therein, the player is "upgraded" and receives residuals just like everybody else when the commercial is run. When this happens unexpectedly the producer is required to send a new contract to the player indicating that rather than being employed as an "extra" as planned the player's performance has become "principal".

Voice-Over people are much in demand in Hollywood and New York for all kinds of commercials. These folks are either attractive natural voices which sponsors feel will appeal to the broadest possible demographics in all sections of the country, or they are voice-trick people who can sound like a neworn baby or a wizened old man, a dog or cat or an automobile's carburetor if asked to. They also include dialect specialists who are authentic-sounding but who can still be easily understood in the dialect by "Middle America" audiences.

There are casting categories which are always most in demand. "Housewife" women, with no long hair and clean, un-madeup looks, are always one of the biggest lists in commercial agents' books. They sell everything from vacuum cleaners to lemonade, from detergents to window blinds and from feminine products to toothpaste. When they go on interviews they never dress fancily.

"Dads" and "Sportsmen" are two more categories in demand all the time, They turn down second cups that aren't Yuban; they slurp beer while a well known sports star talks in the foreground; they jump into the air beside Toyotas; they scowl when turned down for bank loans at all but that one more lenient bank; and they finally agree that the one oleomargarine does actually taste like butter. When these guys go on interviews their agents usually ask them to wear open-neck plaid shirts and casual pants. They usually have parted hair, by he way, if they're Caucasian, and neatly clipped hair if they're Black.

Then there are the "Coke and McDonald's" kids and teens. They're usually fairly thin, not fat---because otherwise they might appear to have gotten that way from too many Cokes or too many McDonald's fast food things. They're clean-looking, with geat smiles and "up" personalities. Again, these kids don't dress up for commercial interviews. They should be "just out of school and thirsty or hungry" young Middle Americans. Freckles can be a big plus.

The "Senior Citizens", being the largest sector of our population now, are also used more and more. They need something outstanding, though. The less "professional" they appear the better. Many older women have found themselves plunged into commercial acting careers suddenly by being picked off the street because of their smile and have soon found themselves turning that special smile on the Sparkletts water man as they hand him a cookie, or looking shocked at a dog food package changing its label right beore their eyes, or scandalizing their old women friends by running by on the sidewalk for their health, or even walking up to a counter and demanding "Where's the beef?"

Older men are usually "Grandaddies" telling their grandsons that Alpo is better than that other kind; telling their daughters that their brand of English muffin is the best after all; or being told by the druggist that Anacin is better in six ways.

The "High Fashion" type category dances or sips wine in a bistro under soft lighting, applies Ultima II in front of a mirror or walks by some gawkers on the sidewalk in that special bra. No perfume or hair product would be without its favorite model spokesperson. They're never anything but gorgeous and, yes, they *do* dress to the nines for commercial interviews. How can they be "worth" Clairol or demonstrate how soft Johnson & Johnson Baby Powder is if they're not beautiful?

The thing that most other commercial types have in common is that they must appear in interviews to be "just off Main Street" rather than just off Fifth or Madison Avenue. Just out of the five-and-dime in Wymore, Nebraska or Azusa, California is best.

Then there are the *Comedians* and *Comediennes*. They can be anything at all....and are. In recent years a lot of humor has come into commercials. Nyquil requires a veritable tongue-twister of an actor to say what he should have gotten at the drugstore but didn't; those "other" banks where the loans are always turned down require some marvelous deadpan players; the "other" transmission repair places require convincing tongue-in-cheek, put-on actors; and Winstron Tires turning down all the gimmick peddlers who approach the desk of Big Sam require some fantastic let-down expressions that comedians excel at. One actor has risen swiftly to stardom by simply leaning his big nose into a fish-eye camera lens and making a bore of himself until a car window is wound up and pins him.

Some fine commercial actors are signed with agents who represent for both "theatrical" (motion picture and television roles) as well as "commercials", but most of the really successful commercial folks advise that unless the agency is large enough to have a special department handling commercials while other departments handle other things it's best to be signed with a strictly commercial agency. The commercial production offices and advertising agencies are usually in parts of the city far from the motion picture and television studios and production centers. Certainly a one person agency head can't hope to cover film and television casting and still cover the commercial field effectively too.

Also, commercials are cast by representatives---usually account executives---from advertising agencies that represent client's products. Those representatives of large sponsors' products, in advance of coming to Hollywood for casting, make their first calls to strictly *commercial* agent....usually agents with whom they especially like to deal when casting. It would be very unusual for these out-of-towners to give first calls or for that matter any calls at all to the agencies that handle both theatrical and commercial clients unless the *Commercial Departments* of those agencies are the main departments at those agencies.

Upon signing with a commercials agent you'll have to furnish that agency with your list of commercials done in the past and those currently running or on holding fees toward possible resumption. This is damned important! There's the dreaded word "*conflict*" in the commercials world. A "conflict" occurs when you have an automobile commercial running somewhere---even if not in major markets at the time---and you'd like to do that commercial for another maker's car or transmission repair or auto horn or something. While you may not think there's any conflict the producer certainly may think there is, and you won't get the commercial or even be sent out for it. Betty Crocker conflicts with a local or regional bakery. California Cellars wine can be a borderline conflict with Schlitz Beer or Dr. Pepper. McDonald's certainly conflicts with Mightyburger, but it's also borderline with any other fast food item.

Your commercials list is studied by the agent and continually updated very carefully as you do more, to protect you from the big trouble you can get into if you do conflicting commercials which are in use periods at the same time. When you've been released from a commercial and the producr has assured your agent that it won't be run again, then you're free to do those productions' commercials which would have been "conflicts" before....but normally the subsequent producer won't want to risk the reviving of that earlier commercial anyhow.

You're hired for a commercial when you accept a call to work or receive a script or a contract or a promise of employment with date thereof or even without.

Once hired, you must remember that the commercial definitely has you, even if you should suddenly be offered a nice guest starring role in a series with work dates that conflict.

Some years ago one of the author's actor clients, scheduled to do three Jantzen commercials on Monday and Tuesday of the next week, on Friday got a guest starring role in the "*Future Cop*" series at Paramount which would begin shooting on Tuesaday. The commitment to the Jantzen commercial---even though no paper had been signed---under SAG rules had the actor firmly, unless a contract was already in hand on paper from "*Future Cop*" and of course no actual contract had been signed yet.

The actor decided to risk violating the SAG rule and do the guest starring role for his acting career's sake, since he wasn't hurting for money after doing scads of other commercials. His agent---this author---had to get on the phone to New York---after hours there, with offices closed---and on an emergency basis get him out of the Jantzen commercial with the head office of Jantzen in New York. It wasn't easy. The actor could actually have been brought up on charges by SAG and sued by Jantzen, but as it turned out he wasn't, because Jantzen frequently used him, liked him and felt they'd like to use him again someday. You must be aware of the special conditions pertaining to how you become committed to a commercial as opposed to being committed on paper for regular film and television roles.

It's said that commercial agents have their "A" and "B" lists, by the way. It's easy to understand that these agents must make deisions, each time calls come in, as to which of their clients will most likely stand the best chances of getting the commercials if sent out; which ones should never be sent out on the regional, wild spot or test market commercials at all; which ones will most likely handle well the requirements thrown at them in particular interviews; and which ones are borderline as to behavior at such interviews. Some of the agents' clients are sent out almost every day. Some sit for long periods between calls and are probably on the agents' "B" lists for some reasons.

However, if you want to go on a lot of interviews and maybe get a lot of commercials, the bottom line that we'd recommend is to get with a top _commercials_ agency, even if you have to be on its "B" list till it gets to know you better. It's better to be on the "B" list of a top agency that gets many, many more calls from commercial casting people than it is to be on the "A" list of a small agency that tries to handle both "theatrical" and "commercials" and gets about one commercial casting call every six months.

The commercials field, like any other field, respects its _specialists_ and like any other field doesn't like to waste precious time fiddling with those agencies that don't specialize in signing the best available commercial talents, that don't keep staffs that understand the differences among the different kinds of commercials, that don't understand the special language and terms used in calling for standard commercial types, and that don't maintain special accountants that know how to keep track of residuals, standard commercial use periods, holding fees and other agency responsibilities that are unique to commercial agencies and are gobbledygook to many primarily "theatrical" agents who try to wear two hats and do a poor job of it.

There are many, many of the smaller agencies in Hollywood that prefer to sign all clients for _all_ kinds of possible employments, just in case the client may get lucky through their own efforts or contacts and with no work by the agent manage to land a Class A National commercial or some other form of nicely paying employment. Many of these agencies have no ability to handle, no knowledge of or contacts in, and in fact no interest at all in the commercials field. There's absolutely _no_ value in signing with these agencies to be represented for commercials. Theatrical, maybe, if everything's right. But the commercials field is so specialized that you're wasting time if you think this kind of agency can handle you for that field.

In fact, if the agency is pretending it's really involved with commercials, yet is a small, one-person office, there's no possible way that agent can handle you for both theatrical and commercials and it might be a shrewd judgment that if the agent even pretends he or she can handle both effectively that agent is misrepresenting its representation and might not be trustworthy in other matters either. Keep looking.

Bottom line: If you feel you have top potential for commercials, don't settle for an agency that handles both "theatrical" and "commercials" unless it's definitely known and respected for both. Some are. Look till you find one of these or else insist on having a separate commercial agent.

Chapter Twenty-Two

Your Own Holding Company...
For Holding Onto Your Earnings

If and when you reach the point in your career where there is a fairly sure and fairly continuous flow of income in the six or seven figure bracket---no matter the source from which it comes, it's time to change your operating status.

Some remain "stars" for long periods and still wind up with little money left at the ends of their lavish lifestyle careers. What they haven't thrown around foolishly, often self-indulgently, during their boom years, they sooner or later have to drain for keeping up appearances when the leaner years come, as they do come for many.

But some---usually those who've been smart enough to have good financial advisors during their boom years---have followed the good advice they've gotten from those advisors and incorporated themselves by forming what are called "*Holding Companies*" *or* "*Loanout*" companies.

Holding companies are formed by many top-income people---whether actors or other professionals---for, literally, the purpose of "holding" onto as much of their top-income-period money as they can.

When a holding company's corporation is being formed, you'll probably want to be the President; your wife or daughter or grandfather can be Vice President of the corporation and your infant son or daughter can be the corporation's Secretary of record...if he or she can sign at the bottom of the paper. An adult member is of course best for Treasurer, though, so they can at least sign their name on double-signature checks drawn on the corporation's account.

It's simple to call for the forms to be sent out to you by the Office of The Secretary of State for your city or county and come out with an established corporate "holding company".

Your corporation can then "loan you out"....and receive those big checks for your services as a corporation employee. After contracts are negotiated between your corporation---not you personally---and the companies that want to employ you, it---the corporation---is committed to furnish your services. The checks, when they arrive, are deposited in the corporation account and you are issued checks from that account in whatever amounts you as President determine to be your rightful salary from the corporation. As President, you certainly have the right to tell the Treasurer what to pay you.

A corporation can hold onto lots more than an individual can. It's able to legitimately write off more expense items for business operation, equipment, rental of space, services, a company car or two for your exclusive use and other things like advertising, promotion, business trips, etc. A more limited number of these can apply if you're an individual, unincorporated taxpayer receiving those large salaries and residuals, production points and other special benefits of taxable kinds.

The majority of the top stars have "loan-out" (holding) companies. The studios and production companies are accustomed to being notified that all contracts are to be signed by a corporate officer, if not actually the star himself as that corporate officer, and that all checks are to be made out to the corporation rather than to the star.

Corporate entities have more legitimate and acceptable tax shelters available to them than do individuals. Corporations can spend venture capital on projects----film and television projects included----that would not be tax-deductible for individuals. Large undertakings in parnership with studios on films to star the corporation's president are easier for corporation lawyers to work out than for your very qualified personal attorney. Amortization of original investments is easier to handle in tax terms, and your personal staff is more easily and more feasibly enlarged.

It's an important thing to consider if things start popping for you all of a sudden...and that's generally how they happen in Hollywood. Today's famine is often tomorrow's feast. But if you don't have your own holding company during peak income periods the reverse can be true later.

Chapter Twenty-Three

The Top Rungs
Of The Career Ladder
Are Very Slippery!

The time may come---in fact will come for many readers---when you're steadily receiving some form of "Starring" billing whenever you work. It will feel like you're finally making it to the top. But by industry standards you'll still have a long way to go.

You see, there are "bottom stars" as well as "top stars". A *Bottom Star* is someone who has had their shot at the whole ball of wax and has blown it in some way, but still has that residual face-recognition and name-awareness that pulls those different forms of "starring" billing. At least the industry knows who you are, even if the public still calls you "Whatsizname", knowing they've seen you in many roles but not being able to remember your name.

Your face and your talent are still worth good, top roles in television series episodes or in "also starring" roles in decent motion pictures. It doesn't necessarily mean that you've slipped backward if you're a "bottom star"....it simply means that you're *not moving still higher* as rapidly as you may have at one time. You've fallen into a treading of the water in the same position over a long period. There are reasons, usually, for this temporary or sometimes permanent stagnation.

You may not have changed agents when you should have, after finding out that your agent wasn't as skillful a negotiator as you needed at some point and some opportunities were missed. You may have failed to exploit a series starring role by getting a press agent to blow you up further in the public's eyes while you had your big chance. You may have failed to push for better and more involvement in a series when you knew that you were one of the regulars actually carrying the series in popularity and ratings. You may have been too eager to accept pennies when you could have had dollars along the way, or you may have been one of those actors who considered your roles more important than your billing and your salary, ignoring the unfortunate fact of Hollywood higher-ups measuring actors' worth in terms of these two yardsticks. You may have taken off for Tahiti after that one major picture and spent all your savings, feeling you had earned the trip, and been out of the country for too long while people were calling for you and your agent was committing suicide because you weren't available here in Hollywood.

Or you may have left that wonderful, caring agent who had built your career and handled it skillfully into good starring roles then saw you answer the siren call of a large, prestigious agency that offered you the moon but had actually seen your star rising swiftly and threatening the position of one of its top actors, so secretly persuaded you into its stable so that agency could keep you out of the running for its favored client's roles. There are several stories of this happening.

Or you may simply be one of those people who, for one reason or another, just isn't recognized as having any special spark, any uniquely magnetic personality, any sex appeal or any of that craziness that major studios recognize as big boxoffice potential because of escapades that, one after another in a constant stream, get into the tabloids and create curiosity.

Although called a "star" in the industry, you may be of absolutely *no* value at the boxoffice and as a result have a low "*TVQ Rating*" as well.

The TVQ---which everybody denies exists at all---is a very real thing. This author has seen it---in computer printout--- countless times. It's published in secret and used in secret. Through assertedly polling the public, an organization back east determines how many people polled even know your face, whether they like your work and personality and whether they would want to see you in more things. Top stars who continually play leads must now have "*high TVQ*" ratings. Those who don't simply don't help get bank financing for pictures or insure network ratings enough to work as often in series, whether as regulars or guest stars.

SAG has tried in every manner possible to stop the TVQ evaluation of actors, since its ratings are highly questionable and it is, in reverse, actually a "blacklist"---or a "whitelist" that has the same effect on too many very fine actors' careers if they're not high in those TVQ numbers. In the cold, computerized world of today, though, the TVQ isn't going to go away, even though network executives continue to assure all of us that it already has.

The TVQ is responsible for many, many actors with enviable talents remaining in this "bottom star" level over longer periods of time than they would have to otherwise. It has nothing to do with their talents. It has nothing to do with the job market. It only means that their public recognition---and those damnable TVQ respondents, whoever and wherever they are polled---have prevented those actors from becoming "bankable"---for film financing---or at least not being "ratings risks"---from network series standpoints, and therefore they're never on the top of the list for consideration for the plums.

In the "bottom star" level you're still getting excellent billing, almost always in the main titles and on separate cards, in TV guest appearances and even occasionally in major films. You're sometimes sent out on personal appearance tours for the films you've recently appeared in. You're being wined and dined by producers asking you to read their scripts. You're being granted more and more special accommodations when you work---whether on a studio lot or on a location shoot. And your agent is actually turning down some things which are being grabbed up by has-been stars and this year's blossoming favorites.

It's really not a bad position to be in, even if you have to stay there forever. There are many people who do just that...never becoming major boxoffice stars or names on John W. Public's lips or in gossip columns...always remaining "Whatsiznames" whose faces but nothing else are well known. They work regularly in excellent roles, but the public can't tell you who they are.

Certainly, the next step up is the hardest of all to break into.

THE BOX-OFFICE STAR!

How many real boxoffice stars are there in the world at this time? Not too many. Each person who arrives at the door of this hallowed hierarchy must (1) bring audiences of all ages into theatres and produce revenues for Gulf & Western or Coca-Cola or some other owner of one of the big studio lots and production companies; (2) get fan mail enough to keep one secretary or several secretaries busy tabulating the studios' own individual versions of the TVQ list; (3) keep his position through pressagentry salaried by himself rather than by a studio as it used to be handled; (4) pretend to be worth millions more than he actually is, so publicity is promoted saying his salary for each motion picture or television series lead is the highest in history; and (5) be able to say "no" to more pictures than he says "yes" to without worrying about a mortgate or six figure bank loan coming due; and (6) be willing to sit idle for months on end until his agent and manager can agree to let him read the next picture which will guarantee the desired role, the desired billing, the desired salary---by then probably well up in the seven figures level---and the right supporting cast, over which our star should have some contractual control by then.

Often the name will now appear *above the title* on prints of the picture and in all space (newspaper and magazine) advertising and on all billboard advertising. Sometimes producers eager for his services will have offered "points" in the production---a "net profit-sharing" device which has become suspect in recent times because of "creative bookkeeping" (chicanery) on the part of studios and releasing and distributing companies. When "points" are finally accepted in lieu of salary dollars out front, "net" should be a dirty word and not appear in the star's contract. "Net" points mean that after both legitimate and possibly illegitimate---even flat out crooked---"expense items" involved in production, pre-production, post-production, studio services and facilities, the obtaining of a releasing organization, the obtaining of a distributing organization, and the providing of many prints for theatre rentals, the actor may see only a few pennies...seldom many of the anticipated (promised) big dollars!

In this level, scripts are turned down with regularity. The actor and his agent stay up nights and have big hassles as to which scripts will help his career, and the other script offerers can simply ask and be told "No."

Money ranges too widely in this "Top U. S. Boxoffice Star" category to even estimate it here. You get what you can, after lengthy agent negotiations and all the propaganda your press agent can manufacture to help the agent's position in bargaining.

When a picture shoots on location you can get---and should certainly have it in your contract that you shall receive---huge per diems, the best available hotel accommodations, big expense accounts, your personal staff transported to the location and maintained there for you, a car for your private use, special concessions such as the right to leave the location to return to Hollywood for a day or two when Polaroid or Rice Krispies needs you to do another commercial for which you have that long term "spokesperson" contract, or the right to take a week off between certain specified dates to race at Daytona.

When you reach this position it might be wise to be represented by an agency which also has a good Literary Department. To reach this point in the first place, you're probably already with one of the Goliaths.

The Literary Department of an agency represents Writers' Guild members who write screenplays of all kinds, and the agency which has such a department is often the "packager" (putting script, producer, director and talent together for the picture). It's a family affair, often---with the writer's original script being sent to the *star* (another agency client) to get comments and some indication that the script is something the star would like to do; sometimes the star contacts a *director* (who's also handled by the agency) and they huddle about the script's chances, after which sometimes the writer revises the screenplay with the star's and director's wishes in mind, and the whole project---the script, with a director and a star both eager to do it---is then taken to the head of the agency, who assigns a *producer* (another of the agency's clients), who takes it to the studios and production companies to get it produced or takes it to the bank to obtain financing as an independent project.

These "packages" are bankable or not---meaning that they have enough going for them out front that a production company can get bank financing on the strength of those names committed to participate if the project is produced.

In other words, such an agency---if it handles Writers, Producers and Directors and is therefore probably also a WGA-franchised "packager"---can act as an entrepreneur, bringing together all the elements of the proposed production. In the end all that has to be done---with the script written, the star committed to do the starring role and the director available subject to the wishes of whoever can be gotten to produce it, is to find that important "whoever", the producer. If the star is of sufficient boxoffice appeal magnitude the finding of the producer is easy. He or she is also a client of the same agency.

More and more these days, feature films are produced under these exact circumstances. The big agencies' actor client lists are assuredly consulted out front when scripts are initially submitted by one of the agencies' writers, and it's not infrequent that top starring roles occur in that manner for people just breaking into boxoffice starring levels----simply because they're clients of the agencies handling the scripts.

Of course at this "top U. S. boxoffice starring" level the decisions of which scripts and which roles to accept are critical. Notice that word "accept". There are plenty of scripts submitted when someone is a boxoffice draw. There are production companies clamoring for signatures on contracts, many of which have to be turned down for one reason or another.

At this point it should be *major motion pictures and nothing else*. To special guest star on television might indicate that the star needs money. The name is always *above the title* except in some special case where it doesn't work for the main titles format of the series---which of course will be seldom, because this level of star, not the script, is the drawing power for the film by then. Ask for the moon and it will probably be given unto you, over and above the astronomical salary you'll receive. The production company will be very aware that it's _your name_ which, once committed to the project, enables them to get the bank financing. It's _your name_ that will get much publicity for the picture even before it goes into release. It's _your name_ which will bring people swarming to the boxoffice. You are the film, and they'll be happy to show their gratitude in almost any manner you may ask.

There's still another level, though. And you'll hardly know it when you get there.

TOP INTERNATIONAL STAR!

There are few differences between a "top U. S. boxoffice star" and a "top *international* star". It's only a few million dollars difference in salary. And you've already been getting the best treatment anyone can give you before you arrive at the level where everyone in Europe, England, Austraila, South Africa and the Orient also knows who you are and sees all your films.

The main difference is that in addition to many more requests for interviews with columnists of *The New York Times*, *Newsweek*, *The Inquirer* and *People* in the U. S. there will now be invitations to spend a few weeks touring Japan for your fans there or making a good will jaunt to China or Outer Somewhere-or-Other. Also, the pace of meetings with business managers, stock brokers, PR people, photographers, producers, agents, personal managers and Las Vegas gambling casino heads will be quickened.

Your several apartment complexes and condominiums in Manhattan will demand some of your attention between times, as will your diamond mine stocks in Africa. Sometimes you'll simply take a vacation to get away from it all and do a *film!* You'll be tied up in court cases, with your lawyer making most of the appearances to help you avoid autograph seekers, when you're suing Universal, Paramount, 20th Century-Fox, Columbia and other studios to try to collect the "points" in productions which have been far less, after "creative bookkeeping" in studio offices, than you know they should be.

You'll be so busy, as a top international star, that you won't be able to concentrate effectively on the current filming and will swear to confidantes that you're going to retire.

But you're on top, and the world knows it. It's sweet revenge---if that's what's important by then---on the people back in your little home town who swore you'd be a failure because you couldn't do anything but act while your brothers were out selling farm machinery and raising families. Those folks won't know, back in your old home town, that you're probably going to AA meetings under court order after a long period of alcoholism brought on by stress; taking sleeping pills to sleep at night because of the many industries and companies you have stock in, the many ex-wives or ex-husbands you're paying alimony to (ever since finding out that they only married you in the first place for your money and influence), and the IRS controversies you're embroiled in; or the fact that with all your success you get lonely once in a while and wish you could be living quietly back in that small town, surrounded by good friends and neighbors rather than the hangers-on who may be your only real pals by now.

Most of you will never reach that pinnacle of success at the top of the acting ladder, but if you do, take a moment and look back and reflect on how simple and happy your life was when you were still on the bottom rung.

STAYING ON TOP ONCE YOU GET THERE

While some may be able to skip most of the upward climbing described in this book and make it to the top in one big leap through some fluke or lucky break or miracle of casting genius, directorial omniscience, producer cunning, promotion saturation and boxoffice windfall...it's the _staying_ there that matters in the long run.

There are many "overnight sensations" who fade within twenty-four hours or so. There are those jokes about how swiftly fame can slip and careers fade. One of these---often quoted in Hollywood especially---is: "Who's John Whatsizname?".....".Get me John Whatsizname!".....".Get me _a_ John Whatsizname!".....".Get me a _young_ John Whatsizname!".....and finally, again, "Who's John Whatsizname?" The circle can move swiftly for some.

To stay at the pinnacle of top stardom over a long period you'll have to be willing to say no to about 90% of the scripts brought to your managers. You'll need a _script reader_ to do the hours and hours of reading and then report the outstanding possibilities to you for your own reading. You'll need to have somebody scouting for scripts you can option or purchase outright so _you_ can produce them yourself to insure that _nobody else_ will get them.

You'll need to fake romances, divorces, sexual triangles, fan club events and fights with producers to stay in the scandal sheet columns so you'll be on the tips of housewives' tongues. Even when nominated for an Academy Award you'll have to deplete half your bank account inserting big, full-page ads to publicize the nomination and promote your chances of winning another statuette.

You'll have to practically move your press agent into a guest cottage on your estate because you need to be with that aide so much of the time. You'll need to forego any and all private life most of the time to afford clamoring interviewers all those requested hours of your time.

You'll be paying big salaries---to press agents, office staffs, officers of your private corporation and several lawyers to handle libel and copyright suits. You'll be paying six-figure commissions---10% to your agent and between 15% and 50% to your manager (on that contract signed so many years earlier that had all those escalation clauses in it), and you'll be getting letters every day from starving actors, abandoned mothers of fourteen, stray and runaway kids who've seen your films and think you look like a soft touch. Charity organizations of all nature will be hounding you regularly for charitable donations and appearances or public service announcements to contribute your help on fund-raising drives.

In other words, you'll be so busy staying on top that you'll have a hard time remembering that once you just wanted to be an actor. But it's the name of the game. Once you get there, you, like everybody else who's been there, will try your damnedest to stay.

There are no top stars who feel secure in their gilded aeries. They've become accustomed to top star treatment....not only by fans but also by people in the industry. It's a heady experience, and one that doesn't go away easily. Nobody wants to hecome a "has-been"!   But it can happen. And once an actor reaches that top position and can hang onto it for a while it's worth all the foregoing problem experiences just to stay there. If you're one of those who's able to get to that lofty place someday, savor it while you can.

Chapter Twenty-Four

So...Do You Still Want
A Hollywood Film Acting Career?

If, after all this---and after learning that our streets aren't paved with gold and our trees don't grow money, also that you can starve for a long time before getting a single break---you still want to come to Hollywood, you probably will sooner or later.

If you're that determined, then it's best to not put it off "till the right time comes" or "till the kids grow up" or "till I can leave Mom alone" or till anything else. Wait too long and, if and when you do come, people will wonder where you've been and why you didn't head this way earlier in life to begin your career on a professional level if that's what you've really wanted.

Everybody, everywhere, would come to Hollywood to act in films if they thought they had a chance. You're in a very small minority if you haven't dreamed of it and thought "Someday!"

But if you're one of those who *absolutely has to come* to Hollywood---because that's what you want more than anything else, and because you know you're qualified to compete in one of the toughest rat races there are....then hop in the car or on a plane and come.

At least you'll be one of those who---after reading this book and getting some of those other publications referred to in an early chapter---will know much more about what you're getting yourself into and what to do with what you've got to offer than hundreds of thousands of others who've come.

I wish you success. Also luck. You'll need a lot of that, no matter what.

ADDENDA

Terms Film Actors
Need To Know

Although there's no law that says actors must know a lot of the technical terms used in the filming process, it often gives some feeling of security to know what all those technicians, the director, the cameraman and others are talking about in what might otherwise sound like a lot of mumbo-jumbo. The following terms aren't all, by any means, but they're probably the ones the actor will profit most from understanding and having available for use when they're helpful:

ADDED SCENES: Additional filming for which a cast member is called back to shoot additional (new) footage after a picture is completed.

ANSWER PRINT: The print that comes back from the Lab ready to be copied in many "release prints" for theatres, television networks and stations.

ASSISTANT: The First Assistant Director...more often called "The First".

ATMOSPHERE: The extras.

BACKSTEPPING: A method of hitting marks, not all that dependable.

BACKGROUND: Either actors, extras or scenery behind foreground players.

BLUES: Blue (usually first revision) pages of the script.

BOOM: The sound crew member who controls the mike extended above the actors' heads; also the "boom" from which the mike is suspended.

BOUNCING: Bouncing up and down by actors. A no-no quickly stopped.

BUZZER: The buzzer on a set that with a long single blast quiets all noise around the set, either on a soundstage or on an exterior location; also the buzzer that with two short blasts signals "all clear", the shot is finished and noise is permissible.

CU: This, in a script, indicates "closeup" shot of the actor's face or something else.

CAMERA CAR: The car that has a camera mounted on it for filming car chase and other traveling car shots.

CAMERAMAN: The Director of Photogaphy, or the Cinematographer. He sets up shots requested by the director, or shots of his own suggestion, checks lighting, lenses and filters, operates the camera during rehearsals of shots and sometimes also during actual filming of the takes.

CALL: The actor's call with details of when and where and to whom the actor is to report for filming.

CALL SHEET: Published by the Production Department, showing all work calls for cast and crew, planned filming locations, scenes to be shot and equipment needed.

CHALKS: The marks made around the actor's feet during the rehearsal of a shot. His "marks".

CHARACTER DESCRIPTION: This is almost always found at the *very first appearance* of the character in the script.

CHEATING: A slang expression for what actors playing foreground must do when playing a scene with actors standing behind them.

CHECK AUTHORIZATION FORM: What you've signed for your agent to send to Payroll Departments when you work that directs that your paycheck be mailed to the agency for deducting of the agent's 10% commission before issuing you the agency's own check to you for the balance.

CLAPBOARDS: Mostly called "Slates", the two-boarded slates that are clapped loudly in front of the actor's face or an object just as a shot is starting, so the visual "marker" (identification information) on the work picture can be synced up in the Sync Room for the running of both work picture and dialogue track, synchronized, in "dailies".

CLEAN ENTRANCE, CLEAN EXIT: Being all the way out of the shot either before walking into it or when exiting a shot.... "clean" meaning all the way out or in.

CLOSEUP: A shot including little more than the actor's face.

COMMERCIAL COMPOSITE: The usually two-sided photo print of actors seeking commercials, with one large photo on the front and several "in character" shots on the back with the actor in wardrobe, using props, in various locations that suggest what the actor is right for.

CONTINUITY: The person who on a complex. many detailed shooting is responsible for the "matching" of all details in all sequences of shots.

CONVERSION RATE: A contract provision that can if desired convert a day player's daily salary rate to a three-day or weekly rate which will not be as much as the same amount of work period at the daily rate would be.

CO-STAR: The billing level which immediately follows "Starring" in opening or end credits of films and television.

COVERAGE: Additional takes of scenes from other angles; reaction shots; closeups; medium shots; closeups of hands doing something; a clock ticking away, etc.

COVERING: Accidentally covering another actor or something else by an actor.

CUT!: This is yelled to stop a shot in progress or finished.

CREW: The technicians of all kinds....Cameramen, Sound Crew, Lighting Crew, Grips, Drivers, Makeup, Hairdresser, etc.

DAILIES: The previous day's "rushes" (all takes), synced up for early morning or sometimes lunch break viewing by the Director, the Producer and perhaps others.

DAILY: The contract for an actor hired for either a single day of work or the type of contract for an actor who's to be paid at a "daily" rate rather than a "weekly" rate.

DAY PLAYER: An actor who customarily plays one-day engagements.

DEAL MEMO: The draft of a series player's contract sent by the producer to the actor's agent representing the tentative terms of the series contract proposed.

DIALOGUE DIRECTOR: Usually a friend of the director who knows his or her tastes, who "runs scenes" with actors before time for their actual filming and reports to the director to save time when some problems are evident that the director won't yet know about.

DOWNGRADING: In a commercial, if someone expected to be a "principal" (face recognizable in the finished commercial) becomes unrecognizable in the final version of the commercial.

DUPE NEG: What the actor asks a Photo Reproduction Lab to make up from which 8x10's can be duplicated.

DISSOLVE: A slow disappearing of one scene and the slow emerging of another shot, marked in editing and accomplished in the Lab. The actor should anticipate that the end of the scene will involve some silent footage before "Cut!" will be called by the Director at the end of the shot, or after "Action" at the start of a shot.

DOLLY: The mount for the camera, or the action when the camera moves toward, away from or with the scene's action.

DOUBLE: Does stunts and hazardous actions while made to appear to be the actor.

DRIFTING: An actor drifting from one position in a shot to another, usually blocking something by doing so.

DRIVE-ON: Permission to drive the actor's own car onto the lot and park near where shooting is planned, or even next to the soundstage itself.

DROP-PICKUP: A Screen Actors Guild concession that allows actors to work one day, be paid, then be called back after a period of time to resume a role.

DRY RUN: A rehearsal before filming a shot.

DUBBING: The adding of music track, sound track and special sound effects in the post-production work on a film. Also refers to an actor "dubbing" of a different language over the original dialogue track.

EDITOR: The man or woman who cuts the film together in the "cutting room".

END CREDITS: The lists----usually the character names with the actors who played the roles; the crew members' titles and names; etc.

EPISODE: A single show segment of a continuing series.

EST. SHOT: This is a suggestion to the Cameraman of an "establishing shot" to *establish* a place, a building or something else.

EXECUTIVE PRODUCER: The head honcho of a production company or one of the top producers for such a company. He or she plans projects, assigns them to Supervising Producers for handling and then rides herd on the projects from inception through to completion.

EXT.: In the scene description, means "Exterior".

FAVORED NATIONS: This is the standard phrase guaranteeing that no other player will receive a higher salary in the motion picture or in a television series production than the actor to whom "Favored Nations" is contractually promised.

FEATURED: This is the billing given to the less important roles in film and television. It normally follows the "Co-Starring" billings in end credit listings.

FINAL CUT: This is what finally meets the approval of the producer, director and technicians before it's dubbed (with the adding of music track, special sound effects, etc.) and sent to the Lab for answer printing.

FIRMING: The "setting" (official hiring) of the actor to definitely play the role.

FIRM START DATE: The date a production company promises to an actor as the date of starting the actor's employment.

FIRST: See "Assistant" and "First Assistant Director".

FIRST POSITION: The position where an actor is directed to be located for the start of a shot.

FIRST TEAM!: The call for the actors to return to the set for filming as the "Second Team" (their stand-ins) are retired after the setting of lighting for a shot.

FITTING FEE: Extra payment for having to go to the Wardrobe Department or elsewhere to be fitted for wardrobe.

FORCE MAJEURE: The clause in a contract which allows the producer to stop production, whether expecting to resume or not, under certain unexpected or catastrophic conditions.

FOREGROUND: Action closest to the camera.

FOREIGN FILMS: Films produced by production companies based in foreign countries...over which SAG has no jurisdiction!

GOLDEN TIME: That overtime which is still later than simple overtime, time-and-a-half and double-time hours used in figuring cast and crew pay.

GREENS or **GREEN PAGES**: Usually the set of third revision pages of the script, to be substituted for like-numbered pages previously received.

GRIPS: The crew members who move, hold and carry things on the set.

GUARANTEE: The minimum employment period guaranteed the actor in a contract.

HAIRDRESSER: Combs out and touches up women's hair.

HEADS: What "closeups" are sometimes called.

HEADSHOTS: Actors' professional photos, usually of just the head.

HIGH HAT: A low to the ground camera mount.

HOLDING FEE: A fee paid an actor to keep the actor available until something starts, resumes or airs.

HONEY WAGON: The portable john truck on locations.

INSERT STAGE: Where "cutaway" shots are made that involve things like a hand holding a note, a clock ticking, a hand ringing a doorbell, etc.

INT.: In the scene description, means "Interior" shot.

INTERMEDIATE CUT: That working cut of a picture prepared when a director or producer wants to see some changes prior to "final cut" preparation.

KILL THE BLOWERS!: The yell to turn off airconditioners on a soundstage set.

LAPEL MIKE: The small microphone hidden somewhere on an actor who doesn't speak loudly enough for ideal recording of speeches or when it's impossible to have a boom mike hanging close over the actors' heads in a shot. Actors talking as they walk along sidewalks are often fitted with lapel mikes.

LEFT FRAME: To your right when you're facing the camera.

LINES: The speeches of your role in the script.

LIP-SYNC: Actor lip-syncing lines synchronously with silent footage running on a screen.

LOCATION: Shooting that's anywhere outside the studio lot, even if on a nearby street.

LOCATION CASTING DIRECTOR: The person who calls for interview the actors and extras, local residents of location areas where films are shooting, and handles their casting and first day work call details.

LOCATION MANAGER: When a film is preparing to shoot at a distant, usually out of state location, the Location Manager is in charge of the small cadre of personnel sent out to prepare everything---housing for staff, crew and cast members; use permits for shooting at planned locations; scouting of more locations in the area; rounding up of local crews, etc. During the actual filming, the Location Manager is still in charge of such details.

LONG SHOT: When action is distant from the camera.

LOOPING: Re-recording dialogue while listening to a playback of original dialogue recorded with action on the set, to produce better dialogue track. The actor is sent to the "Looping Stage" for this.

(M.O.S.): In scene description, means "Music or Sound" rather than dialogue track.

MAKEUP: Either the Studio Makeup Department or the man or woman on the set who does the job.

MARKS: Chalk marks or tapes on the floor or sidewalk to mark feet positions the actor is expected to start on, to walk onto or stand on for a shot.

MASTER: A shot which usually includes large or moving action. One of the very first shots taken of a scene. The actor must remember all details of movement, position, etc., because he must duplicate them skillfully in the additional shots of portions of the same scene when they're done later.

MATCHING: The art of duplicating all actions, positions, handling of props, etc., in additional shots of same scenes.

MEAL PENALTY: When meal breaks don't come after filming for periods specified by SAG, a meal penalty is assessed over and above the actor's salary for the day.

MEDIUM SHOT: Shows most of your body, sometimes wih others in the shot also.

MERCHANDISING: The actor's contracted share in items sold or licensed by production companies that bear his or her likeness and/or his or her character's likeness in a role.

MILEAGE: The amount paid an actor for gas mileage when he or she drives own car to location.

MINIMUM: The term used to indicate that the actor will receive the SAG-regulated minimum salary and no more. (It's standard for actors to receive "minimum plus ten" or "scale plus ten" so the agency can receive its ten percent.)

MIXER: The Sound Crew member who controls the volume levels of sound recording---to maximize dialogue and minimize other sounds or noise.

MORALS CLAUSE: The clause that authorizes the firing of an actor if he or she does something during filming that offends public standards.

MULTIPLE CONTRACT: A not often issued contract nowadays, employing an actor to appear in several pictures for a studio or production company over a period of time.

MUST JOIN: Station 12 at the Screen Actors Guild reports to casting people that a proposed cast member is a "Must Join", meaning that he or she must come to SAG and join before being allowed to work. Also, actors are called by SAG "Must Join" people if they have perhaps done their first film under the *Taft-Hartley Law* and must join SAG prior to their next employment in a SAG-signatory film.

NUMBER ONE POSITION (or "**FIRST POSITION**"): The "marks" position where the actor is to start for a shot.

(O.S.): When this appears with a character's speech it indicates that the speech is heard "off screen".

ON A BELL!: Called out when ready to make a take. Then comes the long buzzer sound signalling "Quiet!"

ON OR ABOUT: This is the phrase used to cover the production, when setting an actor for a role, a little more flexibly as to actual working date in case of some problem delaying shooting start for the actor by a day or so.

OPENING CREDITS: The credits---usually Producers, Director, Stars' names---at the start of a film or television program.

OPERATOR: The Assistant Cameraman, who usually rides the camera dolly and does the actual filming after the setup and framing is readied by the Cameraman or Director of Photography.

OPTION: The production company's option to use the actor within a contracted period of time.

OUT TAKES: The extra prints of shots which were filmed but which aren't cut into the film in editing.

OUTGRADING: Removing an actor totally from a commercial in the final version.

OVER THE SHOULDER SHOT: A shot in which most of the frame is devoted to an actor's face or something else while perhaps part of a head and shoulder of someone frames the edge of the shot in the foreground.

OVERLAPPING: Talking too soon after any other sound, or moving too quickly, leaving no room for cutting with scissors by the Editor.

PAGE NUMBERS: The *page* numbers are the numbers at the top right corner of script pages, usually followed by a period.

PANNING: When camera frame moves from one actor or object to another or when action is filmed in moves from one point to another and the camera follows the move.

PARTICIPATIONS: The series actor's contracted share in net profits realized by the series.

PER DIEM: The meal allowance the actor receives for meals when on location if they're not furnished by the production company.

PICKUP: The re-shooting of a part of a scene wherein something wasn't satisfactory.

PILOT: The usually two-hour series episode used to first obtain a series pickup by a network. Often telecast as a two-hour Movie of The Week by a network or special two-hour program prior to the series' start. Pilots that don't achieve network pickups are often run as Movies of The Week to recoup some of their production costs.

PINKS: The pink (usually second revision) pages of the script.

POV: This stands for "Point of View". The camera takes the actor's place; films what the actor is supposedly looking at.

POST PRODUCTION: The work, such as editing, dubbing, printing, etc., remaining to be done after all of a film's shooting is finished.

POWDER DOWN!: The call for Makeup to come to the set and powder the actor's face to prevent or eliminate any perspiration shine.

PRINT: There are successive "prints"....Work Prints, Rough Cuts,

Intermediate Cuts, Final Cuts, Answer Prints, etc....in the post-production stage of a film.

PRINT!: What the Director calls out when a shot has satisfied him, to direct that that shot be "printed" for probable cutting into the picture.

PROCESS STAGE (or simply **PROCESS**): The two connected soundstages where a mockup car is filmed going along a street that is projected on a giant screen behind it, or actors cower before a tiger which is leaping down upon them but is actually on film projected behind them.

PRODUCER: Sometimes the head honcho himself, in total control of the project; sometimes under the supervision of an Executive Producer...but in any event always the most actively and continually in charge of the project.

PROPS: The person who handles hand props on the set is called "Props".

RECURRING ROLE: A role which returns from time to time in a television series rather than being on a continuous contract basis.

REGULAR or **SERIES REGULAR**: A series starring or co-starring role that appears in all or most episodes of a series.

READY: This means completely ready for shooting, in makeup and wardrobe, at a designated spot.

RELEASE PRINT: The print of the picture which is sent out to theatres, television networks and stations.

RESIDUALS: What the actor receives when motion pictures, telefilms and commercials are rerun.

REST PERIOD: On location filming projects, the number of hours the actor must be allowed for rest between work periods.

RETAKES: Shooting of same scenes again, usually due to problems.

REVERSE or **REVERSE SHOT**: A shot from a totally reversed angle from one shot earlier.

REVISIONS: Script change pages to be substituted for similarly numbered pages in the script.

RIGHT FRAME: To your left as you face the camera.

ROLL 'EM!....SPEED!....SCENE TWO, TAKE SIX! are typical last calls usually heard before the Director calls out **ACTION!** "Roll em!" means to roll camera and sound, interlocked. "Speed!" (or an electronic beep) signals that both camera and sound are rolling together at the right speed for recording action and dialogue properly. "Scene Two, Take Six!" would be what "Slates" calls out hurriedly just before clapping the clapboards in front of the actor. All is then ready for the Director to call "Action!"

ROUGH CUT: The first spliced-together version of the film which the Editor shows to the producer and the director for their approvals and suggestions.

SAG ELIGIBLE: This means an actor is eligible to join SAG at any time he chooses, having done a picture without joining or being otherwise qualified under current SAG regulations for membership.

SCALE: The minimum SAG salary for a day player is referred to as either "Minimum" or "Scale".

SCENE NUMBERS: The numbers running down the sides of script pages.

SCREENING: Usually means the showing of a film with the producer, the director and many other department heads present, for any suggestions or to simply show the film to department people and guests.

SCRIPT SUPERVISOR (or **SCRIPT**): This person times each shot, checks all details for matching with other shots of the same scene, corrects dialogue errors, records data, then at the end of all filming hands that script over to the Editor as the record of all footage of all scenes available for cutting into the picture.

SECOND (or **SECOND ASSISTANT DIRECTOR**): The staff member who is in charge of the cast members at all times.

SEPARATE CARD: Actors' agents try to obtain billing for their starring players on *separate card*, with no other actor's name appearing in the frame at the same time.

SHARE CARD: This means that two or more leading cast members' names will appear in the opening credit frame at the same time.

SHOOTING SCHEDULE: Production Department sheets showing scenes to be shot, locations planned for their filming, when they're planned, equipment needed, crews required and cast members involved.

SIDES: Casting offices supply "sides" (a few pages of dialogue) to actors, for their preparing to read for roles, rather than complete scripts. SAG requires that such "sides" be made available for actors to pick up at least 24 hours prior to their reading appointments.

SIGHTING: The most reliable manner of "hitting your marks" by finding intersecting points on both a nearby and a more distant object.

SLATES: He or she holds the clapboards in front of your face and claps them when a shot is ready to begin; also rides the camera dolly continually, all the while adjusing focal depth.

SLOPPING: An actor "slops" when his role isn't finished on the day expected and he is to continue the next day or on another day.

STAND-INS: The folks who literally "stand in" actors' positions while lighting is being set. They're called "Second Team", while the actor is a "First Team" member.

STATION 12: That office at Screen Actors Guild which must be checked with by the Casting Office to determine that an actor is a SAG member and is paid up in dues and can be set for a role.

STICKS: The tripod on which a camera may be mounted out on locations when camera dollies and laid tracks aren't practical.

STILLS, STILL BOOK, STILL DEPARTMENT: Still photography by the Still Photographer made on a set is printed into the film's Still Book and is available in the Still Department for actors to look at for the purpose of choosing prints they'd like to order.

STOP DATE: The date the production company promises to be finished with the actor.

STUNTMEN, STUNTWOMEN: They fight, fall from buildings, get shot, etc., in hazardous sequences, while made up and wardrobed to look like the actors they represent.

TAFT-HARTLEY: The Law which allows actors to do their first film roles without having to join Screen Actors Guild.

TAKE (or **SHOT**): What's filmed between the words "Action!" and "Cut!".

THREE-DAY: The three day contract for a television role. (There is no three day contract for motion pictures.)

TIMESHEET: What the Second Assistant Director has the actor sign on the set upon arrival to show time or arrival and upon release at the end of the day to show time of dismissal.

TOP OF THE SHOW: Television series announce to agents that there is a top salary figure beyond which no actor will be paid.

TRAVEL TIME: The time during which an actor is required to travel to a remote location.

TRIMS: Pieces of film clipped out of footage by the Editor for alternating characters' faces and their dialogue in sequences during the cutting together of the picture. The actor's closeups of dialogue or action sequences are each filmed in continuous takes, but in editing other actors' faces, dialogue and action into the same scene those moments when the other actors' faces are cut into the film will mean there's a piece of the first actor's footage that becomes a "trim".

TURNAROUND: The period between completion of a television series' production for the season and the notification by the production company that it plans to continue or resume the actor's employment.

TWO SHOT: A shot, medium or otherwise, which includes two characters.

UPGRADING: When an actor has worked in less than a "principal" role in a commercial but is later "upgraded" into a recognizable face in the final version of the commercial and will therefore receive residuals.

VOICE-OVER: An actor's voice, when his face doesn't appear on screen.

WARDROBE: Either the person who handles your wardrobe, or your wardrobe for the role you play. It's usually hung in the closet of your dressing room before you arrive, ready for you.

WEATHER PERMITTING: The phrase used in issuing actors' calls when the weather is questionable but shooting is planned.

WEAVING: Drifting from side to side in a shot and causing problems for the cameraman trying to hold the actor in frame.

WEEKLY: The term for the contract of an actor who is hired for one or more weeks on a picture, rather than being hired on a "daily".

WESTERN: Usually means the Western Costume Company. Actors are instructed to "Go to Western" for fittings of wardrobe which the Studio

Wardrobe Department doesn't have available.

WHITES: The original pages of the shooting script (the white pages).

WILD LINES: Lines said into a mike, on or off the set, as lines only (without picture). They're for adding to the track in a dubbing session.

WORK CALL: Usually the details of where, what time and to whom the actor is to report for the following day's filming.

WORK PRINT: This is the first actual print of a picture after the "final cut" phase, especially when there's more work anticipated to be done in editing before dubbing of additional sound and music.

WRANGLER: The horses' straw boss on western sets. The man or woman who checks to see whether you know how to get on and off and what you're supposed to be able to do when riding. If you don't know enough, a "Riding Double" is immediately called for by the Wrangler.

WRAP: At the end of a day's shooting "It's a wrap!" is called to signal going home time. At the end of a picture's final filming it's the signal for breaking out the Wrap Party champagne.

WRAP PARTY: Usually held on a soundstage with catering. The occasion for everybody to breathe sighs of relief and forgive everybody.

Examples of Actors' Résumés
in the Industry-Recommended Form

This résumé layout is recommended for the actor or actress who _has_ a number of film and television credits as well as theatre background.

JAMES HARPER

SAG / AFTRA / Equity

Height: 6' 1"   Warner / Phillips Agency
Weight: 160 lbs.   Helen Phillips (212) 650-2111
Hair: Dk. Brown
Eyes: Spooky Grey

MOTION PICTURES

DEER VALLEY	Jake, The Hunter (Co-Starring)	Columbia (90)
WALLABEES	The Out Back Hermit (Featured)	Univ. (89)
THE LONG WALK	Juniper, the AWOL (Top Featured)	Lorimar (88)

TELEVISION

BITTER SEED	Paul, The Cellmate (Co-Starring)	NBC MOW (90)
FANTASY CHILD	William, The Threatener (Cameo)	CBS MOW (90)

THEATRE

Leading roles in **JUNO & THE PAYCOCK, WELL BORN, PSYCHICALLY SPEAKING, BOYLAN & SON**, Circle Players, Off Broadway NY; Summer Theatre, 4 seasons at Ogunquit Playhouse, Maine (1985-1988)

COMMERCIALS

List Upon Request

MISCELLANEOUS SKILLS   **TRAINING**
Most Field Sports, Team Roping,   Neighborhood Plhs. (NY)
Heavy Equip. of All Kinds   Uta Hagen (2 Yrs)

This form of résumé might ideally serve a newcomer who has no film or television credits yet but who has much theatre background:

Deborah Cramden

Equity

Height: 5' 6"   Tel. Messages: (310) 275-8298
Weight: 110 lbs.
Hair: Flax Blonde
Eyes: Soft Lavender

THEATRE

A DOLL'S HOUSE	Nora (Title Role)	Greenwich Playhouse NY, '87
DESPERATE JOURNEY	Maybelle (Lead)	ANTA Theatre NY, '86-87
HELLO OUT THERE	The Girl (Lead)	National Tour for CFI, '88

and **many seasons of Summer Theatre** in top roles, at Keene Summer Theate, Long Island Players (Bridgehampton), Ephrata Star Playhouse, Boothbay Theatre, etc.

MOTION PICTURES

None Yet....Just Starting in Hollywood in 1991

TELEVISION

Same...None Yet

COMMERCIALS

Many Non-Union Commercials in New York for
Local and Regional Market Products and Services

MISCELLANEOUS SKILLS   **TRAINING**

Wordprocessing & Computer Skills,   Sanford Meisner (4 Years), NY
Mountainclimbing, Snake Dancing,   Lawrence Parfke (Hwd), Now
Gemologist, Horticulturist, Ecol. Nut   Jeanne Hartman (Reading)

Examples of Ideal Cropping
of Actors' Professional "Headshot" Photos

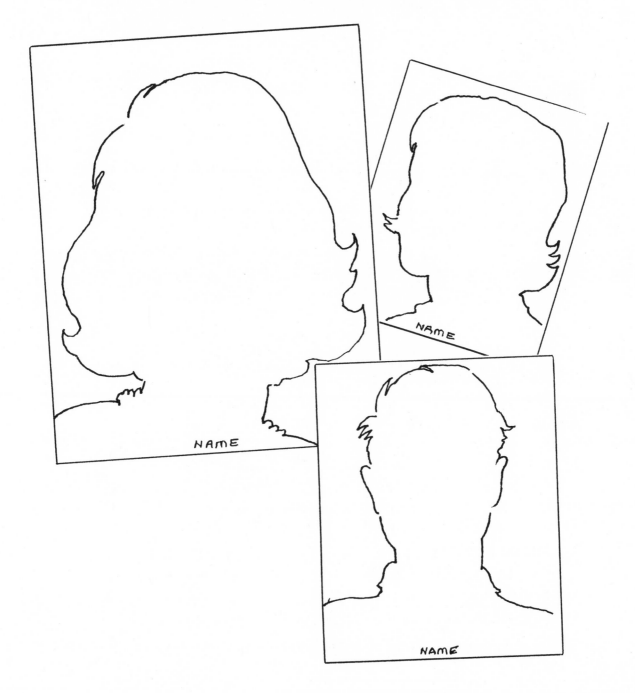

Examples of Photo Arrangements for Reverse Side of Commercial Composites

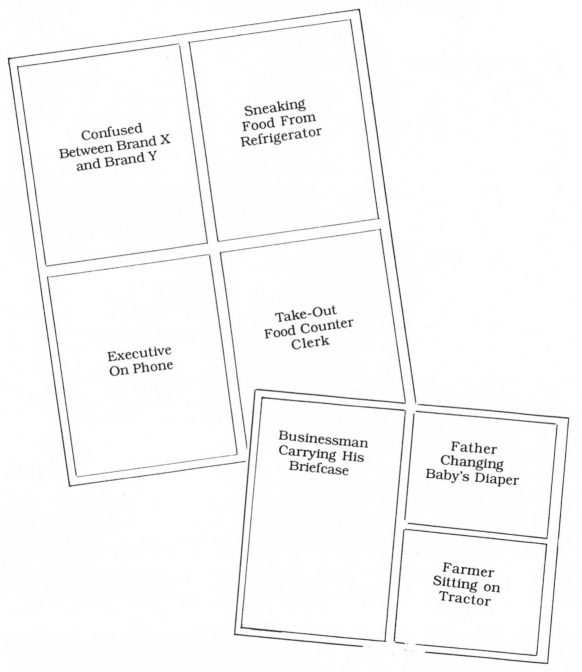

Samples of The Very Short Notes
The Industry Really Prefers

To An Agent, Seeking Representation:

I'd like you to consider representing me. My photo and resume are enclosed. I'd be happy to come for interview at your convenience. I'll call in about a week to check for your decision.

To A Casting Person, for General Interview:

I'd appreciate your granting me a General Interview at your convenience. My photo and resume are enclosed.

To A Production Company Regarding Casting:

I'd appreciate an opportunity to read for a role in your upcoming film "....(Title)....". I'm an (here put anything that qualifies you, <u>underlined and in bold print</u> if your typewriter or wordprocessor has it, such as **EXPERT HORSEMAN**, **QUICK DRAW GUNMAN**, **LICENSED SMALL PLANE PILOT**, **STOCK CAR RACER**, **EXPERT SCUBA DIVER**, etc.)

To Any Industry Person, Inviting to a Theatre Performance:

I'd appreciate your coming to see my performance in "...(Title).." at the ...(Name)... Theatre. A flyer is enclosed. If you'll call me with what night you can come I'll leave two complimentary tickets at the boxoffice in your name.

To Industry People Asking Them To Watch A Television Role:

I hope you'll see my performance as <u>Billy Joe</u> in the Hallmark Hall Of Fame movie "<u>The Phineas Connection</u>" next Thursday, the 20th at 8PM on CBS. Producer Jon Epstein says I did an outstanding job!

Questions To Ask When Getting Photographer Quotes

Sitting Fees:
    Head Shots:
    Commercial Shoot:

Deposit Required? If so, How Much?

When Payment Due:

Any Charge for Cancellation?

Shoot Indoor?   Outdoor?   Both?
    Types of Backgrounds?

Wardrobe Guidance Povided?   Any Charge?
Makeup Help Provided?   Any Charge?
How Many Wardrobe Changes Included?

Number of Proofs for Head Shots?   For Commercial Shoot?

Proofs How Soon After The Shooting Session?

Are The Negatives Released?

Prints How Soon After Proofs Returned with Selections?

Number of 8x10 Prints Included for Headshots?   For Commercials?

Are Prints Standard Border or Bleed?

Charge for Each Additional 8x10 Desired?

Some Recommended
Acting Study Programs

While the reader may want to review the complete list of study facilities, coaches and teachers by picking up the current quarterly issue of *__The Hollywood Acting Coaches And Teachers Directory__* at one of the performing arts bookstores, as the founder and for three years the first president of The Acting Coaches And Teachers Association this author feels himself eminently qualified---from personal acquaintance with and knowledge of most of the acting study community---to make the following recommendations in the interest of time-saving and lengthy searching on the part of the readers of this book:

For Acting Study, Most Types And Levels

With apologies to those whose names or organizations don't ap - pear in the following list through unintential omission, here is a list of coaches, teachers and facilities where the highest quality has been consistently maintained in the teaching of **Acting Technique** for Beginning, Intermediate and Professional Actors in Hollywood:

William Alderson, Joel Asher, Martin Barter, Stephen Book, Ron Burrus, Vincent Chase, Jeff Corey, Robert Ellenstein, Lev Mailer, Allen Garfield, Bruce Glover, Maria Gobetti, Lelia Goldoni, Estelle Harman Actors Workshop, Lorrie Hull, Paul Kent (at the Melrose Theatre Assn.), **Jack Kosslyn, Ned Manderino, Daniel Mann, Sanford Meisner, Allen Miller, Eric Morris, Jose Quintero** (when in Hollywood), **Tracy Roberts, Delia Salvi, George Shdanoff** and **Guy Stockwell.**

For **Acting For The Camera**: **Film Actors Workshop, Film Industry Workshops Inc. (FIWI).**

For **Comedy Coaching**: **The Groundlings, Stanley Myron Handelman, The Harvey Lembeck Comedy Workshops, Second City LA, Sandi C. Shore.**

For **Commercial Acting Training**: **Randy Kirby's Commercial Workshops, Tepper-Gallegos Workshops.**

For **Cold Reading Coaching (Film and Television)**: **Jeanne Hartman**, first and foremost among the many coaches that include such coaching in their over-all programs.

For **Auditioning For Theatre**: Certainly **Michael Shurtleff, Gordon Hunt, Jill André** and also the aforementioned **Jeanne Hartman**.

For **Dialects Coaching and Accent Elimination**: Some leaders certainly stand out: **Robert Easton, Dr. Lillian Glass, Larry Moss** and **David Alan Stern's** wonderful tapes, available in actor bookstores.

For **Voice-Over Coaching**: **Louise Chamis, Halvey Kalmenson, Mel Welles, Dave Sebastian Williams.**

For **Musical Theatre Training**: **David Craig, Derek Graydon, Robert Hanley, Devra Korwin, The Los Angeles Civic Light Opera Musical Theatre Workshop, Warren Lyons, Roy Rogosin** and the **Vocal Power Institute** of **Elizabeth Howard** and **Howard Austin**.

Note:

Although the foregoing list has been updated in 1996--at least to the limits of the awareness of this writer, at the time when the reader sees the list there will doubtless have been a few of the above teaching programs that have been discontinued, more created, so the reader should not rely wholly on this list and should obtain a then current copy of **The Hollywood Acting Coaches And Teachers Directory** at either Samuel French or another actors' bookstore in Hollywood, or by direct order from the publisher, Acting World Books, Post Office Box 3044, Hollywood, CA 90078. At the time of this writing, the cost is $15., but---constantly expanding at each Updating time---the price must be checked at the time of purchasing.

UPDATINGS AND CHANGES

Union regulations, minimum salaries, standard contract clauses, addresses, phones and just about everything else involving the actor change over periods of time. You may want to use this and the next four pages for making notes of the changes you want to remember. (Additional changes can be inserted on additional blank pages.)

Updatings and Changes, cont'd:

Updatings and Changes, cont'd:

Updatings and Changes, cont'd:

Updatings and Changes, cont'd:

PEOPLE WHO'VE SEEN MY WORK

It's easy to forget who attended your showcase or theatre performances, confirmed that they watched a television performance or saw you in a film, watched an office audition scene or may know your work from an acting workshop or special class. These acquaintances with your talents can be important for your agent to mention when suggesting you for roles, or for you to mention when contacting the people directly. For that reason, on this and the next page, keep records, so you won't forget as time passes. (Add more blank pages if necessary.)

PRODUCTION OR WHERE, WHEN?	ROLE OR WHAT I DID	WHO ATTENDED OR SAW MY WORK

People Who've Seen My Work, Cont'd:

281

COMMERCIAL RESIDUALS / AGENTS OWED COMMISSIONS

The agent representing the actor at the time when the actor does a commercial for which he or she will receive residuals over periods of time is the agent to whom the actor owes commission whether that agent is currently representing the actor at such later date or not. It's sometimes difficult for the actor to remember, at such later time, which of perhaps several agents was involved at the earlier time. For that purpose, you may want to keep a record , on this page, of all commercials you do and the agent of record at the time when they were done. (Add additional pages as necessary.)

COMMERCIAL   **DATE OF SESSION**   **AGENCY REPRESENTING**

BIRTHDAYS TO REMEMBER

It's nice to have your birthday remembered. Whether we're a casting director friend, a director friend, an agent friend or perhaps a trade paper or daily newspaper columnist friend, those who remember our birthdays are special people. It's a reminder that we matter to them, but it's also a reminder <u>about</u> them! Why not keep these dates handy on this and the next page?

Birthdays To Remember, Cont'd:

INDEX

290